Heidegger's Gods

NEW HEIDEGGER RESEARCH

Series Editors:

Gregory Fried, Professor of Philosophy, Suffolk University, USA
Richard Polt, Professor of Philosophy, Xavier University, USA

The *New Heidegger Research* series promotes informed and critical dialogue that breaks new philosophical ground by taking into account the full range of Heidegger's thought, as well as the enduring questions raised by his work.

Titles in the Series:

Making Sense of Heidegger, Thomas Sheehan
Heidegger and the Environment, Casey Rentmeester
After the Greeks, Laurence Paul Hemming (forthcoming)
The Question Concerning the Thing: On Kant's Doctrine of the Transcendental Principles, Martin Heidegger, translated by Benjamin D. Crowe and James D. Reid (forthcoming)
Heidegger's Gods: An Ecofeminist Perspective, Susanne Claxton

Heidegger's Gods

An Ecofeminist Perspective

Susanne Claxton

Published by Rowman & Littlefield International Ltd
Unit A, Whitacre Mews, 26-34 Stannary Street, London SE11 4AB
www.rowmaninternational.com

Rowman & Littlefield International Ltd. is an affiliate of Rowman & Littlefield
4501 Forbes Boulevard, Suite 200, Lanham, Maryland 20706, USA
With additional offices in Boulder, New York, Toronto (Canada), and Plymouth (UK)
www.rowman.com

British Library Cataloguing in Publication Data

A catalogue record for this book is available from the British Library

ISBN: HB 978-1-7866-0242-8
PB 978-1-7866-0243-5

Library of Congress Cataloging-in-Publication Data

Names: Claxton, Susanne, author.
Title: Heidegger's gods : an ecofeminist perspective / Susanne Claxton.
Description: Lanham : Rowman & Littlefield International, 2017. |
Series: New Heidegger research | Includes bibliographical references and index.
Identifiers: LCCN 2017000655 (print) | LCCN 2017005619 (ebook) |
ISBN 9781786602428 (cloth : alk. paper) | ISBN 9781786602442 (electronic) |
ISBN 9781786602435 (paper : alk. paper)
Subjects: LCSH: Heidegger, Martin, 1889-1976. | Ecofeminism. |
Environmental ethics. | Phenomenology.
Classification: LCC B3279.H49 C534 2017 (print) | LCC B3279.H49 (ebook) |
DDC 193—dc23
LC record available at https://lccn.loc.gov/2017000655

™ The paper used in this publication meets the minimum requirements of American National Standard for Information Sciences—Permanence of Paper for Printed Library Materials, ANSI/NISO Z39.48-1992.

Printed in the United States of America

Table of Contents

Chapter One

Introduction to the Project

Numerous attempts have been made and are made daily to better understand our current realities, to make sense of our human existence, to lay bare the meaning and import of our experiences both collective and individual. Such attempts, made in earnest and with the utmost sincerity, can easily overwhelm even those with the most adept powers of reasoning and the most resilient emotional being, and even more so if one considers the vast number of approaches, disciplines, thinkers, traditions, and perspectives from which one might begin such thinking.

Thoughtful persons tend to agree that in some way or another human existence at present seems sorely afflicted. Things are just not right or as they should be, ought to be, might be, or could be. Something is amiss, something is missing, something is wrong. Whether we are looking at cases of human rights abuses, social-political injustices, current environmental crises, worker exploitation, existential alienation, gender inequality, loss of community and inter-human connection, or any other of the myriad problems currently afflicting us, it appears that human beings either have never known or have somehow forgotten how to fully *dwell*. Human beings seem to know not how to meaningfully exist as that which we are in the context of all that exists and to which we are intimately related. This project presupposes this to be a readily observable and recognized phenomenon to which the project itself is a response both in the sense of providing deeper understanding and in the sense of offering a possible means of amelioration.

While I will not argue for the theoretical supremacy of my approach, I believe that the approach will speak for itself in terms of its being meaningful, useful, illuminating, and somehow making a difference. My methodology might be described as an ecofeminist Heideggerian phenomenology or perhaps an eco-phenomenological Heideggerian feminism. Whatever labels may ultimately be assigned, the reality *is* a closely woven fabric, as Merleau-Ponty once wrote, and thus the relevance of each and every part and method will show itself, I trust, to the mindful reader. Some may ask: How does one use phenomenology in a critique if phenomenology, by definition, is merely descriptive? I reply: As an approach to existence, phenomenology reveals to us new and different ways of being that the dominating points of view eclipse and deny, and these phenomenological revelations are transformative.

Human beings are transformed when their perceptions are broadened, when their perspective shifts. Broadened perceptions and new perspectives indeed do present new options prescriptively. Thus, both critique and possible new solutions result from the phenomenological approach for which I advocate. Additionally, while phenomenology is clearly a crucial part of epistemology, it is also intimately tied to metaphysics and may be argued to itself be a form of spirituality precisely because its diligent and mindful practice can unconceal that which may otherwise remain hidden or concealed.

In *Being and Time*, Heidegger writes, "For the analysis of Reality is possible only on the basis of our having appropriate access to the Real."[1] This project aims at discovering, explaining, and putting to use that which constitutes an "appropriate access to the Real." As I will endeavor to show, a proper understanding of the practice of phenomenology in an attempt to encounter truth, also properly understood, can free us from the shackles that prevent the realization of alternatives to current supposed and limited options, options that are themselves some of the very things preventing the attainment of fuller *dwelling* in intimate relation to self, others, and nature.

In this project, the path down which I will travel takes its start in Chapters 2 and 3 with an examination of the thinking of Martin Heidegger and his passionate engagement with the Greeks. I place great emphasis upon what I take to be one of the most central concepts of his thinking, the concept of truth understood as *a-letheia* and the idea of the concealed and the unconcealed. Heidegger held that the Greek's unique mode of and relation to Being was contingent upon this particular understanding of truth, and it was due to this particular understanding of truth and Being that the Greeks experienced their unique existence.

In exploring Heidegger's thinking, I will direct attention to specific suggestions he makes that may help set us on our own path to achieving a mode of being in the world that, although not the mode possessed by the Greeks, may perhaps be equally or more glorious. Such an end result becomes possible when we understand that such glorious greatness and fulfillment of being is neither something found only in some linear past now gone forever, nor is it something to be found in some linear future toward which we inevitably move. Rather, it is something always and continuously present, awaiting unconcealment, awaiting revelation by means of a special negation, the negation of our nihilistic mechanistic materialist mindset, our long-entrenched ways of conceptualizing self and others, our denial of immanent divinity, our reduction of humans, animals, and nature to mere resources awaiting optimization, in short, the negation of our "modern" mode of being.

This negation, this saving cessation, brings about that which may be understood in one sense as an emptying of mind, the creation of the necessary condition for the flowing-in of that which is itself the source of all meaning and glory, as well as the cultivation of what Heidegger calls *meditative thinking*, a thinking that is indeed the necessary condition for our attainment of full *dwelling* in the *Fourfold* as mortals, upon the earth, beneath the sky, and in communion with the divinity.

This negation of which I speak may be understood to be synonymous with Heidegger's concept of the "clearing" [*die Lichtung*] that allows Being to reveal itself anew and thus new understanding to take place. Through the explorations involved in this project, I will show why it is correct to understand that, for Heidegger, *a-letheia*, *physis*, and Being are the same. I will show why it is that Heidegger esteems the poet and the artist in the ways in which he does. I will demonstrate how a proper return to myth and art is the means by which the transcendental realities that constitute the phenomenology of our embodied existence may be better understood. Such an understanding, in turn, may allow us to come to fully *dwell*, to live full lives, rich in meaning and value, for art and myth are not just necessary tools for better living but are important means that are glorious ends in themselves. I should point out here that even the use of terms like "means" and "ends" can be somewhat misleading in that they presuppose a metaphysics that places a limitation upon what is, in essence, a fullness beyond measure.

In Chapter 4, I will introduce the philosophy of ecofeminism, laying out what may be understood as its four core tenets, the four sides of the frame, so to speak, that comprise the framework that is the ecofeminist critique. I will explain how each of the four operates as a crucial part of the whole. In doing this, I will show the ways in which meaning and value, as the crucially important realities they are, are indeed manipulable and manipulated within our current paradigm, this current epoch of human existence. Those ideas, once established, will prove important in making clear the connections that will be established in later chapters between ecofeminism, specific ideas of Giorgio Agamben, and those of Heidegger. I will also take a look at some particular ideas developed by Nietzsche in his criticism of Christianity that can serve to further enlarge perspective in their strong resonance with certain ecofeminist and Agambean ideas. The ideas set forth in my thinking about Nietzsche's thought become relevant again in Chapters 6 and 7.

In Chapter 5, I will examine a specific figure in Judaeo-Christian mythology, the mythological figure of Lilith, through the lens of philosopher Giorgio

Agamben and his brilliant and illuminating concepts of *homo sacer*, the *state of exception*, and the *hinge*. I will show how Agamben's ideas on the foundation of sovereign power provide insight into how we have arrived at certain of our own current realities. My analysis of Lilith via Agamben will further establish how Heidegger's ideas on myth are indeed relevant and how a return to myth, with an aim toward understanding what a careful study thereof unconceals, may assist us in pursuing full *dwelling*. I will make clear the connections between Agamben and previously set forth ideas, and I will employ Agamben's insights throughout the remaining chapters. I will link up Agamben's particular concept of the *state of exception* as the *hinge* with the ecofeminist critique of dualisms, and, perhaps more importantly, I will employ Agamben's concept of the *hinge* in Chapters 6 and 7 in order to provide us with a means of escape from the prison of the binary, the binary itself being that which is the greatest imprisoning conceptual institution of our current epoch.

In Chapter 6, I will return to Nietzsche and Heidegger, as well as the thinking of two particular contemporary philosophy scholars. I will explain an important eco-phenomenological difference between Nietzsche and Heidegger, as articulated by Iain Thomson, and argue that this difference, when understood properly, easily lends itself to the ecofeminist project in that it offers us a *transcendental ethical realism* that is definitely not a part of your average *anthropocentrism*. Moreover, I will demonstrate that this alternative is also one that allows us to avoid the pitfalls that are revealed in a critique of *ecocentrism*.

In revisiting the ecofeminist perspective, some specific terminology and concepts relevant to this project will be explored and employed via the work of Trish Glazebrook in order to bring together ideas that aid in moving beyond the binary of *anthropocentrism* and *ecocentrism* to a third alternative previously concealed, an alternative that has been obscured by the common discourse and metaphysics prevalent in environmental ethics. This third alternative I term *Daseincentrism*, and I argue that a proper understanding and embrace of *Daseincentrism* is the means by which fullness of *dwelling* may be achieved.

The final chapter will wrap up the journey by coming round full circle to connect back again with Heidegger and critical ideas laid out early on. In doing so, the ways in which we have indeed gained a clearer and more concrete sense of what *meditative thinking* looks like, its importance for *dwelling*, its connection to myth, and the role that myth and art can and do play for us will be made clear. It will then be possible to envision a new world in which we may all fully *dwell*, a world made possible precisely by the overcoming of dualisms and binaries, long-entrenched ways of understanding our realities, as well as by the unconcealing discovery, via this eco-phenomenological

Heideggerian feminism, of the third alternative to the binary of *anthropocentrism* and *ecocentrism* that I term *Daseincentrism*.

Is the path I take linear and to the point? No. It cannot be. But, as will hopefully become clear as we progress, by no means are any of the steps wasted. There is not a simple and straight path by means of which this journey can be made, as I hope to show via the various vantage points from which I will be taking in the view along the way, a view that, when seen from the differing vantage points, reveals how understanding is increased through multiple perspectives and thereby thus demonstrates the need for continuous augmentation, organic, and dynamic as it is.

This is a broad project. In undertaking to make my thoughts and ideas comprehensible, I will endeavor to be as clear as possible. I will examine the views and ideas of various thinkers and traditions with an aim toward taking what is most enlightening from each and putting it to use in order to better illuminate a new pathway of understanding. In other words, "Rather than endlessly restaging the old debates between the masters … we do better to follow the spirit of the eco-phenomenological movement by working creatively to appropriate their thinking for ourselves."[2]

In order to further assist the reader in getting a better sense of the path I will be taking, it may best be understood as my describing a *cure*, describing the *symptoms*, making a *diagnosis*, and then returning to a discussion of the *cure* in a more in-depth sort of way. It is my thinking that only in an adequate exploration of the ideas presented in the next two chapters (which are indeed constitutive of the *cure*, but not wholly sufficient) are the *symptoms* able to be recognized as the *symptoms* that they are. In other words, only by establishing a basic understanding of truth as *a-letheia*, how it relates, for Heidegger, to both Being and *physis*, along with its role in the functioning of the *Fourfold*, are we rendered able to recognize certain *symptoms* as such, and thus, come to see the *diagnosis* as accurate. This in turn allows for a fuller understanding of what the *cure* looks like both theoretically and practically as presented in the final chapters.

NOTES

1. Martin Heidegger, *Being and Time*, trans. John Macquarrie and Edward Robinson. (New York: Harper and Row, 1962), 246.
2. Iain Thomson, "Ontology and Ethics at the Intersection of Phenomenology and Environmental Philosophy," Inquiry 47:4 (2004): 400.

Chapter Two

Heidegger and the Greeks

A-LETHEIA

The Greeks, for Heidegger, are exemplary. Their way of living and mode of existence, as Heidegger understood them, were ontologically unique. They existed and lived with and within something that was exceedingly vital, perhaps even better understood as superlatively vivifying, yet they did so without explicitly articulating it. They did not analyze it, nor did they seek to conceptualize and intellectualize it as a modality of existence, since that would require the existence of other modalities as well as a consciousness of them.

The Greeks, in particular, the Pre-Socratics, as Heidegger understood them, were blessed with what we can think of as an innate situatedness within Being that allowed them to experience existence in the fullest way possible. Paradoxically, this required them to be subject to what modern thinking might see as a special oblivion of sorts. It was this very special oblivion that allowed them to exist in such close proximity to the source of intelligibility, to that which Heidegger understands as having been in continuous withdrawal from humankind ever since. This vital thing that has continued to retreat into the realm of the obscure has by no means, however, ceased to exist. Rather, it has become concealed, hidden, occulted, obscured, but in a very real sense it is no less immanent to the intelligible order that it continues to make possible.

The idea of something existent yet always partially hidden is, in fact, central to the Greeks' own conceptualization of truth. The idea of that which is present yet partially concealed is what constitutes the Greek concept of truth understood as *a-letheia*, literally translated from the Greek language as "truth" and with the understanding that it is also literally "un-forgetting" or "un-concealing," as *lethe* means "a forgetting, forgetfulness" in the Greek.[1]

Understanding truth as *a-letheia*, with its particular metaphysics of truth and its understanding of the nature of reality, is of paramount importance to Heidegger's thinking, derived as it is from a phenomenology of existence. The idea of truth as that which is real and present yet always partially concealed, I contend, is in fact a single thread that runs throughout and unifies a great deal of Heidegger's most original thinking.

The essential notion of concealed and unconcealed, as that which characterizes all that is most central to human existence, is integral not only to the concept of truth, or *a-letheia*, but also, as I will attempt to show, to virtually every other of the most intriguing concepts in Heidegger's thinking, such as the relationship between "earth" and "world," the *Fourfold* of earth, sky, divinities, and mortals, his understanding of *poiesis*, art, poetry, and the poet's relationship to the divine, to the thinker, and to humanity as a whole, as well as myth itself and myth's rightful place, according to Heidegger, as central to human life in the attempt to attain to full *dwelling*.

Moreover, it is my view that, for Heidegger, *a-letheia*, *physis*, and Being are the same. In what follows, I will attempt to demonstrate that throughout his lifetime of thinking Heidegger endeavored to bring this to awareness, to demonstrate by various means that although the legacy of the modern philosophy of consciousness is to regard the human *logos* as the measure of all that is, the reality is that "The *Logos* is accordingly something hearable, a kind of speech and voice; but manifestly not the voice of a human being."[2]

In the spirit of Heidegger's emphasis on the active receptivity of *Gelassenheit* or "releasement," I believe that an endeavor to make sense of some of the more seemingly esoteric strands of Heidegger's thought is made easier if we first open ourselves to receiving this concept of the integral nature of concealment with unconcealment and allow it to be our guiding word, so to speak. This concept that we are attempting to fathom in a general way, if understood and accepted, will in turn allow us to see how it permeates, inheres within, or otherwise weaves together in essence the various aforementioned important concepts in Heidegger's thinking.

Perhaps before attempting to spell out what it is, I should be clear on what it is not. This idea of concealed and unconcealed should not be thought of as a pair of opposites. It should neither be thought of as thesis and antithesis, nor as a proposition and its negation. Rather, it may be thought of as a pair of interdependent complements, but without the notion of a distinct dividing line between the two which constitute the "pair." Perhaps a more realistic imagistic conceptualization would yield something like a circular continuum on which at each of the two 180-degree points one would find what we call "concealment" and "unconcealment" while in between would be all manner of degrees of the two in their intermingling and integral interrelatedness.

To offer an example and analogue in more physical and material terms, one may try to better grasp truth as *a-letheia* or unconcealing in a practical manner in the following way: Imagine you are standing in front of a tree. You want to know about the tree. You want to know the *truth* about it. Well, you can undertake to very diligently pursue a view of all its parts, inside and out. However, notice that when you are looking at one part of the tree, a different part of the tree is not necessarily available to your view. The hidden part is not any less true or any less real, but it is concealed. When you move to bring a concealed part of the tree into view, thus bringing it into unconcealment, another part of the tree becomes concealed from your view. The roots may even remain perpetually concealed. Additionally, and as is well-understood, what is unconcealed about the tree in winter is very different than what is unconcealed in the spring. Thus would all of your efforts to fully unconceal the truth of the tree at any point in time necessarily fail. The relevance of time here is not to be dismissed. While this example and analogy may be helpful, the crucial difference between a tree and truth is that the former is in a certain sense finite, and the latter, as will be explained in more detail soon, is infinite.

Heidegger's embrace of and emphasis upon the Greek conception of truth as *a-letheia* is exceedingly important to him because his own understanding is one in which everything is ultimately constituted by this essential reality of concealed and unconcealed. Of course, for Heidegger, the Greeks, especially the Pre-Socratics, were special not only because this essential fullness of understanding was their lived reality, but also because they lived it without making it explicit, analyzing it, and setting it forth conceptually in conscious opposition to something else. This is a crucial point to be understood.

The very unique and special situation that the Greeks occupied in relation to this matter, although it can never be recovered now that it has been lost, is a situation that Heidegger believes may be approximated by means of proper understanding and effort, albeit with a few obvious differences. Regarding the unique situation of the Greeks in terms of their relationship to *a-letheia*, or concealedness and unconcealedness, what Heidegger says in the following is very important and quite clear:

> [F]or the Greeks the mutual counter-essence of *aletheia* and *lethe* was experienced originally. We might therefore expect that this essential correlation between *aletheia* and *lethe* would also, in a correspondingly original way, be thought through by the Greeks and posed in thinking. This expectation is not fulfilled. The Greeks never did explicitly think through *aletheia* and *lethe* with regard to their essence and the ground of their essence, since already, i.e., prior to *all* thinking and poetizing, these pervade the to-be-thought as its "essence." The Greeks think and poetize and "deal" *within* the essence of *aletheia* and *lethe*, but they do not think and poetize *about* this essence and they do not

> "deal" with it. For the Greeks it suffices to be claimed by *aletheia* itself and to be encompassed by it.[3]

Here I see that Heidegger understands the Greeks as having existed in intimate relation to this central aspect of existence but in a way that might best be described as an existence of purely unreflective awareness and experience. In other words, the Greeks were not engaging in reflecting upon their unreflective awareness and experience and thus analyzing it or contrasting it with something else. In this regard, the Greeks could be described as immersed within or simply being in flow with that reality. The distinction between what I am calling "being in flow with that reality" versus being engaged in a reflective awareness upon it may be understood by thinking of what it is like to engage in an activity of embodiment versus what it is like to reflect upon that engagement.

Let me preface here by acknowledging that while such an analogy is far from perfect and is indeed more ontic than ontological, it can nonetheless help one to begin thinking in the right direction. For example, it is one thing to ride a bicycle and quite another to think about riding a bicycle. When one rides a bicycle, there is clearly at play matters of physics, balance, gravity, and motion, as well as many other material matters such as path, obstacles, weather, and wind. However, while one rides a bicycle within the reality and operation of any and all of these things, riding a bicycle does not require that one explicitly think through any of these things. Moreover, riding a bicycle may well be made much more difficult if one attempts to think about doing it and do it at the same time. The same can be said for any number of embodied activities of a certain sort, such as snow skiing, skating, snowboarding, dancing, swimming, and so on. What is relevant here, again, are not the analogues per se, but the idea that riding a bicycle in no way requires one to explicitly think about riding a bicycle. Reflecting upon it, "dealing" with it, is in no way necessary for doing it, for experiencing it. For a bicyclist, gravity is a given. Gravity, like *a-letheia*, need not be discussed, analyzed, theoretically understood, or thematically explained in order for it to be operative. As Heidegger would say in good phenomenological fashion, gravity is prior to all thinking about riding a bicycle. Thus, as is true for many activities of embodiment, one may ride a bicycle with only a purely unreflective awareness and experience of that which may "pervade the to-be-thought as its 'essence'," as Heidegger would say.

Before saying more on this, perhaps it is best to refresh with something from Maurice Merleau-Ponty's *Phenomenology of Perception* to help make clearer my meaning:

> The world is there before any possible analysis of mine, and it would be artificial to make it the outcome of a series of syntheses. ... When I begin to reflect

> my reflection bears upon an unreflective experience; moreover my reflection cannot be unaware of itself as an event, and so it appears to itself in the light of a truly creative act, of a changed structure of consciousness, and yet it has to recognize, as having priority over its own operations, the world which is given to the subject, because the subject is given to himself. The real has to be described, not constructed or formed. Which means that I cannot put perception into the same category as the syntheses represented by judgements, acts or predications.[4]

There are many aspects of existence that, as such, are best understood not as "judgements, acts or predications" but as "perceptions." The aforementioned activities of skiing, dancing, bicycling, and so on, may be understood to fall into this category. For a better understanding of the idea of an activity of embodiment being a "perception," Merleau-Ponty offers an example of someone who learns to use a walking-stick. He makes very clear that once the stick is familiar as perceptual habit, it becomes an extension of the hand, and the world of feelable things now begins not with the hand but with the end of the stick.[5] It is my contention that these ideas articulated by Merleau-Ponty are precisely what Heidegger has in mind regarding the Greeks' relation to *a-letheia*. The Greeks did not construct *a-letheia* as a result of a series of syntheses. Rather, they perceived *a-letheia* as truth fundamentally. It was the world given to them. It was familiar as perceptual habit. It was the real to be described.

Again, as Heidegger expressed in the above quotation, the Greeks lived within *a-letheia* and *lethe* without reflecting upon it and conceptualizing it, especially in contrast to something else. Being, understood as *a-letheia*, was simply part of what Merleau-Ponty would call their perception. Their existence within and awareness of *a-letheia*, without reflection thereupon, occurred in the same way that one encounters the world as unreflective experience or the way in which one engages in an activity of embodiment without reflecting upon it or the way in which one uses a stick as an extension of the hand as a means of simple perception.

It seems clear to me that this is precisely what Heidegger has in mind when he stresses in the above quotation that the Greeks thought and poetized *within* the essence of *a-letheia*. There was no reflecting upon that unreflective awareness and experience, no conceptual analysis thereof, and no attempts to understand and articulate it. *A-letheia* was the real, as Heidegger put it; it was the world which was given to the Greeks. And that is precisely what Heidegger means when he says that the Greeks did not "deal" with *a-letheia* but *dealt within it*. Of course, for us, being already engaged in reflection upon our unreflective awareness and experience as heirs to the problematic metaphysics of modernity, the best we can do is try to imagine what it would be like to not so much deal with concealedness and unconcealedness but to deal within it, for clearly in our modern and late-modern worlds, we have already been subject to that "changed structure of consciousness" and put in a position where we must "deal" with it. In agreement with Heidegger, I contend that the key is to return as best we can to an encounter with the real so as to describe it as it is and take our start from there.

In a most erudite and astute work of scholarship, Richard Capobianco sets forth an understanding of Heidegger that is in perfect keeping with my own. He makes very clear in his book *Heidegger's Way of Being* that Heidegger indeed understood *a-letheia*, *physis*, and *Logos* as names used by the Greeks to refer to Being. His careful and insightful translation of certain works in the *Gesamtausgabe*, which are yet to be translated into English, is of immense help in making clearer ideas articulated by Heidegger in works more commonly explored. Central to Capobianco's thinking, as to my own, is a concern that much of the recent scholarship on Heidegger has reduced Being to mere meaning-making on the part of human beings. Capobianco writes:

> To be sure, for Heidegger it is the case that the human being is the "shepherd of Being," "the guardian of Being." That is, we are always reminded that our access to Being is only through our Dasein—and for this reason it may be fair to say that his thinking remained broadly "phenomenological" to the end—but if so, his *enrichment* of phenomenology lay precisely in his giving a full accounting of the "phenomenon," of the "claim of Being," on the human being and our meaning-making. Nevertheless, Being itself as "ever-living" emergence became of such overriding concern to Heidegger that he sometimes explicitly stated that the "truth-ing of Being" not only *exceeds* the relation to the human being but is also *altogether independent* of that relation.[6]

It is this idea of Being as "ever-living" emergence that is what is at play in the Greeks' use of the terms *a-letheia*, *physis*, and *Logos* when speaking of Being. And in returning to the above quotation from Heidegger in which he seeks to show what it was that set the Greeks apart from all that came thereafter, more clearly shown is the legacy of the metaphysics that has dominated Western thinking since that time, that is, the legacy of shifting the source of meaning from Being to the human being, the legacy of reducing the *Logos* to the *homologein*.[7]

Regarding the way in which Heidegger uses these relevant terms and how he understands them as having been used by the Greeks themselves, it is instructive to consider that throughout his lifetime of thinking Heidegger returned again and again to an emphasis upon the primacy of Being and the inescapable nature of Dasein in relation thereto, a relation that is subordinate. Heidegger articulates this idea in many places, and many of these quotations will be used throughout this project. In an Addendum to the *Parmenides* lecture, Heidegger makes it clear when he says:

> Only because Being and the truth of Being are essentially beyond all men and humanities, can, and therefore must, the "Being" or "non-being" of man be at stake where man as historical is determined to the preservation of the truth of Being.[8]

In Heidegger's estimation, it was the Greeks preservation of the truth of Being that set them apart. While Plato may have inaugurated a new epoch that was later further entrenched by Descartes, an epoch in which there was a shift away from the continually emergent nature of Being, that is, Being's *presencing*, and toward a metaphysics that sought to establish presence via a subject and an object, for Heidegger, the Greeks were utterly enveloped by Being understood as *a-letheia*, *physis*, and *Logos*. Capobianco captures this nicely when he writes:

> In "Time and Being," Heidegger brought the language of "letting" and "giving" to the forefront, but, again, the core matter of his thinking remained the same: the movedness (*Bewegtheit*) of all things into and out of presence. It had always been his claim that if we were able to truly "hear" the Greek language, then we would be able to discern this "movedness" in the *Ur*-words *physis, Logos, hen, aletheia* ... the Greeks never proferred what we now so routinely refer to as a "metaphysics of presence" because they never lost sight of the *presencing* of all things, even if they could not thematize this as such.[9]

The Greeks' failure or inability to "thematize" this crucial *presencing* is precisely why Heidegger viewed them as possessing such a unique and important relation to Being/*a-letheia*. Moreover, it was in the subsequent thematization that unfolded in the modern epoch that Heidegger saw the thinking of Being go awry. While more will be said as I go along about *physis* and *a-letheia*, I want to focus briefly on Heidegger's understanding of *Logos* and the way in which this relates to the analytic of Dasein set forth in *Being and Time*.

In *Being and Time*, Heidegger sets forth "the twofold task" of working out the "question of Being." Indeed, as is commonly understood, pursuit of the question of Being requires first an analytic of Dasein. As Heidegger explains, an analytic of Dasein is the "first requirement in the question of Being."[10] Once this has been shown "proximally and for the most part," the Being of Dasein will be shown in a "preparatory fashion."[11] Heidegger quickly points out, however, that what is revealed thereby is incomplete and provisional. He says of such an analysis of Dasein:

> It merely brings out the Being of this entity, without Interpreting its meaning. It is rather a preparatory procedure by which the horizon for the most primordial

> way of interpreting Being may be laid bare. Once we have arrived at that horizon, this preparatory analytic of Dasein will have to be repeated on a higher and authentically ontological basis. We shall point to temporality as the meaning of the Being of that entity which we call "Dasein." … In thus interpreting Dasein as temporality, however, we shall not give the answer to our leading question as to the meaning of Being in general. But the ground will have been prepared for obtaining such an answer. … We have already intimated that Dasein has a pre-ontological Being as its ontically constitutive state. Dasein *is* in such a way as to be something which understands something like Being. Keeping this interconnection firmly in mind, we shall show that whenever Dasein tacitly understands and interprets something like Being, it does so with *time* as its standpoint. … In order for us to discern this, *time* needs to be *explicated primordially as the horizon for the understanding of Being, and in terms of temporality as the Being of Dasein, which understands Being.*[12]

While a great deal of scholarship exists in which the above, or at least parts of it, are explored, I want to focus on two primary elements: (a) the way in which "the analytic of Dasein will have to be repeated on a higher and authentically ontological basis," and (b) the relevant meaning of the idea that "time needs to be explicated primordially." It is my understanding that what this means is that the analytic of Dasein first reveals the ontic character of Dasein in its *average everydayness*. From such an understanding, *time* is understood as the standpoint from which Dasein understands and interprets Being. From here, time may be "explicated primordially," and the analytic may be repeated on a "higher and authentically ontological basis."

It is my view that what Heidegger seeks to reveal through the primordial explication and the repetition of a higher analysis remains the same throughout the lifetime of Heidegger's thinking. Although he continually sought for new ways to express his ideas, employing different terminology at different times in an effort to direct thinking away from what he saw as problematic or dogmatic and toward the thought of Being that he himself ever pursued, it is my contention that from the beginning what Heidegger sought to show was the truth of Being as *a-letheia*, *physis*, and *Logos*. And while Heidegger only went so far in *Being and Time*, careful attention to the threads sown there and continued in his subsequent thinking reveals that he unceasingly sought to show that while Being reveals itself to Dasein by means of the openness of Dasein to that revealing which in turn necessitates the resultant articulations of those understandings by Dasein, Being itself is always something more.

In much of contemporary Heidegger scholarship, it seems that the very thing Heidegger wished to make clear in his lifetime of thinking has been lost or forgotten in that Being has been reduced to mere meaning and the making of meaning on the part of human beings. The idea of Being as that which exceeds any given meaning and is itself that which makes meaning possible has become lost or forgotten; it has been concealed.

In an otherwise very insightful book, Taylor Carman says plainly, "Does this schematic sketch of the inquiry and its formal distinction between being and the meaning of being entail any substantive or systematic distinction between them? I think not … for Heidegger, being is constituted by the meaning of being, so that an understanding of being is in effect the same as an understanding of its meaning."[13] This far too common reduction of *Sein* to *Sinn* is simply not in keeping with Heidegger's own thinking, speaking, and writing on the matter. In fact, it appears to me as quite myopic and perhaps somewhat narcissistic. On this issue, Capobianco writes:

> [T]he matter of Being has been almost entirely left behind. … [I]n the work of other recent Heidegger commentators, the question of Being has been transformed into the question of "meaning," and the "meaning-making" activity of the human being has taken center stage in the scholarship. In these accounts, *Sein* is reducible to *Sinn*, and Heidegger's thinking is brought so close to Husserl's that there remains hardly a trace of the profound and fundamental difference between the two approaches that Heidegger insisted upon. To be sure, Heidegger was intensively concerned with human Dasein's "languaged" relation to Being … [but] his paramount concern was with the *primacy of Being* in relation to human Dasein.[14]

To better understand what is meant by the *primacy of Being* mentioned by Capobianco, it is instructive to consider his examination of the *Logos* and its relation to the human *logos* or *homologein.* Capobianco writes:

> The German title of the 1944 lecture course, *Logik. Heraklits Lehre vom Logos*, already gives us to consider that Heidegger's focus is on Heraclitus' "teaching" (*Lehre*) as it issues forth *from* the primordial *Logos*. What emerges distinctly in these elucidations is that Heidegger's concern is first and foremost with bringing into view and affirming the primacy of Being as the primordial *Logos* in "relation" (*Bezug*, *Beziehung*) to the *logos* of the human being.[15]

In a wonderful chapter of his book, the chapter called "This *Logos* is Being Itself," Capobianco argues brilliantly for his understanding of Heidegger via an examination of this particular work of Heidegger's that has yet to be translated into English. Through careful and thoughtful explication of the content of Heidegger's 1944 lecture course on Heraclitus, Capobianco demonstrates that Heidegger did indeed have a pre-metaphysical understanding of *Logos* as Being. And, moreover, that Heidegger's understanding of the nature of the relationship between human beings and Being, between *homologein* and *Logos*, is one in which human beings "glean" or "gather" (Greek *legein*, German *lesen/sammeln)* through their reaching out and bringing back from Being, through their open receptive and appreciative "hearing" of *Logos*. Capobianco writes, "According to Heidegger, as he translates and reads Fragment 50 … Heraclitus tells us that for us to truly 'gather,' which is 'knowing,' we must be able to 'hearken' (*horchen*) in humble silence (*gehorsam*, obediently) to the primordial *Logos* and what it 'says'."[16]

For Heidegger, Being can never be reduced to human being or the meaning-making of human beings. And here, again, is why Heidegger so favored the Greeks, especially the pre-Socratics, and why he sought incessantly to show how and in what ways their thinking of Being had been largely forgotten but desperately needed to be reclaimed.

While the first steps of the path toward real thinking necessitate the analytic of Dasein, the thinking of Being is not reducible to Dasein, and as Heidegger's thought unfolded over the course of his lifetime of thinking, this seems to me to be one of the most important ideas he attempted to make clear. Thus, Capobianco notes that in 1941, Heidegger wrote, "At times, Being needs the essencing of human being, and yet Being is never dependent upon existing humanity."[17] And as Capobianco carefully and painstakingly demonstrates in his work, to miss what are the most constituent concerns in Heidegger's thinking guarantees a missing of the mark of his thinking entirely. Capobianco writes:

> He [Heidegger] is perfectly clear that the *Erfragte*—that which we are seeking in our questioning beyond metaphysical thinking about beings in their beingness—is Being itself. … Furthermore, he clarifies this point in a way that stands in even starker contrast to the position of those contemporary commentators who argue that it is Dasein and Dasein's constitutive meaning-making or coping-activity that is the core concern of his thinking. Heidegger tells us that Being itself as the primordial *Logos*, "the pre-metaphysical *Logos*," is not "any kind of activity of human saying or stating" (277). This is crucial. The essencing of *Logos* is not reducible to formal statements or assertions or propositions or any form of meaning; *nor is it reducible to any kind of human "saying"* (*Sagen*). Simply put, the primordial *Logos* is not reducible to any activity of the human being.[18]

I will now return to exploring a bit more the concept of *a-letheia* and the nature of concealment and unconcealment as it appears in Heidegger's thinking and attempt to provide other means of thinking about this concept. I believe it can be instructive to consider ideas regarding "truth" set forth by Jean-Paul Sartre in his work *The Anti-Semite and the Jew.* Despite Heidegger's need to distinguish himself from Sartre in his "Letter on Humanism" and his well-founded criticism of Sartre's excessive subjectivism (which I understand as Sartre's failure to acknowledge that he was indeed "claimed by Being"), there is yet within Sartre's own thinking about the nature of truth as articulated in this particular piece of writing certain ideas I see as helpful to further understanding *a-letheia*.

In his book, Sartre attempts to explain what is it that makes an anti-semite an anti-semite, or more generally, what makes a bigot a bigot. His explanation involves the workings of a cluster of specific fears that together serve to create a bigot by means of the bigot's own response to them. Central to his explanation, however, is the very concept of truth itself, and the way in which a bigot fears truth. Sartre explains that the bigot longs for impenetrability and stasis due to his fear of change and his subsequent need for something immutable. But to say that the bigot fears truth in general is to miss the more subtle but crucial reality of the situation, that is the phenomenological experience of truth itself. Sartre explains that the bigot fears not the content of truth but its very *form*, for the form of truth, according to Sartre, is infinite.[19]

The encounter with the infinitude of truth is perhaps phenomenologically akin to facing death or to gazing into the abyss in that each of these are encounters with something necessarily beyond comprehension and adequation. By contemplating such things, one can gain some perspective as to how one experiences existence itself. Of course, it is important to point out here that in so far as one accepts this characterization of the nature of truth as infinite in form, it is done in conjunction with the recognition of the finitude of one's own capacity and perspectives in the face of that which is apparently inexhaustible and beyond total comprehension. To speak of truth as infinite in its form in this way is to avoid hypostatizing the concept while preserving the phenomenological experience of it.

The anti-semite or bigot, for Sartre, is someone who wishes to be in possession of complete and immutable truth because he simply cannot deal with the prospect of the truth not being finite. The bigot's fear-driven modality of being simply cannot entertain the prospect of the truth not being something that he may possess in totality, especially in so far as he desperately needs something unchanging upon which he may rely in order to quell his fears and anxiety.

As Sartre explains, the bigot is afraid of freedom and longs for the security that he believes comes from submission or perhaps even enslavement to an unwavering truth. Sartre makes clear that a bigot will even ignore evidence that points to an error in his beliefs or thinking, so frantic and thorough going is his need to be right and in possession of the truth. Thus, from a Heideggerian perspective, the bigot may well be said to forego authentic being-toward-death and to refuse "to learn." Of course, as I stated, understanding and accepting truth as infinite presupposes an acknowledgment of the finitude of one's human existence, and such an acknowledgment entails the idea that what would indeed constitute being rational is that one have an attitude of openness toward the perpetual unconcealing of truth since truth exceeds oneself necessarily.

It is my contention that the dynamic experience described by Sartre as the emergence of truth as finite content from truth in its infinite form is the very play and movement that constitute the unconcealing and concealing that is *a-letheia*. Such dynamism and mutability are the conditions that allow for truth, as that which is infinite in its form, to perpetually reveal itself in different ways, as that which is finite in its manifest content. Such an idea is captured in Iain Thomson's *Heidegger, Art, and Postmodernity* when he states: "For, it remains possible for being to continue to become newly intelligible only if it cannot ever become fully intelligible."[20]

As mentioned above, Sartre explains that the reaction of the bigot, when faced with truth as infinite, is to misuse reason. Sartre stresses that a bigot, as such, misuses reason in a very real sense in that he takes his hypothesis as truth and interprets all evidence in its light, ignoring, and outright dismissing any evidence that would call into question his own beliefs. Sartre says, "[T]hey wish to lead the kind of life wherein reasoning and research play only a subordinate role, wherein one seeks only what he has already found, wherein one becomes only what he already was."[21] This reduction, what can be understood as an erroneous simplification of infinite truth to finite knowledge, is precisely what Heidegger seeks to avoid in pursuing and developing the ideas that are most central to his thinking, all of which are tied to the concealed and unconcealed.

Thus, Sartre, in his understanding of both truth as infinite and healthy reason as something "open" and "receptive," is in agreement with certain views articulated by Heidegger. There is within Sartre's own thinking, it seems to me, an awareness of the inestimable importance of understanding truth as essentially constituted by the concealed and unconcealed. To live in accordance with such truth, for Heidegger, is "to learn," and Sartre's description of what constitutes a "reasonable man" is in keeping with a description of what it is to be able "to learn," as set forth by Heidegger in his *Introduction to Metaphysics*. For Sartre, a reasonable man is open, tentative even, in his point of view, in that he recognizes that his held opinions and views are continually subject to revision given new experience, discovery, and thinking. This proper use of reason, for Sartre, is in grave contrast to the way a bigot employs reason.[22] The subtlety and nuance of such an idea is revealed when Heidegger says:

> To know means *to be able to learn*. Of course, everyday understanding believes that one has knowledge when one needs to learn nothing more, because one has finished learning. No. The only one who knows is the one who understands that

he must always learn again, and who above all, on the basis of this understanding, has brought himself to the point where he continually *can learn*. This is far harder than possessing information.[23]

I think that the concept of truth understood as *a-letheia* makes incredible sense precisely because it resonates with so much of our lived experience. It provides a key to understanding certain phenomena of existence. It reveals how things that we may merely sense as being connected are indeed interwoven despite our inability to see and touch each thread. It explains the sense one may have that there is a connection between things even though the connection is seemingly existent behind a veil, just out of reach, and beyond the possibility of any prehensile capture that would render it fully and completely comprehended or apprehended in a manner fitting a "modern" understanding.

There is a particular word used by Heidegger in both *Elucidations of Hölderlin's Poetry* and *Hölderlin's Hymns "Germania" and "The Rhine"* which he takes from Hölderlin's poetry that captures these ideas; that word is *Innigkeit*. Translations of the term include "sincerity," "ardor," and "intimacy," and much thought has been given to the ways in which Heidegger uses the term and the ways in which it is best understood in order to capture his meaning.

In an interesting essay, "Translating *Innigkeit*," Peter Warnek offers a treatment of the concept. In discussing Heidegger's views regarding translation and interpretation, Warnek brings up the important distinction made by Heidegger between "earth" and "world." Warnek writes, "What is at issue in such translations is not simply the experiences these words should convey, but rather the world itself for which these words and the experiences opened up by them play a constituting role."[24] This notion that "world" is conditioned and so never reveals to us everything is a key part of understanding *Innigkeit* as "the belonging together of the strange," according to Warnek. Moreover, this understanding of the world as conditioned allows us to see how the concept of *Innigkeit* captures what I believe is the core of Heidegger's thought regarding the reality of Dasein as explained through the concept of the concealed and unconcealed.

Warnek points out that, for Heidegger, *Innigkeit* is a *Geheimnis*, and that it is not to be understood simply as the "mystery" of being but "as the way in which human *dwelling* is *grounded* in a hiddenness, or, said otherwise, the way in which the human world belongs to the earth."[25] Of course, the notion that human *dwelling* is grounded in a hiddenness is just another way to speak of the pervasive nature of the concealed and unconcealed. I will examine this further by looking at Heidegger's discussion of the *Fourfold*, its oneness, and its relationship to *dwelling*.

DWELLING AND THE FOURFOLD

In his essay "Building Dwelling Thinking," Heidegger tells us: "By a *primal* oneness the four—earth and sky, divinities and mortals—belong together in one."[26] Heidegger emphasizes the "primal oneness" here because, as he goes on to explain, no one part of the *Fourfold* is ever thought without the other three, yet we might easily forget to give thought to "the simple oneness of the four."[27] Heidegger explains that mortals assume their rightful place in the *Fourfold* by means of *dwelling*. He goes on to make clear that mortals indeed have a unique role to play in their *dwelling* in that they "safeguard the Fourfold in its essential unfolding."[28]

In *dwelling*, mortals *save* the earth. Heidegger says: "To save properly means to set something free into its own essence ... Saving the earth does not master the earth and does not subjugate it."[29] This notion of *saving* as setting something free into its own essence may be understood more fully in light of something Heidegger says in his "Letter on Humanism." There he says: "To embrace a 'thing' or a 'person' in their essence means to love them, to favor them. Thought in a more original way, such favoring means the bestowal of their essence as a gift. Such favoring ... can let something essentially unfold in its provenance, that is, let it be."[30] To save the earth, mortals must first orient themselves toward it in such a way that the essence of the earth is recognized. In order to recognize the essence of the earth, mortals must understand that the earth does have an essence. The first step in doing this involves an understanding of the earth as an inexhaustible source of meaning that is nonetheless inherently beyond complete comprehension. Of course, this is in no way the same as saying that the earth (or our world) has limitless resources.

The idea that the earth is an exhaustible source of meaning and that it is necessarily beyond total apprehension is yet another manifestation of the relevance of *a-letheia* and the operation of the concealed and unconcealed. For Heidegger, fullness of *dwelling* presupposes an understanding of the nature of earth and in contrast to the world. The essentially concealed nature of earth is safeguarded in the fullness of *dwelling*. And indeed, while human beings can and inevitably do seek to know more and more, those who may be said to be *in the know* are some of the first to assert the limits of what is and can be known of earth at any given point in time. While a thing may be rendered intelligible and thus become part of world, earth itself is never unconcealed.

In his essay "On the Essence of Truth," Heidegger says, "Philosophical thinking is gentle releasement that does not renounce the concealment of being as a whole. Philosophical thinking is especially the stern and resolute openness that does not disrupt the concealing but entreats its unbroken essence into the open region of understanding and thus into its own truth."[31]

Thus, for Heidegger, the fullness of *dwelling* cannot be obtained without this understanding. And despite the errors that mark the modern epoch and human beings' confused understanding of truth and their relation thereto, Heidegger never stopped trying to help make such errors clear to us. Heidegger understood precisely how the truth of truth had become eclipsed since Plato. Moreover, he understood how such errors, how such forgetfulness of *a-letheia*, prevents Being from appearing to us primordially. Thus, he says, "Because sheltering that clears belongs to it, Being appears primordially in the light of concealing withdrawal. The name of this clearing [*Lichtung*] is *alētheia*."[32]

While Heidegger's distinction between earth and world serves a specific purpose in his thinking, his use of the term "earth" in his essay "Building Dwelling Thinking" does have implications for thinking about the concept of *dwelling* and what that may look like or entail in terms of ecology, environmental science, environmental ethics, and other related areas.

The notion that the earth "conceals" is not just a philosophical idea, but is also an idea at work in ecology, as well. In his well-known book, *A Sand County Almanac*, Aldo Leopold discusses the prevalence of scientism among the masses, and he explains what may be understood as something indicative of an epochal shift that is occurring in terms of how we now understand the unfolding of history. Leopold writes:

> The ordinary citizen today assumes that science knows what makes the community clock tick; the scientist is equally sure that he does not. He knows that the biotic mechanism is so complex that its workings may never be fully understood. That man is, in fact, only a member of a biotic team is shown by an ecological interpretation of history. Many historical events, hitherto explained solely in terms of human enterprise, were actually biotic interactions between people and land. The characteristics of the land determined the facts quite as potently as the characteristics of the men who lived on it.[33]

In the above passage, Leopold makes a few different and relevant points. He says that an average citizen may mistakenly hold as true the scientistic claims that, (a) science has a monopoly on truth, and (b) science has or can have all the answers regarding the earth. This scientistic error in thinking on the part of many is related to the hubristic idea discussed earlier in terms of truth being understood as something finite and wholly attainable. Leopold also points out that the scientists themselves know their limitations. It is not uncommon to hear those in the various fields of science say that in answering one question, ten other new questions arise. One of the basic precepts of "Understanding Science" according to UC Berkeley is "Science is continually refining and expanding our knowledge of the universe, and as it does, it leads to new questions for future investigation. Science will never be 'finished.'"[34]

In the above quotation, Leopold also points out that the way in which we formerly understood and reported history was to see history as simply the unfolding and result of the actions of humankind. This *anthropocentric* understanding of things has now been replaced with a more informed understanding of the unfolding of history as a dynamic interaction "between people and land," or as Heidegger might phrase it, between earth and mortals. For, as has been stated, the "earth" is not merely a set of resources to be optimized, despite numerous attempts by mortals to make it so. The earth holds within it possibilities that finite human beings simply cannot know or predict with any kind of certitude or accuracy.

To think through this idea more deeply, consider what Leopold says in the following excerpt, continued from the above quotation. Relevant is the application of the idea that earth, as concealed, is to be distinguished from world, as unconcealed:

> Consider, for example, the settlement of the Mississippi valley … it is time now to ponder the fact that the cane-lands, when subjected to the particular mixture of forces represented by the cow, plow, fire, and axe of the pioneer, became bluegrass. What if the plant succession inherent in this dark and bloody ground had, under the impact of these forces, given us some worthless sedge, shrub, or weed. … We are commonly told what the human actors in this drama tried to do, but we are seldom told that their success, or the lack of it, hung in large degree on the reaction of particular soils to the impact of the particular forces exerted by their occupancy.[35]

What happened in the Mississippi valley may be understood as an example of the idea that some part of that which was concealed and hidden within the earth emerged into unconcealment, resulting in a new world, and this occurred through the dynamic interaction of mortals and earth. Indeed, the idea that land, or "earth," is not merely a thing, but is itself a being, a part of Being, and thus interacts with other beings, is an idea quite common to much of the literature in ecological and environmental philosophy today.

Similarly, we are also coming to understand that many of the diseases that afflict human beings are also the result of actions taken by human beings that degrade, damage, devastate, or otherwise violently or carelessly affect the earth, and they are most properly understood to be the result of the interaction of the two. Through the actions of deforestation, urban development, animal agriculture, and a host of other human activities, humans create deadly situations by creating the very conditions for the flourishing of disease. An article in the *New York Times* on the ecology of disease says, "AIDS, Ebola, West Nile, SARS, Lyme disease and hundreds more diseases that have occurred over the last several decades—don't just happen. They are a result of things people do to nature."[36] The study is published in the Proceedings of the National Academy of Sciences (PNAS). In a well-researched article published in *The Telegraph* in November 2009, Geoffrey Lean reported:

> Do felling forests, slaughtering wildlife, cramming animals into inhuman factory farms, and the general trashing of the natural world make you sick? There's growing evidence that environmental degradation increases the spread of killer diseases and causes new ones. Indeed, a report concludes that it poses "the greatest public health challenge of the 21st century" ... Published by two blue-chip, Washington-based bodies—the Worldwatch Institute and the United Nations Foundation—and written by Dr. Samuel Myers, a practising physician who teaches at Harvard, the report concludes that, "more often than not, disruption of historical land cover," such as through deforestation and intensive agriculture, "seems to boost the risk of disease exposure" ... [Consider] schistosomiasis, infecting some 200 million people worldwide, second only to malaria in its devastating effect. An upsurge of the disease in Cameroon was traced to deforestation, because a snail harbouring the parasitic worm that causes it flourished in the cleared habitats. Another big outbreak was spurred on by overfishing in Lake Malawi, depleting the fish that ate a similar snail. And sleeping sickness spread in parts of West Africa because coffee and cacao plantations, which replaced natural forest, provided ideal habitats for the tsetse fly.[37]

Additionally, climate change is also having some repercussions no one could have predicted. One result is the thawing of ice that has been frozen for centuries or millennia. In March 2014, the BBC World Service Science and Environment reporting division wrote, "An ancient virus has "come back to life" after lying dormant for at least 30,000 years. ... It was found frozen in a deep layer of the Siberian permafrost, but after it thawed it became infectious once again. The French scientists say the contagion poses no danger to humans or animals, but other viruses could be unleashed as the ground becomes exposed."[38]

I do think of these phenomena as demonstrating the way in which the earth, as concealed, is in dynamic interaction with human beings, and how it gives rise to new worlds unconcealed, for good or ill as humans would evaluate it, when the four of the *Fourfold* interact.

I suggest that Heidegger's urging us to the attainment of full *dwelling* can be understood as the means to "the cure" for such diseases, or at least the elimination of conditions that give rise to them. A proper orientation toward the earth entails, at the very least, an attitude of respect and reverence toward nature, and an appreciation and understanding of nature, of our worlds, and of the earth, as being made up of both unconcealed and concealed truth. Our desire as human beings should be to stand in appropriate relation thereto so as to experience the emergence of significance. Awe and wonder, as well as harmony, are no doubt inherent within existence when mortals fully *dwell*.

The attitude toward the earth, that on one hand acknowledges our worlds and their limited resources and yet on the other hand preserves its status as an endless source of meaning, is one readily embraced by certain ecologists and environmental thinkers, including proponents of deep ecology, such as Arne Naess and Warwick Fox. These deep ecologists understand that such an attitude is an intuition, that is, a view that itself cannot be proven, although it must be understood to arise from and be grounded in phenomenological experience.

In other words, such deep ecologists share an understanding of the value of nature that results not from a process of reasoning alone, but from direct experience of nature and an inescapable sense of appreciation for and connectedness with it. As Warwick Fox puts it, "The experience of commonality with another entity does imply a sense of similarity with that entity, even if this similarity is not of any obvious physical, emotional or mental kind; it may involve 'nothing more' than the deep-seated realization that all entities are aspects of a single unfolding reality."[39] Such a realization is akin to what I believe Heidegger to have in mind when he emphasizes that mortals fully *dwell* only when they safeguard the *Fourfold* in its unfolding, when they engage in *meditative thinking* so as to correctly direct their *calculative thinking* toward the kind of building that is appropriate to full *dwelling*.

Unfortunately, various models of "stewardship" in ecology and environmental philosophy presuppose certain of these ideas to various degrees but more often than not are themselves built upon an *anthropocentric* metaphysics. And while the view of deep ecologists, like Naess and Fox, is one that preserves the earth as valuable in itself and safeguards it, as we will see in Chapter 6, such a view has its own problems. However, the deep ecology view does acknowledge the earth as finite in the relevant ways but also sees it as an infinite source of meaning beyond the full comprehension of human beings, and thus it denies long-standing *anthropocentric* pretensions. It recognizes the interrelatedness and interdependence of all beings and the limits of our human finitude.

The crucial and timely relevance of such thinking, thinking which arises out of a phenomenological experience of the world and in turn gives way to the kinds of intuitions required if humankind is to continue and to flourish as part of the *Fourfold*, is emphasized by many thinkers from diverse disciplines. Historian Theodore Roszak wrote in the 1970s:

> Ecology stands at a critical cross-roads. Is it, too, to become another anthropocentric technique of efficient manipulation, a matter of enlightened self-interest and expert, long-range resource budgeting? Or will it meet the nature mystics

on their own terms and so recognize that we are to embrace nature as if indeed it were a beloved person in whom, as in ourselves, something sacred dwells?[40]

I believe that the question posed by Roszak asks if we will adopt the kind of view that Heidegger sets forth in his notion of *saving the earth* by means of full *dwelling*. Will we forego the common *anthropocentric* views that have long been standard by embracing that which is held dear by the "nature mystics" and return to an understanding of the essential oneness of the four of the *Fourfold*? Again, the *elucidations* upon Heidegger's thinking offered by Capobianco reveal these connections. He writes:

> There is, perhaps, an element of "Nature mysticism" (or *physis*-mysticism) in these reflections, and understandably it is not for all philosophical tastes. Nonetheless, this is precisely the kind of resonant reflection that is distinctively Heideggerian, and some patience is needed in order to appreciate what he is seeing in his saying. ... It is apparent that he is offering a richly poetical philosophical account of all-that-is. We discern in what he is saying his fundamental understanding of Being-*physis*-Nature as the one-and-only, temporal-spatial unfolding of all beings and things. All things (*panta*) emerge out of, issue forth from, the One (*hen*), but, assuredly, the One (Being) is no "being," no "principle," apart from the Many. ... All beings, in their own particular way, have this relation-as-belonging to the primordial *Logos* that lays them out and gathers them. In this way, according to his vision, all beings, including human beings in a special manner, move along the Way as "reaching out and bringing back" within the Open/Way (Being-*physis*-*Logos*). ... Alas, I suppose that one either "sees" this along with Heidegger, or one does not.[41]

Indeed, like Capobianco, I am convinced that one either has the eyes to see these things or one does not. One either hears or one does not. One is able to learn or one is not.

I will now return to looking at more of what Heidegger says in "Building Dwelling Thinking." There he says that in *dwelling* mortals "receive the sky as sky. They leave to the sun and the moon their journey."[42] Heidegger explains that in *dwelling* the mortals open themselves to the sky and its movements as the integral part of the *Fourfold* that it is, accepting what it is in itself and accepting it as part of the One of which they themselves are also part. They do not seek to exert control over it, but, as Heidegger tells us, "They leave to the seasons their blessing and their inclemency."[43]

In *dwelling*, mortals attune to the flow of the natural world and adapt themselves to it. In receiving the sky as sky, mortals bring themselves into harmony with the natural world. They attune themselves to the rhythms of existence, the ebb and flow of natural phenomena. By means of an attitude of openness, an attitude that allows for the reception of reality, mortals are able to recognize the patterns and movements in the sky. Such an understanding allows for the harmonious existence of the mortals within and as part of the *Fourfold*. Possession of the proper attitude toward earth and sky, an attitude that we will later come to see is comprised of what Heidegger calls *knowledge* and *tenderness* (*Wissenschaft und Zärtlichkeit*), is what ushers in the possibility for a greater understanding of existence and the attainment of full *dwelling*.

Perhaps it is in the mortals' relation to the divinities that we are presented with what may be thought to be the most esoteric and difficult to comprehend of the relations existent within the *Fourfold*. While there are quite possibly numerous ways to interpret Heidegger on this point overall, I believe that there are some specifics that are rather apparent and easily understood when considered from the appropriate points of view. About the relation, Heidegger tells us:

> Mortals dwell in that they await the divinities as divinities. In hope they hold up to the divinities what is unhoped for. They wait for intimations of their coming and do not mistake the signs of their absence. They do not make their gods for themselves and do not worship idols. In the very depth of misfortune they wait for the weal that has been withdrawn.[44]

Most fundamental to the relationship between mortals and divinities is the way in which mortals are essentially in what may be called subjection to the divinities. It is important here to not reinscribe the modern metaphysics of subject and object. Care must also be taken so as not to construe this "subjection" as some kind of enslavement or demeaning degradation. Rather, it should be conceived metaphorically. Mortals, by their very nature and essence, are subjects of the divinities and subject to their divine expression. This way of capturing the nature of reality is indeed metaphorical and makes clear the central importance of myth, but perhaps more importantly, it is a way to capture and express the phenomenological experience of the embodied being of mortals.

When one reflects upon any of a number of unreflective experiences that make up the repertoire of human experiences, experiences that seem to emerge independent of choice or will, experiences that seem to seize the individual, like a possessing spirit, experiences such as rage, passion, joy, and so on, this way of conceptualizing the experience is apropos. For example, one does not reflect and thus choose to experience joy. When one experiences joy, one experiences joy as a being in subjection to joy. When one experiences terror, one experiences terror as a being in subjection to terror.

If we bear in mind Heidegger's assertion that the *Fourfold* is itself one, we may contemplate the interdependence of and essential link between each of the four of the *Fourfold*. The nature of this interdependence between mortals and divinities is such that it can be understood as on a par with the operation of nature (*physis*) itself. In other words, we should understand that there are natural "laws" that determine the ways in which the interdependence between mortals and divinities plays out. To say that, however, is not to imply that mortals are able to necessarily discover and catalogue all such "laws." For any such "laws," being another part of truth or *a-letheia*, would also be subject to the interplay of the concealed and unconcealed. What's more, if we do indeed grasp this interrelatedness and understand things in this way, we must forego any conceptualization of the divinities as *supernatural* or *otherworldly*. The divinities, as one of the four of the *Fourfold*, are not outside, above, or beyond the other three of the four. The *Fourfold* is itself one, as Heidegger tells us, and yet it is four: earth, sky, divinities, and mortals. To conceptualize the divinities and their operations as supernatural or otherworldly is to fundamentally fail to understand Heidegger.

The idea that mortals are to "await the divinities as divinities" is the way in which mortals are in subjection to divinity. Here, again, the mortal should not be understood as a *subject* in relation to an *object* that is divinity which would imply a relationship between them that sets up the mortal as a consciousness and the divinity as a thing to be represented therein. Nor is the conception rendered correct by positing that the divinity is a *subject* that relates to a mortal as an *object* and for the same reasons. To say that mortals are in subjection to the divinities is best understood by thinking more deeply about how best to understand the term *subject* and the way it is defined. In looking at the very meaning of the word, I see that *to be subject* to something is simply *to be open or exposed to the force* of that something. Thus, for Heidegger, mortals are open or exposed to the force of divinity. Mortals, in recognizing this as true, are able to wait for the *intimations* of the divinities, as Heidegger tells us. In other words, mortals wait for those manifestations by means of which the divinities make themselves known. Such manifestations will be *intimate* in that *intimacy* is the nature of the relationship that holds between mortals and divinities. In reflecting upon the word *intimate*, its forms, and its etymology, I can perhaps make clearer my meaning.

The infinitive verb *to intimate* means *an act by which someone or something makes itself known*. One may *intimate* in hopes of being intimate or achieving intimacy. The Latin verb *intimare* means *to make known*, *to impress upon*, and the adjective *intimus* means *the most inward* or *most within*. For Heidegger, in the German, the word is *Innigkeit*. For an *intimate* relationship to hold between two beings or things there must exist on the part of both beings both the active and the receptive or passive element.

The active aspect of this relation may be understood as being willing and able to truly *intimate* that which is most inward to the other. In the case of conscious beings, one must be *intimus* in one's own thoughts, words, and actions and thus truly reveal that which indeed is *the most inward* and offer it to the other, thereby having a being toward the other that is *intimare*.

The receptive or passive aspect may be understood as assuming an orientation toward the other such that one is able *to be impressed upon* by the other's being, a being that is itself *intimare.* One must be open to the knowing of the *intimus* of the other; that is, one must be open to receiving that which is *the most inward* or *most within* the other. Thus and only is the reciprocal relation that is intimacy achieved. Much more will be said about what it looks like for this to play out between a mortal and a divinity in the next chapter. And, as we will see, those characteristics that Heidegger terms *knowledge* and *tenderness* (*Wissenschaft und Zärtlichkeit*) are crucial for the occurrence of *intimacy*, and for Heidegger they are given their fullest expression in the person of a poet and his unique relation to divinity.[45]

Heidegger also reminds us in the above-quoted passage that the divinities are in no way *made* by the mortals. Rather, the divinities are best understood as being given as what they are, and, as we will see, some of the clearest articulations by means of which the divinities may be understood are found in myth. Mortals do not *make* the divinities. Nor do mortals worship idols, Heidegger tells us. The divinities are rightly said to not be idols in that they are not *mere appearances* or *representations*, either mental or material, manufactured from the imaginations of mortals.

As will hopefully become clearer as I proceed, it is the divinities who bring to mortals an abundance of rich experiences by means of their existence and interrelatedness, and we can conceptualize these divinities as transcendental realities, elements, or principles. Thus, when Heidegger says, "In hope they hold up to the divinities what is unhoped for," he puts us in remembrance of the wisdom of Heraclitus.[46]

Heraclitus wrote, "Unless he hopes for the unhoped-for, he will not find it, since it is not to be hunted out and is impassable."[47] The implicit truth in this statement is, once again, the assertion of that fundamental idea of inexhaustible meaning, of the always partially concealed nature of reality, of the importance and meaning of the finitude of mortals and their relation to the infinite form of truth, that is, to Being itself. Thus, this fundamental recognition of the finitude of mortal existence and the acknowledgment of the existence of something more, something which is itself the source of meaning, coupled with an orientation of openness toward it, is what allows for the very possibility of more than what Heidegger calls "the merely actual." The very notion of the *unhoped-for* points us toward that which is concealed yet is very much in the realm of possibility.

What is most relevant, it would seem, in what is said by both Heidegger and Heraclitus is that that which is in the realm of the possible necessarily exceeds all our expectations, for the realm of the possible is infinite and we, as mortals, are finite. Thus, not even in our most vivid imaginings can we ever conjure up an expectation fit to match our anticipation. This is precisely how it is that we can and should, as mortals, hope for the unhoped-for. We could say that it is against the loss of the *unhoped-for* that Heidegger makes his plea for us to understand the danger of *average everydayness* in *Being and Time*, when he writes:

> This leveling off of Dasein's possibilities to what is proximally at its everyday disposal also results in a dimming down of the possible as such. The average everydayness of concern becomes blind to its possibilities, and tranquilizes itself with that which is merely "actual." This tranquilizing does not rule out a high degree of diligence in one's own concern, but arouses it. In this case no positive new possibilities are willed, but that which is at one's disposal becomes "tactically" altered in such a way that there is a semblance of something happening.[48]

What Heidegger describes above is not only the loss of hope for the unhoped-for but a fundamental foregoing of *dwelling* that occurs in such a way that one is unaware that it is happening since one is operating under an active illusion of sorts. One becomes highly involved in the day-to-day realities of existence, so much so that nothing beyond those mundane cares and concerns is even possible, yet one feels very much like one is working hard, moving forward, aspiring, living.

Regarding *dwelling*, Heidegger tells us that mortals "initiate their own essential being—their being capable of death as death—into the use and practice of this capacity, so that there may be a good death."[49] Heidegger explains that we are not to understand him here as saying that death is some "empty nothing" that is for all mortals the goal. Nor are we to understand Heidegger as casting some sort of nihilistic wet blanket over the whole of *dwelling* itself. Rather, in recognizing *death* as the actuality and capacity that he understands it to be (an integral part of *physis*) and thus instituting its "use and practice," death is realized as an integral part of those inevitable transformations that occur in mortal existence for mortals in their being as mortals and as one of the four of the *Fourfold.*

As Heidegger first made clear in *Being and Time*, being-toward-death is constitutive for Dasein. However, not all Dasein are authentic in their being-toward-death. In terms of Heidegger's above assertion that mortals can put death into use and practice, he alludes to authentic being-toward-death. Perhaps a simple way of capturing his thought is to say: *Life is Death.* In other words, life itself depends upon and is made up of death, both literally and figuratively.

This idea is most easily observed in the cycles of nature: day into night into day, spring into summer into autumn into winter into spring again, the process of growth, fruiting and flowering, withering, dying, and decaying that is the essence of all living things. Life itself in all its parts is made up of continuous changes, concealing and unconcealing, and all of these changes may be understood as "deaths" in that something that was no longer is, something that is will inevitably cease to be.

Death, as a regularly occurring event, may well be thought to be the most fundamental manifestation that is the play of the concealed and unconcealed. When one understands death for what it is, accepts it, and accustoms herself to it as the necessary and recurring event of existence, as the event that not only brings to an end a path, a plan, a project, a phase, a relationship, or a life, but also as the event that by its very nature makes possible the birth of something else, then one is truly on her way to "a good death." One has achieved an authentic being-toward-death and can *dwell* fully.

As most are well aware, death, in Heidegger's thought, is central. Understanding the centrality and importance of this concept is necessary in order to grasp the concept of *dwelling* in its fullness. One need not read more than a few choice lines of Heidegger here and there to know that he has something much broader and deeper in mind when he uses the term "death" than the simple expiration of a life.

While elaborating on the oneness of the four of the *Fourfold*, he writes: "The mortals are the human beings. They are called mortals because they can die. To die means to be capable of death as death. Only man dies, and indeed continually, as long as he remains on earth, under the sky, before the divinities.[50] For Heidegger, mortals, as Dasein, are in a unique position (this becomes more relevant and discussed in a different way in the final chapters); they are the only beings for whom existence itself is an issue. This idea was discussed earlier regarding the way in which human beings are *homologein* in relation to the primordial *Logos*. Mortals have as central to their existence care, finitude, and an awareness of the way in which they are thrown into a temporal-spatial existence to travel through potentiality toward an inevitable end.

While all living things perish, mortals alone have a capacity to put into practice their ability to honestly and openly confront death in all its manifestations and occurrences and in doing so make themselves able to attain "a good death." And as Heidegger stressed when he said that doing this was in no way to "make death, as empty Nothing, the goal," putting this capacity into use and practice ensures fuller and richer *dwelling* in that the practice itself is a necessary means to it.

Again, Heidegger tells us that the four of the *Fourfold* is one. In order to facilitate our understanding of the idea of the four of the *Fourfold* as parts of that which is primally one, Heidegger's explanation of the Greek term *peras* is both helpful and important. About the Greek *peras*, or *boundary*, he says, "A boundary is not that at which something stops, but, as the Greeks recognized, the boundary is that from which something *begins its essential unfolding*."[51] If we apply this idea to the concept of the *Fourfold*, we can see that Being, understood as the primal one that is the *Fourfold*, could not *begin its essential unfolding* as the *Fourfold* without the *boundaries* that mark the four of the *Fourfold* into the four that they are.

I wish to emphasize the relevance of Heidegger's stress upon the importance of the Greek *peras*. To understand more fully, I want to look at some related Greek terms. The various words that share in the root, be they verb, noun, adjective, adverb, or participle, all involve the notion of that which is finite, limited, and with a distinct end or a finish.[52] The Greek participle *peperasmenos*, for example, is a word that appears often in Aristotle, such as in his *Physics*.

In a discussion of Aristotle's use of the word in his critique of Zeno, Cherubin and Mannucci write, "Similarly, *peperasmenon* is often translated as 'finite,' but it may equally well mean 'limited', 'definite', or 'determinate'."[53] This is in critically important contrast to *apeiron*, a word very important in ancient Greek thought and appearing often, as well. The meaning of *apeiron* is that which is indeterminate, indefinite, and without limit. Keeping these ideas in mind, it is easy to conceive of *peras* as that which renders something determinate or delineates something as such. This is in contrast to *apeiron* as that which is indeterminate. Thus, it is clear to me exactly why Heidegger would emphasize the importance of *peras* since such a boundary is indeed that which allows something to unfold and become that which it is.

Seeing that the *peras* or boundary is that which marks out each of the four, we can understand that the boundary is *not* something rightly understood as separating, dividing, cleaving, or severing into four what was one, given that that which is one, as such, is itself necessarily determinate, definite, and finite. In other words, there must already be more than one in order to have one. Rather, the *peras* or boundary should be understood as that which allows form to be given to what would otherwise be limitless and thus without form, it is that which allows Being to unfold in its essence as beings, as the *Fourfold*. This idea takes on even greater significance when we look at it in the light of a few other concepts that are central to ancient Greek thought and Heidegger's thinking, as well.

BOUNDARIES, CHAOS, AND INTIMACY

Endeavoring to understand the relationship between a few related and important concepts in ancient Greek thinking and the place of *peras* among them, there is an important discussion of the concept of *Chaos* in an essay by Drew Hyland I want to consider. Hyland undertakes to show that the real impact of Hesiod's claim that "first of all came Chaos" is experienced only when the original Greek conceptualization of the word Chaos is understood. He argues that while our modern English understanding of Chaos as a "primal soup" or "an unintelligible, undifferentiated, unarticulable condition" is one that fits nicely with accounts from other cultures and even seems to prefigure the ideas of Anaximader, such an understanding of the word is not really in keeping with its original Greek meaning. Making use of the research and the work of others, Hyland explains that the word Chaos means something like *a gap, a yawn, a separation.*[54]

Hyland proceeds to make the case that the questions and assumptions that seem to naturally follow from such an idea, however reasonable they and the presuppositions they indicate seem to be, are nonetheless in error. Hyland says: "Almost from the time the original meaning of Hesiod's *chaos* as gap or separation was taken seriously, the question was asked, and answers ventured, as to what the entities were that *were separated* by Chaos."[55] Hyland goes on to work his way through the different proposals that have been made regarding the idea of preexisting entities separated by Chaos and to show how each one, however long-held and dearly loved it may be, simply does not fit with Hesiod's actual words.

In attempting to diagnose the widespread error, Hyland cites the work of three different scholars of ancient Greek philosophy: Miller, Bussanich, and Cornford. Hyland writes, "[T]hese views assume that if Chaos is a gap or a 'between', it must be a gap in something that *precedes* (or is at least co-primordial with) Chaos, and that 'something', Miller suggests, 'implies a pre-existing undifferentiated field'."[56] It is this very notion, the notion that a gap or separation necessarily presupposes the existence of an undifferentiated field, that Hyland believes is an error. On this point I agree, for Hesiod asserts that "first of all came Chaos." Hyland writes:

> Difficult as it may be to understand, however counter to our intuitions that if Chaos is a gap or separation it must somehow *separate something*, I suggest we should take Hesiod's Greek in the passage under consideration to be indicating this truly remarkable thought: that Chaos, gap, separation, *comes before, is prior to, any pairings that it might subsequently separate. Difference precedes and is the condition for sameness or identity. The "between" somehow precedes the binaries that it distinguishes.*[57]

Before I follow up on this notion of a "between which precedes the binaries it distinguishes," I wish to first follow up on Hyland's suggestion regarding the view he attributes to Bussanich via a quote from Bussanich that Hyland employs in his essay. In Hyland's reading of Bussanich's essay, I think Hyland slightly misunderstands the view developed by Bussanich.

From page 216 of Bussanich's essay, "A Theoretical Interpretation of Hesiod's Chaos," Hyland quotes, "Relying on a literal reading of the text and on later conceptions of Chaos, many scholars have identified Chaos with the gap between heaven and earth. But it is unlikely that a gap between two cosmic masses could exist before the masses themselves." While this quote serves Hyland's purpose, I think it does misrepresent the overall view articulated by Bussanich since Bussanich does not ultimately hold that Chaos is to be understood in this way.

I would argue that Bussanich articulates his main point when he writes in his essay, "The name Chaos symbolizes the initial stage of pre-cosmic reality—a yawning chasm or abyss. Since it stands at the beginning of things, it cannot be envisioned according to the laws of perspective or dimension."[58] Given the way Bussanich fleshes out his view in his essay, I believe Bussanich's understanding of Chaos is a bit more nuanced than what Hyland allows. While it is possible that they are both ultimately saying the same thing, I believe that in considering these subtleties our understanding of Heidegger is enriched.

While Hyland seeks to put forth an understanding of Chaos not as a thing itself or as a something that presupposes the existence of any *things* but rather as something like the very concept of *difference* that would itself in turn allow for the existence of things, Bussanich seems to develop an understanding of Chaos that makes it neither a thing (or a something that presupposes any other things) nor merely Hyland's concept of *difference*.

Bussanich writes, "Since its function is cosmogonic, Chaos must be defined as undimensional or principial space, an articulated nothing: it is the barest indication that there is a qualitative something, from and in which cosmic differentiation occurs."[59] This is where I see what may well be the most important difference in the respective views of Hyland and Bussanich and where Bussanich may be understood to think just a bit further than does Hyland.

For Hyland, Chaos is difference. For Bussanich, Chaos is the opening up that allows for difference. No doubt, certain ideas that are so centrally important to modern philosophy, such as that of *substance*, serve to render even more difficult attempts at understanding Chaos in this context. While Hyland's analysis of Chaos is insightful and reveals important understanding of the concept, Bussanich offers an understanding that is better in keeping with certain ideas being developed overall in this project when he writes, "Speculation on the first things is the response of the imagination when finite experience confronts a transfinite reality, in this case the origin of the cosmos."[60] That which Bussanich refers to as a *transfinite reality*, I believe, is intimately tied to that which comprises the very heart of this project and to the very notion of truth as *a-letheia* and its essence of concealed and unconcealed. Furthermore, I contend that it is the response of the imagination when finite experience confronts a transfinite reality that gives rise to the articulation of myth itself, for many of our phenomenological experiences in existence as human beings point us to the concealed and unconcealed, and in response, we are given naturally to the kind of imaginative speculation that gives birth to myth.

In thinking about the understanding of Chaos attributed to Hesiod and explored by Hyland, it is understandable how some might see it as unreasonable to propose that *difference* itself precede everything else. However, such thinking, when scrutinized, is the result of metaphysical presuppositions that themselves should call out for further thinking. Someone may thoughtfully ask, "How can a concept, the concept of *difference*, coming into existence, be the necessary condition for the coming to existence of beings/things? Wouldn't there need to be a being from which beings come?"

The ultimate point, however, is missed in such questioning in that it matters not whether there was a being or whether there was nothing since being*s* can only emerge once there is the possibility for *difference* itself. To my mind, this is undoubtedly intertwined with the Greek concept of *peras* explained earlier in that the existence of distinction and difference themselves is the necessary condition for plurality. Thus, I believe we can accept that Chaos came first and simultaneously recognize that it does not matter whether there was being or whether there was nothing before that time in that either way it was a homogeneity about which such a designation as *one* or *sameness* would not even apply since the very concepts of *one* or *sameness* presuppose plurality and difference, if not as prior, then at least as co-temporal/co-primordial. You must have at least two to say that they are the same, and in order to have two, there must exist *difference*.

Moreover, the designation "one" cannot exist except in contrast to "not one," and the "not one" cannot be "nothing" in that that does not present a contrast to "one" since both are homogenous. Thus, there must be at least "two" in order to recognize "one." And this is where, I believe, Hyland's thinking stopped a bit too soon in that he only reasoned up to the necessity of *difference*, which, while an important discovery, calls out for further thinking.

This very interesting concept of *difference* as the condition under which differentiated being may manifest ties with the concept set forth at the outset as central to so much of Heidegger's thinking, the concept of *a-letheia*, or the concealed and unconcealed. The concept of the concealed may be understood as analogous to the concept of difference in that there is a tendency of reason, it would seem, to draw an inference from the assertion of either of these concepts that then, as an assumption, is taken as a presupposition, albeit in error. That is to say, just as one might take the positing of *Chaos as first* as indicating the preexistence of an undifferentiated field or a holistic entity or undifferentiated substance that subsequently is made to possess difference by means of the establishing of the existence of its parts, one may likewise take that which is *concealment* as indicating the preexistence of *unconcealment* as some kind of holistic entity or undifferentiated substance that is made to possess concealment by means of the establishing of the existence of its parts. Such persons then might feel compelled to believe and to pursue, albeit in vain, the acquisition of the truth in total unconcealment, much as they would the establishment of a so-called undifferentiated field. They may then proceed to build great edifices of knowledge on such a false belief.

Concern about such errors is articulated by Trish Glazebrook in her essay, "Gynocentric Eco-Logics," to be examined in the second section of Chapter 6. In her essay, Glazebrook offers a critique of "phallic logic" as a system and way of thinking in that there is within it a presupposition of truth as a totality, a finite something capable of being fully penetrated, dominated, and subsumed by that given system of logic and thus is rejected all possibility of the existence of something that exceeds its totalizing apprehension.

In returning now to that understanding of Chaos which Hyland referred to earlier as "a between that precedes the binaries which it distinguishes," I want to consider also the concept of *peras*, along with Warnek's take on *Innigkeit*. In doing so, I see connections previously concealed begin to move into unconcealment. Hyland's conceptualization of Chaos as "a between that precedes the binaries which it distinguishes" is an illuminating idea and for a number of reasons. It is very much amenable conceptually to Heidegger's understanding of *peras* as "that from which something begins its essential unfolding," and it relates to Heidegger's concept of *Innigkeit*. Holding in mind the idea of *Chaos as first*, it is interesting to look at something else said by Warnek in his essay, "Translating *Innigkeit*." Warnek writes:

> The task of translating *Innigkeit* thus demands the translation of the movement of translation itself, the thought of the *difference* that joins all things together … the translation of *Innigkeit* as the belonging together of the strange already says the difficulty of thinking and saying this word. … The strange, therefore, has to be thought neither as what belongs nor simply as what does not belong; the strange is rather strange precisely in the belonging together that would preserve the strange, the strange as strange. … *Innigkeit*, according to Heidegger, does not simply name all things, but names the granting of things in their discrete difference and oppositional relation, the difference as it holds all things together.[61]

"The difference as it holds all things together," it seems to me, is closely related to the concept of Chaos understood as *a gap or separation* that itself came first. Thus, it appears that Hesiod's conception of *Chaos*, as spelled out above by Hyland and understood as *difference*, is that which allows for the coming into being and the holding together of all things by means of the establishing of *peras*. This, I contend, is central to understanding *Innigkeit* as *the belonging together of the strange* in that all things would take their being from the coming into existence of this primordial *difference* and thus it would be correct to say, as Heidegger does in quoting Hölderlin, "All is intimate."[62]

Chaos, understood as the gap, the yawn, or the separation, in its coming-into-being, is like the coming-into-being of emptiness or an empty space so that some *thing* or *things* can come into being. And thus it is not that Hyland is wrong, but he stops thinking too soon when he sees Chaos' coming-into-being as merely the coming-into-being of difference itself; in fact, Chaos' coming-into-being is actually the condition for the emergence of both difference and sameness. Thus, Hyland was correct to say, "The between somehow precedes the binaries which it distinguishes." He simply did not recognize that the binaries were difference and sameness and that the between, as Chaos, was what allowed them both to emerge. There is something written by Heidegger in his *Elucidations of Hölderlin's Poetry* that further supports and clarifies my point:

> Nevertheless, Χαος signifies first of all the yawning, gaping chasm, the open that first opens itself, wherein everything is engulfed. The chasm affords no support for anything distinct and grounded. And therefore, for all experience, which only knows what is mediated, chaos seems to be without differentiation and thus mere confusion. The "chaotic" in this sense, however, is only the inessential aspect of what "chaos" means. Thought in terms of nature Φυσις chaos remains that gaping out of which the open opens itself. Nothing that is real precedes this opening, but rather always only enters into it.[63]

And so it seems clear from what Heidegger says here that Chaos is, as I said earlier, something like the emptiness which is necessary for anything to enter therein and to thus subsequently be understood by means of concepts such as difference and sameness. This *gaping*, this "open that first opens itself," would appear to be what Bussanich had in mind when he wrote, "Chaos must be defined as undimensional or principial space, an articulated nothing: it is the barest indication that there is a qualitative something, from and in which cosmic differentiation occurs."[64]

ALL TOGETHER

I can now attempt to weave together in a more simple yet meaningful way the different and important concepts I have been examining in order to establish the conceptual groundwork for the ideas regarding poetry and the gods to be explored in the next chapter. Chaos as the gap or yawn which allows for the coming into being of the "real" came first. Concepts of *sameness* and *difference* emerge co-primordially, and it is only after Chaos that beings or things, about which designations of "same" and "different" apply, come into being. All that does come into being in the gap that is Chaos is enabled to do so by the *peras* or boundary that makes possible such differentiation and allows things to begin their essential unfolding. Their emergence into and out of existence, from Being, from *Logos*, is termed *physis*, and the reality of *physis* dictates what constitutes the essence of *a-letheia*, that is, truth understood as the perpetual dynamic of concealing and unconcealing. And thus it is true to say, as Heidegger does, that "All is intimate" despite our mortal inability to see all at once the interconnectivity of all things. Yet, attaining to full *dwelling* does presuppose the ability to recognize these things, to understand, honor, and acknowledge them. And while we mortals cannot do it in the way that the Greeks did, given our changed structure of consciousness, we can comprehend the meaning of what it is to *dwell* within the *Fourfold*, understanding *a-letheia* and *lethe* as pervading the to-be-thought as its essence, and live accordingly.

I turn now to something else from Heidegger's "Building Dwelling Thinking." Hopefully, it can be experienced with an enhanced perspective on the matter so that more clearly seen is the intimate relationship that holds between the four of the *Fourfold* that is itself one. In Heidegger's description of the little farmhouse in the Black Forest, all the important concepts I have been exploring are at play as manifest in the *dwelling* of mortals, upon the earth, beneath the sky, and in communion with the divinities. Heidegger writes:

> Here the self-sufficiency of the power to let earth and sky, divinities and mortals enter *in simple oneness* into things ordered the house. It placed the farm on the wind-sheltered mountain slope, looking south, among the meadows close to the spring. It gave it the wide overhanging shingle roof whose proper slope bears up under the burden of snow, and that, reaching deep down, shields the chambers against the storms of the long winter nights. It did not forget the altar corner behind the community table; it made room in its chamber for the hallowed places of childbed and the "tree of the dead"—for that is what they call a coffin there; the *Totenbaum*—and in this way it designed for the different generations under one roof the character of their journey through time.[65]

The *dwelling* of the mortals who built and arranged their little house is indicative of their understanding of their place within the *Fourfold*. Demonstrated is their receptivity to the *Fourfold* and their willingness to work within it rather than against it. They did not build their house in such a way as to deny nature or to attempt to master it. Rather, they worked with nature in such a way that they both love and preserve it. They did not choose the site upon which to build their little house based upon their preference for a particular view, one that would perhaps have required even more insulation and fuel to combat the cold. Rather, they chose a site that would naturally afford them protection against cold winter winds, and they designed the little house itself and the pitch of its roof to accept the snow and make the best use of it. Likewise, they chose a site near to a water source rather than insisting that water be somehow directed to come closer to them by means of elaborate mechanisms that require "conquering" or working against nature.

Their very things or belongings speak to the reality of Being as the *Fourfold* and *physis.* Their things acknowledge and pay tribute to the stages and phases that make up mortals' lives, to the central role that death plays in existence, as well as the intimate relationship that holds between the four of the *Fourfold.* The presence of both childbed and tree of the dead points toward the awareness and acceptance of the deaths, the continual changes that comprise existence. By making explicit and honoring death as an integral aspect of life, life is more fully understood, and therefore more fully lived. The various rites of passage, the little deaths and changes that can and will occur, are reverenced and cared for and thus full *dwelling* is made possible.

In our own time and society, I sadly say, such an approach to living is scarcely found. While we very much like to talk about and emphasize all the new beginnings in life, rarely is acknowledgment given to the death or ending that made each new beginning possible. Whether it be the death of a childhood fantasy, such as when one learns that there is no Santa Claus or tooth fairy, or the loss of the illusion that one's own parents are perfect or the death that is the loss of one's virginity or the death that is becoming an adult by means of turning eighteen or the death that is high school graduation or the death that is the loss of that first love or the death that is the giving up of a dream or the death that is a divorce or the death that is a layoff or the death that is becoming a parent or the death that is the onset of aging, few if any of these things are ever acknowledged, honored, mourned, and incorporated into an understanding of life as the intrinsic parts of life that they each may be.

Much less do we truly honor death as that ultimate and final happening in a mortal's life. Our society's practices of draining blood, embalming, applying makeup, extracting eyes, and sewing shut lids and lips belie our professions to any real acceptance and embrace of the reality of death. To place a body that itself has been preserved in a wood and metal strongbox and then place that into a vault in the ground so as to stave off the natural, the inevitable, is upon reflection not only sad but really quite hideous and most assuredly indicative of a complete failure to embrace death as the natural part of life which it is.

In assuming their own proper place within the *Fourfold*, the dwellers of the little Black Forest farmhouse create the necessary conditions for a seamless unfolding of their essence, for the safeguarding of their abode, for the receptivity to the movements of the sky, for the manifestation of the unhoped-for and for their initiation into a good death. And as I hope to show as I proceed, mortals need not make their way alone and on their own. They are provided with encouragement, insight, and edification by means of myth, art, and poetry as they make their journey upon the earth, under the sky, and in relation to divinity.

NOTES

1. Henry Liddell and Robert Scott, *An Intermediate Greek-English Lexicon* (Oxford: Oxford University Press, 1889), 34, 470.
2. Martin Heidegger, 1944 lecture course on Heraclitus, trans. Richard Capobianco, *Heidegger's Way of Being* (Toronto: University of Toronto Press, 2014), 80.
3. Martin Heidegger, *Parmenides*, trans. Andre Schuwer and Richard Rojcewicz (Bloomingdale: Indiana University Press, 1992), 8.
4. Maurice Merleau-Ponty, *Phenomenology of Perception* (New York: Routledge, 2012), x.
5. Ibid., 152.
6. Richard Capobianco, *Heidegger's Way of Being* (Toronto: University of Toronto Press, 2014), 17.
7. Ibid., 83.
8. Heidegger, *Parmenides*, 166.
9. Capobianco, *Heidegger's Way of Being*, 40.
10. Martin Heidegger, *Being and Time* (San Francisco: Harper & Row Publishers, 1962), 37.
11. Ibid., 38.
12. Ibid.
13. Taylor Carman, *Heidegger's Analytic* (Cambridge: University of Cambridge Press, 2003), 16.
14. Capobianco, *Heidegger's Way of Being*, 4.
15. Ibid., 80.
16. Ibid., 89.
17. Ibid., 18.
18. Ibid., 85.
19. Jean-Paul Sartre, *The Anti-Semite and the Jew* (New York: Schocken, 1995), 18.
20. Iain Thomson, *Heidegger, Art, and Postmodernity* (New York: Cambridge University Press, 2011), 76.
21. Sartre, *The Anti-Semite and the Jew*, 18.
22. Ibid.
23. Martin Heidegger, *Introduction to Metaphysics*, trans. Gregory Fried and Richard Polt (New Haven & London: Yale University Press, 2000), 23.

24. Peter Warnek "Translating Innigkeit: The Belonging Together of the Strange," in *Heidegger and the Greeks*, ed. Drew Hyland and John Panteleimon Manoussakis (Bloomington & Indianapolis: Indiana University Press, 2006), 59.
25. Ibid.
26. Martin Heidegger, "Building Dwelling Thinking," in *Basic Writings*, trans and ed. David Farrell Krell (New York: HarperCollins, 1993), 351.
27. Ibid.
28. Ibid., 352.
29. Ibid.
30. Martin Heidegger, "Letter on Humanism," in *Basic Writings*, trans and ed. David Farrell Krell (New York: HarperCollins, 1993), 241.
31. Martin Heidegger, "On the Essence of Truth," in *Basic Writings*, trans. and ed. David Farrell Krell (New York: HarperCollins, 1993), 135.
32. Ibid., 137.
33. Aldo Leopold, *A Sand County Almanac* (Oxford: Oxford University Press, 1949), 240.
34. "What Is Science," University of California Berkeley, accessed August 14, 2016, http://undsci.berkeley.edu/lessons/pdfs/what_is_science.pdf
35. Aldo Leopold, *A Sand County Almanac*, 240.
36. "The Ecology of Disease," *The New York Times*, Jim Robbins, accessed July 4, 2016, http://www.nytimes.com/2012/07/15/sunday-review/the-ecology-of-disease.html?pagewanted=all&_r=0
37. "How Environmental Degradation Harms Humanity," *The Telegraph*, Geoffrey Lean, accessed July 4, 2016, http://www.telegraph.co.uk/journalists/geoffrey-lean/6617282/How-environmental-degradation-harms-humanity.html
38. "30,000 Year Old Giant Virus Comes Back to Life," *BBC News*, Rebecca Morelle, accessed July 4, 2016, http://www.bbc.com/news/science-environment-26387276
39. Warwick Fox, *Toward a Transpersonal Ecology: Developing New Foundations for Environmentalism* (New York: State University of New York Press, 1995), 231.
40. Theodore Roszak, *Where the Wasteland Ends* (New York: Bantam Books, 1973), 400.
41. Capobianco, *Heidegger's Way of Being*, 88.
42. Heidegger, "Building Dwelling Thinking," 352.
43. Ibid.
44. Ibid.
45. Martin Heidegger, *Elucidations of Holderlin's Poetry*, trans. Keith Hoeller (New York: Humanity Books, 2000), 192.
46. Heidegger, "Building Dwelling Thinking," 352.
47. Heraclitus, accessed November 2, 2014, http://home.wlu.edu/~mahonj/Ancient_Philosophers/Heraclitus.htm
48. Heidegger, *Being and Time*, 239.
49. Heidegger, "Building Dwelling Thinking," 352.
50. Ibid.
51. Ibid., 356.
52. Liddell and Scott, *An Intermediate Greek-English Lexicon*, 620–22.

53. Rose Cherubin and Mirco A. Mannucci, "A Very Short History of Ultrafinitism," in *Set Theory, Arithmetic, and Foundations of Mathematics*, ed. Juliette Kennedy and Roman Kossak (Cambridge: Cambridge University Press, 2011), 190.
54. Drew Hyland, "First of All Came Chaos," in *Heidegger and the Greeks*, ed. Drew Hyland and John Panteleimon Manoussakis (Bloomington & Indianapolis: Indiana University Press, 2006), 10.
55. Ibid.
56. Ibid., 12.
57. Ibid.,13.
58. John Bussanich, "A Theoretical Interpretation of Hesiod's Chaos," *Classical Philology* 78:3 (1983), 214.
59. Ibid.
60. Ibid.
61. Warnek, "Translating Innigkeit: The Belonging Together of the Strange," 65.
62. Heidegger, *Elucidations on Holderlin's Poetry*, 224.
63. Ibid., 85.
64. Bussanich, "A Theoretical Interpretation of Hesiod's Chaos," 214.
65. Heidegger, "Building Dwelling Thinking," 362.

Chapter Three

Poetry and the Gods

"WHAT IS THE POET'S OWN?" THE POET AS YOKED TO DIVINITY

I want to begin to think about Heidegger's ideas on poetry and the gods as I continue my endeavor to see more clearly the role these play in mortals' pursuit of *dwelling* within the *Fourfold*. Important writings from which I take my start, writings that will greatly assist in gaining insight into the topic, are found in Heidegger's *Elucidations of Hölderlin's Poetry*, as well as his lecture *Hölderlin's Hymn "The Ister."* I will approach this task by taking my cues from Heidegger in the way he himself follows Hölderlin's lead in selecting the pertinent questions that should be asked and answered. In explaining how he plans to proceed in his undertaking, Heidegger first cites lines from Hölderlin's poem "The Archipelago":

> But because the present gods are so near
> I must be as if they were far away, and dark in the clouds
> Must their name be for me, only before the morning
> Begins to glow, before life glows in its midday
> I name them quietly to myself, so that the poet may have
> His own, but whenever the heavenly light goes down
> I gladly think about what is past, and say—go on blooming![1]

Heidegger follows his recitation immediately by saying: "We are inquiring into the proper character of the poem. It can be experienced if we submit ourselves to the following questions: What is the poet's 'own'? What proper element is allotted to him? To where does the decree compel him? From where does it come? How does it compel?"[2] I will approach these issues by using the five questions that Heidegger himself poses as a guide and starting point for the endeavor.

The first question he poses and with which I will begin is, "What is the poet's 'own'?" For Heidegger, true poets, as such, bear a special relationship to the divinities and serve a special role in the operation of the *Fourfold*. Heidegger makes several statements throughout the essay "The Poem" that indicate the nature of the relationship that holds between poets and divinities, such as a poet being a poet due to his destiny, and the idea that a poet and his poetry are determined, and that the character of the poet's poem is allotted to him. While poets in general have a role to play and serve a unique purpose, Heidegger sees Hölderlin as unique and hence of particular significance because of the fact that Hölderlin's poetry not only "names the holy" but also engages in a kind of poetry that is about the poet, his poem, and *poiesis* itself. Heidegger tells us, "Hölderlin has devoted his poetic activity to the poet and his destiny, and thus to the poem's proper character, its own unique nature."[3]

While Heidegger's conception of his own role as thinker may be understood as analogous to that of the poet in certain regards, it is markedly different in others. While Heidegger sees Hölderlin as a poet who "touches upon the fundamental experience of his poetic activity," Heidegger sees himself, as a thinker, as rendering this fundamental experience accessible to any who are capable of thinking along with him. He tells us, "Until now, thinking has not yet been able to think this experience properly, or to ask about the realm in which the experience is at play."[4]

This is precisely why Heidegger chose to call what he is doing with Hölderlin's poetry *Elucidations* (*Erlauterungen)*, a word which has the sense of the reverberating sound of a bell that has been rung. Heidegger does see himself as *making clear* Hölderlin's meaning and not merely interpreting him. And this is a most relevant distinction when keeping in mind the ideas discussed in the previous chapter regarding the unconcealed and concealed nature of *a-letheia*. For if the meaning and its source, as such, are inexhaustible, possible interpretations are, as well. And Heidegger is not merely offering an interpretation of Hölderlin's poetry but rather sees himself as intimately linked to the meaning of Hölderlin's poetry *as* Hölderlin's poetry. This is accomplished by means of the connection between the two within the *Fourfold*.

As Keith Hoeller points out in his *Translator's Introduction* to Heidegger's *Elucidations of Hölderlin's Poetry*, "[I]t is Heidegger's intent to question the text in terms of the one question which, according to the later Heidegger, no science can ever ascertain: the question of Being."[5] There is undoubtedly an element of revelation that occurs with such elucidations. Hoeller quotes Heidegger as having said during a lecture given a year before the publication of the *Elucidations*, "The poetic turn toward his [Hölderlin's] poetry is possible only as a *thoughtful* confrontation with the *revelation of Being (Seyn)* which is successfully accomplished in this poetry."[6]

As I hope will become clearer as I proceed, "a thoughtful confrontation with the revelation of Being" is precisely what is possible between the philosopher and the poet, both of whom fulfill their respective functions by means of a comportment that is best characterized as receptive and appreciative, possessing as they do both *knowledge* and *tenderness* (*Wissenschaft* and *Zärtlichkeit*), and thus do they open themselves to receiving new understanding from that inexhaustible source of meaning itself which is Being.

"FROM WHERE DOES IT COME?" A CALLING FROM BEYOND TIME

Heidegger explains that the poet's *calling* or *vocation* is to serve in the capacity of poet in the operation and being of *the Fourfold*. The poet is to carry out the task of his *poiesis* and thus mediate between the divinities and the mortals. It is the shouldering of this burden that necessitates the poetic saying. "Until the words are found and blossom, it is a matter of bearing one's burden."[7] It is the poet's very *being* as a poet that compels him to his *poiesis*. Heidegger calls this compulsion a "decree."[8] We should be careful to understand that when the poet is spoken of as being compelled, two things are emphasized: (a) The poet cannot choose to not carry his burden and (b) the burden is one placed upon him and not one he merely assumes.

The decree that is issued to the poet comes to him from the "sphere of the gods" or "the arriving gods who are present to him," as well as from "the present gods who are distantly nearing."[9] Using a phrase of Hölderlin's, Heidegger tells us that essentially the poet is "compelled by the holy" to a *poiesis* that names.[10] To be inspired in this way is not then a matter of choice nor is it something that one could choose to abandon. Rather, it seems that phenomenologically, it is best understood as an impulse to *poiesis* that feels divinely decreed and may even take on an aura of madness or frenzy or a drivenness to accomplish expression even despite personal cost.

In thinking more deeply about answering the question of "from where" does the decree issue, a discussion found in *Hölderlin's Hymn "The Ister"* may assist. There Heidegger says:

> [T]his hymnal poetry is in an essential respect river poetry. The spirit of the river is the poetic spirit that experiences the journeying of being unhomely and "thinks of" the locality of becoming homely. As river, that is, as the journeying, the river can never forget the source, because in flowing, that is, in issuing from the source, it itself constantly is the source and remains the locality of its own

essence. What is to be said in this hymnal poetry is the holy, which, *beyond* the gods, determines the gods themselves and simultaneously, as the "poetic" that is to be poetized, brings the *dwelling* of historical human beings into its essence. The poet of such poetizing therefore necessarily stands between human beings and gods. He is no longer merely a human being. Yet for the same reason he is not, indeed never is, a god. From the perspective of the "between" between humans and gods, the poet is a "demigod."[11]

I want to break down this passage carefully and see what is revealed. Heidegger views the hymnal poetry of his favorite poet in a certain way. He employs the metaphor of a river in order to describe it. He explains that a river in its essence is its flowing, its "journeying," and in its journeying is an element of being "unhomely"; however, the river in its flowing nonetheless retains its essence as the source of the river.

The hymnal poetry and the poet who composes it Heidegger likens to a river. He explains that the holy is analogous to the source of the river, and just as the river retains its essence in its flowing, in its journeying, so too does the poetry that flows from the holy through the gods and into the poet. This is why, for Heidegger, the poet is between humans and gods. Just as the source of the spring that creates the river is what compels the river to flow, so is it the holy that compels the poet, and it is from there that the decree given the poet does issue. And although the poet will be compelled to name the gods, it is the holy itself which is to be poetized and is itself beyond the gods and does, in fact, determine them.

To simplify yet retain the chain that is thus far established, there is first the holy or the source (Being), then the gods, then the poet or demigod, then human beings or mortals. However, as I will soon show in the fifth section of this chapter, Heidegger does seek to make a further distinction in terms of "the gods" by means of employing the Greek terms and concepts that distinguish between *theoi* and *daimones*.

I want to note here again that the poet, as river, cannot forget its source because in its flowing it is its source. This is indeed a rich assertion. The spatiotemporal notions that are present in phrases such as *distant gods are nearing* and *the locality of its own essence* point us toward another aspect of Heidegger's thought that appears throughout a great deal of his work. By fleshing out a little the way in which such phrases should be conceived, understanding is gained. To state it simply, the meaning is most readily conceived when "the holy," "the source," and "the gods" are thought of as existent in some sense beyond space and time although the gods, and perhaps only in their aspect as *daimones* as I will show, do manifest within time. Thus, may they be spoken of as being *near* or *distant*. I will point out that I am speaking here of things that we cannot rightfully hope to unconceal in their entirety.

We are exploring ideas that are born of phenomenological experiences, which themselves point us toward things we cannot see clearly and completely but yet about which we are driven to speculate, to postulate, to imagine, and to seek understanding by whatever means available. Thus is born all myth.

In thinking about the idea of a source that is beyond time and space, I find certain ideas developed in the work of phenomenologist Erazim Kohak of great interest and import in understanding Heidegger. By looking at Kohak's ways of conceptualizing certain phenomena, I hope to shed some light on how we can piece together the ways in which being, space, time, the holy, gods, poets, and mortals can all hang together in Heidegger's thinking.

In his book *The Embers and the Stars*, Kohak undertakes to give an account of that which is the source for the phenomenological experience of what we call "the beautiful, the good, and the true." While he acknowledges and even gives an account of how it is we might come to think of being and time as the same, he sets forth a way of understanding reality that accounts for the phenomena that give rise to that error in thinking but that also gives place to those other phenomena that make up existence, as well. Thus does he undercut the notion that being and time are the same. Kohak writes:

> The categories of the "temporal" and the "eternal," though barely philosophically intelligible today, remain indispensable. The temporal perspective of a sequence of events, the preceding determining that which comes after, does create the illusion of being as wholly contained in time, merely natural in the reductive sense of that term.[12]

Kohak thinks, however, that proper reflection upon experience and the phenomena that constitute it reveal such an illusion for what it is. In speaking about what he calls "the fact of being, the flow of time, and the vision of eternity," Kohak makes the case for what he calls the "three orders of reality." He stresses that distinguishing between the three is crucial in giving an account of the diverse phenomena of experience. He writes, "Whenever in its long history, philosophy confounded them, it ended up in a dilemma, just as it when it sought to isolate one of them alone as real."[13]

To summarize simply his three orders of reality, he says there is the "order of being," the realm in which it is correct to say *it is better to be than not to be* or *it is better that there be something than that there be nothing*. This is the realm of *whatever is, is*. Existence is preferable to nonexistence in and of itself. There is also the "order of time," that realm which has come to dominate our thinking in that it is what is most familiar to us in our average everyday consciousness. It is the realm in which utility becomes relevant and in which relative value may appear. It is in the order of time that a conflict may arise between two beings such that it appears that one must be valued or chosen over the other in some way. Kohak explains that because of our phenomenological experience of existence as being in time, we tend to recognize only this one particular order of reality. There is also what he calls the "order of eternity." Kohak says

> Eternity is not an "other" realm, discontinuous with the order of time, nor an infinite prolongation of it. It really does ingress in time, reorienting the moment from its horizontal matrix of the before and after to a vertical one of good and evil.[14]

While I propose to forego the term "evil" in order to avoid unsavory and irrelevant connotations of religious ideology or any kind of Manichaean metaphysical presuppositions, the notion that eternity is an order of reality or a realm in which what we might call *the Good* exists outside of time is not an unfamiliar idea. For Kohak, it is the realm or order of eternity ingressing in time that allows for an experience of nonrelative value and meaning that is not merely instrumental.

I think that we can see this same idea at play in speaking of the ways in which earth manifests as worlds, as I discussed earlier. Such ways of describing experience are in keeping with the kinds of experiences alluded to in the previous chapter in discussing the *intuitions* of deep ecology and their experientially based notion of the sacred as immanent within nature, always available to perception, even if not being perceived, yet necessarily exceeding our human capacity for a full and totalizing comprehension.

For Kohak, the order or realm of eternity is to be understood as that realm in which exists the beautiful, the good, and the true and from which those things manifest within space-time. That which exists in the order of eternity remains concealed in itself, but is unconcealed in its manifestation within the order of time, and in its unconcealment nonetheless does it safeguard that which remains concealed.

Kohak, much like Heidegger, emphasizes the unique situation of human beings. Humans are the ones who can recognize in the flow of time the intersecting dimensions of eternity, time, and being in that they are themselves a nexus of being, time, and eternity. Kohak says, "A person is a being through whom eternity enters time."[15] I see this as the way in which mortals operate within the *Fourfold*. Mortals, as beings within time, are open to the experience of the transcendental realities here captured by the concept of eternity. Even Peter Warnek, it seems, understands human beings to some degree in this way in his discussion of *Innigkeit* when he says, "What is at issue, therefore, in the *Innigkeit* proper to human life is the way in which that life belongs ecstatically to the nature both that it is and that exceeds it."[16]

In returning to the words of Heidegger quoted from the *Ister* lecture at the beginning of this section and keeping in mind Kohak's articulation of ideas, there is an illumination. For it would appear that Heidegger's "source," his "holy," points us to the same reality as that to which Kohak's "eternity" points us. This is further supported by something Heidegger says in Lecture II of *What Is Called Thinking*:

> Its [the poetic word's] statement rests on its own truth. This truth is called beauty. Beauty is a fateful gift of the essence of truth, and here truth means the disclosure of what keeps itself concealed. The beautiful is not what pleases, but what falls within that fateful gift of truth which comes to be when that which is eternally non-apparent and therefore invisible attains its most radiantly apparent appearance.[17]

I contend that that which is signified by Kohak's term "eternity" and that which is signified by Heidegger's phrase "that which is eternally non-apparent" yet can attain "its most radiantly apparent appearance" are in essence the same and should be understood to transcend time yet appear within it.

This idea is in keeping with Heidegger's understanding of "earth" as transcendent in the sense of earth being that which informs yet exceeds our conceptualizations of it. What is of the utmost importance here, I believe, is that regardless of whether we are examining the relationship between eternity and time or the relationship between the holy and poetry or between truth and beauty or between earth and world or between Being and beings, what rules in each and every case is an intimacy, an *Innigkeit*, a *belonging together of the strange.*[18] And the fundamental truth of this *Innigkeit* is *a-letheia* and its unconcealment and concealment. In other words, a full and total comprehension of that which is signified by the terms under discussion is simply not possible by virtue of the very essence and nature of these things and their relationship to one another.

Any kind of intellectual repugnance one might feel in response to this is likely the result of a bias that has come to dominate thinking. This bias, which will be examined in much greater detail in the next chapter, makes the irrational demand that, in the name of reason, one must be able to render something in totality in order for it to be understood. As should already be apparent from my explorations of Heidegger's own thought, such a demand is in error and is a great stumbling block to real thinking.

We can somehow fathom the *Innigkeit* and what it signifies, and we can properly appreciate it for what it is, despite our inability to subject it to a purely analytic reduction. This reality with which we are contending, this notion of that which is transcendent yet can attain to immanence, that which is in turn unconcealed and concealed, this *a-letheia*, *Logos*, *physis*, Being is that which sustains and informs our experience yet necessarily exceeds it and our capacity for comprehension of it. It holds all things together and is itself the place from which the poet's decree does issue.

"TO WHERE DOES THE DECREE COMPEL HIM?" NAMING

As Heidegger explains, Hölderlin, as a poet, is compelled to name the holy in his poetry. Hölderlin engages in a naming that should not be understood as the bestowal of a name. Rather, it should be understood as a naming that is itself the giving account of an essence recognized for which Hölderlin *knows* the name. This is a very important distinction. And here I see the relevance of Heidegger's discussion of the relationship between the Greek words for "name," "naming," and "knowing."[19] It is interesting to note, also, that the Greek word for "mark," that is "gnoma," is related to these other words, as well. There is also a connection between "onoma," the Greek word for "name," which carries with it the idea of the revelation or manifestation of character via the name itself, and the Greek word "nomos," which is translated into English as "law." I would contend that the poet is marked and thus is compelled by decree and must name according to law that name that he knows which is itself a revelation of the character of that which is present to the poet and being named by him. What follows should make this clearer.

Heidegger explains that Hölderlin, in naming these gods, is not *calling* to them in the ordinary sense of *invoking* them. He does not seek to make them arrive or to hasten their arrival. Rather, he *names* and *calls* them because they are to him, as poet, already present. He names them in a way that is indicative of both the revelation to which he is privy and the inherent obscurity that is entailed in such a revelation given from where the decree to name does itself issue. Thus, in order to "preserve the distance," the poet engages in a naming that names, but it does so "darkly." This is precisely why Heidegger describes the naming as both an "unveiling" and a "veiling."[20]

We should in no way think of Hölderlin as attempting to hide something or attempting to make obscure what need not be so. Again, Heidegger's view is that the poet is compelled to name the holy; it is his burden, his calling, his vocation. In naming the holy, the poet simply offers up what is available to him as poet, and thus the naming veils and unveils not due to efforts or motivations on his part as poet but rather due to the very essence of that which he is naming, an essence, which, when unconcealed preserves its concealment, and keeps hidden and safe its essence in that its source is Being itself, inexhaustible in concepts, time, and intelligibility.

The decree itself and the place to which it compels the poet may be understood as applicable not only to the poet but also to all who are called to *poiesis*. In other words, all true artists are mortals who are themselves channels or conduits for the gods, and the gods connect with the mortals via the realm of the daimonic in order to manifest in the material world, within space and time. It may perhaps be helpful to consider the metaphor Heidegger employs to shed light on the situations of both poet (artist) and thinker. The poet and the thinker "dwell near one another on mountains most separate."[21] Perhaps we should say they are separated by Chaos, but both are called to *poiesis*. "The thinker says being. The poet names the holy."[22]

Here I think it is appropriate to say a few words about *poiesis* and what it is for Heidegger. In his essay, "The Question Concerning Technology," he explains that in understanding the meaning of the Greek word *poiesis* as "bringing forth," and Aristotle's Four Causes are at play in this, we absolutely must distinguish *poiesis* from the kind of "making" that results from modern technology. Heidegger explains that while the bringing forth that is *poiesis* is a revealing that involves the moving from concealment into unconcealment (and for the Greeks *technē* belongs to bringing-forth and thus to *poiesis*), modern technology as a revealing is not at all the *poiesis* of the Greeks. Heidegger says, "And yet the revealing that holds sway throughout modern technology does not unfold into a bringing-forth in the sense of *poiesis.* The revealing that rules in modern technology is a challenging [*Herausfordern*], which puts to nature the unreasonable demand that it supply energy that can be extracted and stored as such."[23] The unconcealing that belongs to this "challenging" results in the reduction of all beings and things to mere resources on standby to be optimized (*Bestand*). "The essence of technology lies in Enframing," Heidegger writes. And ultimately, this Enframing "conceals that revealing which, in the sense of *poiesis*, lets what presences come forth into appearance."[24]

With the above understanding in mind, the *poiesis* that belongs to the poet is indeed to be distinguished from any and all production that belongs to the *technē* of modern technology. Iain Thomson explains this distinction well in his book *Heidegger, Art, and Postmodernity* when he writes:

> Just think, on the one hand, of a poetic shepherding into being that respects the natural potentialities of the matters with which it works, just as Michelangelo (who, let us recall, worked in a marble quarry) legendarily claimed he simply set his "David" free from a particularly rich piece of marble (after studying it for a month); or, less hyperbolically, as a skillful woodworker notices the inherent qualities of particular pieces of wood—attending to subtleties of shape and grain, different shades of color, weight, and hardness—while deciding what might best be built from that wood (or whether to build from it at all). Then contrast, on the other hand, a technological making that imposes a predetermined form on matter without paying heed to any intrinsic potentialities, the way an industrial factory indiscriminately grinds wood into woodchips in order to paste

them back together into straight particle board, which can then be used flexibly and efficiently to construct a maximal variety of useful objects.[25]

The crucial differences between the two modes of *poiesis* and *technē* are clear. Moreover, it is clear also that in the *poietic* approach to the wood there is an element of *theorein* (this Greek term will be explored in detail in the fifth section of this chapter) in that the woodworker contemplates, gazes upon, and considers what is apparent to him and allows the possibilities of the wood to *presence*. This is indeed in marked contrast to a technological approach to the wood that would simply impose upon it a predetermined form and meaning. The woodworker, like the poet, is possessed of those characteristics of knowledge (*Wissenschaft*) and tenderness (*Zärtlichkeit*) so important to Heidegger and his understanding of the poet.

Returning now to Heidegger's understanding of Hölderlin, Heidegger explains that Hölderlin, as poet, views the approach of the gods from a lofty vantage point that is accessible to him as poet but inaccessible to others. Hölderlin is compelled to express the gods' imminent arrival based on their immanent presence to him, and their immanent presence to him is itself due to his being as poet. Here we should recall how Heidegger said that the poet, as river, issues from the source and in flowing *is* the source. Moreover, Hölderlin is compelled to the naming due to what Heidegger would call Hölderlin's *knowledge* (*Wissenschaft*), a *knowledge* to which Hölderlin is uniquely privy by means of what Heidegger would term Hölderlin's *tenderness of being* (*Zärtlichkeit*). Again, this mode of being is that special mode of being attributed to the ancient Greeks by both Hölderlin and Heidegger. I believe Heidegger sees himself as possessing this mode of being, as well.

Heidegger's explanation of the concepts of *knowledge* and *tenderness* are found in the essay "Hölderlin's Heaven and Earth" and are used therein in part to explain the operation of the *Fourfold*.[26] Put simply, *knowledge* is the capacity for thinking that is truly *reflective*, that is, thinking that mirrors what *is*, thinking that is open to what *presences*. *Tenderness* is an orientation toward that which *presences* that is open, receptive, and appreciative. Heidegger describes *tenderness* as a "gladdening-bestowing and a simply-receiving."[27] This is the orientation articulated in the discussion of the dwellers of the Black Forest farmhouse, an orientation in and toward the *Fourfold* that is receptive and responsive to what is. It does not seek to conquer and control but to harmonize and to flow. It does not confine itself to the *merely actual* but is open to the possible. Such an orientation or comportment toward being is that which results from the practice of what Heidegger calls *meditative thinking*. Such an orientation and comportment is the one possessed by the poet and that compels him to the "naming."

"HOW DOES IT COMPEL?" A DESTINAL SENDING

Regarding the decree that compels Hölderlin to his *poiesis*, Heidegger states, "What speaks is the claim which holds sway everywhere in its unspokenness, the claim under which his own poetic activity stands."[28] The claim may be understood as something like Hölderlin's destiny, that is, his *being* as poet. The claim does not need to be spoken in order to hold sway. The claim inheres in Hölderlin's very being, his particular ek-sistence. In his "Letter 'On Humanism'," Heidegger says:

> Metaphysics closes itself to the simple essential fact that the human being essentially occurs in his essence only where he is claimed by being. Only from that claim "has" he found that wherein his essence dwells.[29]

The essence of a human being, for Heidegger, cannot be understood as something purely resultant from his or her own control or will, from some pure subjectivity. Rather, the essence does manifest in the human being in his receptivity to Being, in his capacity to be claimed by Being. And perhaps this is why Heidegger says that the claim speaks in its unspokenness. Heidegger explains what he means by ek-sistence:

> As ek-sisting, the human being sustains Dasein in that he takes the *Da*, the clearing of being, into "care." But Dasein itself occurs essentially as "thrown." It unfolds essentially in the throw of being as a destinal sending.[30]

This idea of a *destinal sending* is the lot of mortals in their relationship to divinities in the *Fourfold* that is one, but it is also the role of mortals in their relationship to the earth and sky. The ways in which any given mortal is interconnected to the other three of the *Fourfold* is not a matter over which he or she has ultimate control, regardless of the desire to believe otherwise. Each and every mortal is "thrown" and therefore has his or her own *destinal sending*. Each and every mortal finds himself or herself existent in and among things not of his or her own making or choosing and possessed of an orientation toward existence that has care as its essence.

None of us chose to which set of parents we would be born, our sex, the era of our birth, the county of our origin, the language we would be taught as children, or the number of our siblings. And we did not choose to care about our existence but rather cannot help but care. Hence, there is indeed a *destinal sending* but not in the sense of some one specific predetermined way in which the mortal should be or should act but rather an inexhaustible array of possibilities at any given moment that may be accessed by an orientation of receptivity and openness to the realm of the possible and by a comportment toward being that does not confine itself to the *merely actual*. Only in recognizing this is full *dwelling* made possible.

Both the poet and the mere mortal, as Dasein, in their *thrownness*, find themselves already among things, between earth and sky, and intimately bound up with the divinities, subject to them, and capable of intimacy with all of it, capable of taking that clearing of being into care and fulfilling the *destinal sending*. In order to fulfill the *destinal sending* successfully, however, one must possess those characteristics, that particular comportment and attunement toward Being, that Heidegger has called *knowledge* and *tenderness*. For a receptivity to the very space and time in which one finds oneself is indeed that which is required not only for harmonious existence within the *Fourfold* but to even begin to engage in what Heidegger calls "thinking." For it is in the practice of thinking, *meditative thinking*, that we can recognize and seek to overcome the tendency to totalization that is built into intelligibility and that disposes each understanding of being to take itself to be the whole story. For as I will seek to further demonstrate, it is that faulty mode of thinking, mere *calculative thinking*, that tendency to totalization, that has thwarted our attainment of full *dwelling* thus far and instead brought us to a place where our annihilation may well be imminent.

To better understand these thoughts on thinking, consider something Heidegger says in his *Discourse on Thinking*. There Heidegger tells us that man is *in flight from thinking*.[31] He goes on to make the important distinction between the two modalities of thought which are possible. He calls these *calculative thinking* and *meditative thinking*. About *calculative thinking*, he says: "This calculation is the mark of all thinking that plans and investigates. Such thinking remains calculation even if it neither works with numbers nor uses an adding machine or computer. Calculative thinking races from one prospect to the next. … [It] is not meditative thinking, not thinking which contemplates the meaning which reigns in everything that is."[32]

This distinction between types of thinking is of inestimable value and critical importance in understanding Heidegger. In terms of various concepts and ideas already explored, *calculative thinking* is the kind of thinking that occurs when one confines oneself to the merely actual, given that it is clearly a modality of thought reckoning only with what is useful, efficient, and productive. It imposes predetermined end goals and makes no place for *presencing*. It is the type of thinking which informs modernity, which rules the *essence of technology*.

Meditative thinking, however, is the kind of thinking that occurs when one does not confine oneself to the merely actual but opens in receptivity to the possible, to what was spoken of previously by both Heraclitus and Heidegger as "the unhoped-for." Additionally, *calculative thinking*, as such, would clearly deal only with that which is part of the unconcealed, giving no thought or place to the concealed. *Calculative thinking* would deal only with those prospects that are known, understood, and apprehended, while *meditative thinking* would be open to the whole of *a-letheia*, to both the unconcealed and concealed.

Considering Heidegger's own words that *meditative thinking* is "thinking which contemplates the meaning which reigns in everything that is," it could only be *meditative thinking* that is open to *a-letheia* as such. *Meditative thinking* necessarily involves that capacity to mirror or reflect that which exists, that which *presences*, what Heidegger calls *knowledge*, as well as that particular orientation of appreciation and openness that makes such vision possible, that which Heidegger calls *tenderness.*

Clear to view also is the relevance of the particular locale of the thinker, the particular place in space and time in which he finds himself, that clearing of being which is taken into care, for this is the point at which and in which meaning gathers. This is shown when Heidegger says:

> Yet anyone can follow the path of meditative thinking in his own manner and within his own limits. … It is enough if we dwell on what lies close and meditate on what is closest; upon that which concerns us, each one of us, here and now; here, on this patch of home ground; now, in the present hour of history.[33]

This quotation brings us round yet again to the very notion of *dwelling* and the way in which building, *dwelling*, and thinking go together. Heidegger's distinction between *calculative* and *meditative thinking* is a crucial part of his discussion of the role and place of thinking in relation to building and *dwelling*:

> Building and thinking are, each in its own way, inescapable for dwelling. … The proper dwelling plight lies in this, that mortals ever search anew for the essence of dwelling, that they *must ever learn to dwell*. What if man's homelessness consisted in this, that man still does not even think of the *proper* plight of dwelling as *the* plight? Yet as soon as man *gives thought* to his homelessness, it is a misery no longer. Rightly considered and kept well in mind, it is the sole summons that *calls* mortals into their dwelling. But how else can mortals answer this summons than by trying on *their* part, on their own, to bring dwelling to the fullness of its essence? This they accomplish when they build out of dwelling, and think for the sake of dwelling.[34]

We are to build out of *dwelling* and think for the sake of *dwelling*, and so we see that thinking for the sake of *dwelling* must indeed entail that mode of thinking called *meditative thinking* in that only in *meditative thinking* are mortals able to think of the real plight of *dwelling*, their "homelessness," as the plight. Thus can they begin to seek their being-at-home. And for those who engage in *calculative thinking* but not *meditative thinking*, full *dwelling* is simply not attainable. This is why Heidegger tells us that "The two [building and thinking], however, are also insufficient for dwelling so long as each busies itself with its own affairs in separation, instead of listening to the other."[35] Here is what I take to be the connection between what a more modern conceptualization might call "theory" and "practice," but with the qualification that what is signified by "theory" is in no way a theorizing constituted by mere *calculative thinking*. We can only attain to full *dwelling* when we first engage in *meditative thinking* that is characterized by what Heidegger calls *knowledge* and *tenderness* so that we may encounter Being in its *presencing* in such a way that we are made able to understand the proper means to which we ought put *calculative thinking* in service of building.

Again, mere *calculative thinking* does not serve the end of *dwelling*. For Heidegger's assertion that building and thinking can listen to one another, and only in doing so can *dwelling* be achieved, points to the way in which the two modalities of thinking, *meditative* and *calculative*, can serve the cause of *dwelling* only when employed in the way proper to each. And thus again is clear the necessity for mortals to be ever able *to learn*.

At this point I want to look at the role and place of mortals' *homelessness* (*Unheimlichkeit*) in Heidegger's thinking as it developed over time. Again, Richard Capobianco provides an exceptional piece of scholarship on this matter in an essay entitled, "The Turn towards Home," as found in his book *Engaging Heidegger*. In the essay, Capobianco traces the evolution in Heidegger's thinking on this matter from the ideas set forth in *The History of the Concept of Time* in 1925 and *Being and Time* in 1927 to Heidegger's reading of *Antigone* in his *Introduction to Metaphysics* in 1935 to Heidegger's re-reading of *Antigone* in *Hölderlin's Hymn "The Ister"* in 1942, and finally to two public talks, his "Memorial Address" in 1955 and his "Messkirch's Seventh Centennial" in 1961.

Rather than restating all the textual evidence that Capobianco cites, I will simply summarize his findings here by quoting directly from the essay's *Conclusion* and encourage the reader to consult Capobianco's text directly for fuller explication.

> In several important texts of the 1920's and 1930's—*The History of the Concept of Time, Being and Time*, and *Introduction to Metaphysics*—Heidegger maintained the position that Dasein is primordially *unheimlich*, "unsettled," and thus also *unheimisch*, "not at home" at the core of its being. However, we discover a significant turning in his thinking towards *home*, especially in the early 1940's. The 1942 commentary on Hölderlin's poem "The Ister" stands out as a bridge text between the early and later Heidegger on this issue; in particular, we find a striking and significant difference in his reading of Sophocles'

> *Antigone* compared with the better-known reading in the 1935 *Introduction to Metaphysics*. In "The Ister" commentary, he engaged both Sophocles and Hölderlin to work out the motif—so prominent in his later work—that human beings are primordially "at home" in Being, the sheltering source and origin of all beings. Even so, in this commentary he continued to maintain that confrontation with the "foreign," with the "unsettled," with the "unhomely," belongs to the very essencing of human beings. The journey home for human beings must pass through the "foreign land"; only those, like Antigone, who resolutely confront the "unsettled" and "unhomely" that we essentially *are*—only these can return home and authentically *dwell* at home in relation to Being. We find yet another development in his thinking on this issue in his work of the 1950's and 1960's. In two representative texts, "*Gelassenheit*" ("Memorial Address";1955) and "Messkirch's Seventh Centennial" (1961), he no longer speaks about "unsettledness" and "not-at-homeness" as belonging constitutively to Dasein's being; rather, he speaks of *das Unheimliche* and *das Unheimische* as afflicting Dasein in the modern technological age. In Heidegger's later view, Dasein must struggle against the prevailing unsettling and unhomely spirit of the present age in order to recover its primordially at-home relation to Being to *dwell*, calm and gladdened, in nearness to Being—Home, Source, and Origin of all beings.[36]

The view articulated by Capobianco in terms of his understanding of Heidegger is precisely in keeping with my own. This project aims specifically to outline ways in which we may indeed recover our primordial at-home relation to Being by bringing into view the ways in which we have succumbed to that unhomely spirit which currently prevails and is part of our Enframing. My own engagement with Heidegger, and specifically with texts such as "Building Dwelling Thinking" (1951), is done with this understanding of Dasein and Dasein's unhomeliness as articulated by Heidegger in his later thinking.

Ultimately, each of us bears the weight of responsibility to attain to fuller *dwelling* as a part of the *Fourfold*. When we link this understanding up with the distinctive way in which a poet bears his unique burden, we see that the poet and the mere mortal, while different in certain very important respects, are best understood not as being different in kind but merely different in degree. What is relevant to the one as Dasein is indeed relevant to the other. The poet, as such, however, may be understood to carry a heavier burden given that the poet is closer to the source and to the gods.

Such ideas become clearer when the way in which the poet serves the *Fourfold* as a whole, serving earth, sky, divinities, and mortals in his role as poet, is recognized. And although the poet and the philosopher may stand on different mountain peaks separated by an abyss, they are intimate, they belong together, they are bound together in Being by the *Fourfold* that is one, and they both have their own roles to play in service thereto.

In his essay "Remembrance," Heidegger writes, "Destiny has sent the poet the essence of poetic activity, and chosen him to be the first sacrifice."[37] And we now have the answer to our guiding question in this section as to how the poet is compelled. The poet is compelled by means of his *destinal sending*, a destiny allotted to him and to which he is bound; it is a destiny for which he was chosen.

"WHAT PROPER ELEMENT IS ALLOTTED TO HIM?" FEELING FOR THE GODS

I now arrive at what is perhaps the most interesting question of the five posed by Heidegger in terms of what I take to be his answer, although that answer, as one might suspect, is not so obvious. Heidegger does have an answer in mind, one that I believe has not before now been adequately unconcealed. And while a measure of obscurity and vagueness must endure if I am to stay true to Heidegger's thought and the nature of *a-letheia*, I will clarify what I believe his thinking reveals.

Hölderlin, as poet, is himself like the Greek gods in that he does not command but points and gives signs. For Heidegger, the poet is himself a *sign*. An earlier quote from Heidegger proclaimed the poet a "demigod" of sorts. In considering the *Fourfold* and the poet's role therein, it is clear that the poet has a specific role to play, a vocation, a *calling*, that is crucial to the interplay and the interconnectedness of all that is part of the *Fourfold*. The poet is a means of connection between the four. In seeking to gain further insight into the nature of the relation that holds within the *Fourfold* between divinities and mortals, and more specifically, divinities and poets, I will look at some lines from Hölderlin. From *The Rhine*:

> The most blessed in themselves feel nothing,
> Another, if to say such a thing is
> Permitted, must, I suppose,
> Vicariously feel in the name of the gods,
> And him they need[38]

From The Archipelago:

> Always, as heroes need garlands, the hallowed elements likewise
> Need the hearts of us men to feel and to mirror their glory[39]

From many lines later in that same hymn:

> For the Heavenly like to repose on a human heart that can feel them[40]

These lines from Hölderlin's poetry clearly assert the intimate relationship between divinities and mortals and set forth the idea that there is indeed a mutual dependency, an interdependency, that holds between the four of the *Fourfold*.

In my attempt to make plain the way in which I think Heidegger understands these things, it is important to make clear that the explanation I will be exploring is one resultant from a purely descriptive phenomenological approach to the question and subsequent reflection thereupon. On the one hand, there is the explanation that arises purely from phenomenological experience, an experience that calls out for thinking, an experience that calls out for the thinker's thinking of being, the philosopher's surmising as to the nature of reality that gives rise to the phenomena constituting the experience. On the other hand, the explanation that arises from our phenomenological experience is one that is also a creative response to those experiences, a *poeisis*, one might say, akin to the poet's naming of the holy, or the artist's rendering of what the holy may look like in manifestation. For if we are to truly understand the way in which all things are intimate in the four of the *Fourfold* that is one, as well as the all-pervading nature of *a-letheia*, that is, the way in which unconcealment and concealment rule, then we must open ourselves to undertaking the endeavor in this way. Otherwise, we resign ourselves to an understanding that is necessarily limited and less than it could be.

In attempting to think about the divinities, to speculate upon the nature of the reality that we point to in speaking of them, it is best to conceive of them not as personalities with histories or as independently existing discrete beings but rather quite simply as *affective aspects of being*. In other words, we should conceive of the divinities as principles or elements, as transcendental realities, as modes or moods, as archetypes that may be known by various names, names that themselves point to or indicate these affective dispositions or elemental principles, such as courage, passion, wisdom, mercy, fear, love, strife, and so on.

Once we understand the nature of divinities in this way and can conceptualize their operation within the *Fourfold*, along with the resultant encounter between divinities and mortals, we render the place and importance of myth easily comprehensible as that which creatively results from the point of view that is the *poietic* phenomenological approach to human existence. This, in turn, allows mortals an enhanced understanding of their place and purpose in the *Fourfold* as they ever learn to *dwell*. In this way, myth itself serves as something like a handbook to existence.

Myth is undoubtedly a way of conceptualizing experiences, experiences that are felt by mortals to be encounters between the mortal and an outside force experienced and perceived as acting upon them. In this way, we gain insight into Heidegger's love of the Greeks, and we understand more fully the centrally important function of myth as enlightening, edifying, and educative in the ancient world. Sense is thereby made of Heidegger's conviction that only in a conscious return to myth and art, to poetic *dwelling* upon the earth, may humankind not destroy themselves and die meaningless deaths. As Heidegger says in an interview:

> Philosophy will not be able to bring about a direct change of the present state of the world. This is true not only of philosophy but of all merely human meditations and endeavors. Only a god can still save us. I think the only possibility of salvation left to us is to prepare readiness, through thinking and poetry.[41]

While both our individual and collective futures are concealed from us, we are able through thinking and poetry, through philosophy and art, through contemplation and myth, to make ourselves open to what is *presencing* and ready for whatever may come, and in doing that, we make possible our salvation, even as the unhoped-for, for it is only by engaging in *meditative thinking* and assuming our proper place within the *Fourfold* and attaining to full *dwelling* that a god could "save us."

Stated in another way, it is in our cultivation of both the practice and appreciation of the aforementioned activities that we enhance our perceptual awareness of our place and purpose as one of the four of the *Fourfold* and thereby "practice death," as Heidegger has spoken of it, which is the means by which we are made able to achieve "that good death," whether that be ultimately realized in annihilation or transmutation via "a saving god." Change is essentially what I am speaking of here. Unless and until we are made able to practice our capacity for receptivity and appreciation and thus fully embrace mythos, ethos, and logos, there is no chance for survival. Unless and until we assume our place in harmonious interrelatedness and forego our conqueror mentality, not even a god can save us.

And what of these gods, these divinities? From a phenomenological approach to the matter, how is it that we should understand them in terms of their interactions with us once we conceptualize them as elemental principles or transcendental realities? While Hölderlin tells us that the divinities "feel nothing in themselves," we must attempt to be clear about what this means. Most simply, I take this to mean that the divinities, as the aspects of Being that they are, are without sentient experience; they are not beings or entities. It would be incorrect, however, to assume that because these principles feel nothing in themselves that they are without affective purpose and power to manifest in concrete material reality by means of influence upon and instantiation through mortals.

Here it is important to keep in mind how both divinities and mortals are part of that which is itself one, according to Heidegger. While we may conceptualize mortals as discrete and separate beings, to stop thinking there is to stop thinking too soon. The divinities, as elements or principles, may be understood in a certain sense to purpose manifestation of their essence insofar as each is what it is and inclines to be so in the nexus of the *Fourfold* that is one. In other words, in their interrelatedness with mortals, mortals are their feelings. And so it is correct to say that the divinities have *need* of mortals so that mortals may *feel* on their behalf in the sense that the divinities as elements or principles intend toward manifestation as an embodied expression thus experienced, thus fulfilling that which is appropriate to each as a given element or principle.

These divinities, these gods and goddesses, these elements, these principles, express the aspects of being that they are, and it is only through mortals that they do so. Only through mortals do the divinities have their share of earth and sky and partake of the gathering of meaning that occurs in the clearing taken into care by the mortals. It is in that clearing, taken into care by a mortal, that the divinities may express as that which they are by means of the *knowledge* and *tenderness* of a given mortal whose comportment toward Being is such that his heart be one that can indeed *feel* and *mirror* the glory of the divinities as the transcendental realities which they are, whether they be fear, courage, passion, lust, envy, fury, joy, wonder, sorrow, and so on. For, from a phenomenological point of view, there are no divinities apart from mortals and there are no mortals apart from the divinities, and neither of these exist apart from earth and sky.

The idea of a mortal human being as conduit for something divine is quite commonplace, whether implicit or explicit, and seems to have always been so to some degree or another when looking at language, literature, art, and myth throughout history and across cultures.

Moreover, if we just simply consult ourselves or other people on our experiences as spectators, we find that when witnessing feats of human greatness, virtually everyone has been witness to something *glorious*, something that may be described as the glorious manifestation of divinity of which I speak. For example, imagine what it is like to witness a great runner doing that at which he or she is great or a spellbinding dancer whose movement entrances and reveals the spirit that moves his or her limbs or a mesmerizing pianist whose playing sweeps us away into that other realm, the realm from which his or her own inspiration comes, the realm which may be understood as the one referenced by Kohak when he speaks of *the order of eternity* or Heidegger when he speaks of the eternally non-apparent appearing as beauty. The phenomena of such experiences point to that transcendental or timeless realm, that aspect of Being that we call divine. Such experiences are ones described as "inspired" in that one perceives and feels what can only be described as spirit animating a body.

Many experiences are of the above-mentioned kind; consider the monumental bravery and heroism of a great warrior as manifested in the heat of battle or the captivating words and gestures of a powerful orator or teacher or the grace, speed, and agility of an athlete on the field. All such experiences of human greatness may be understood as experiences of the glory of divinity manifesting in the flesh. Again, in confining ourselves to the phenomenology of certain experiences, in attempting to simply describe the experience, it is possible to get in touch with that element of the experience of greatness in another that is experienced and felt and often described as an encounter with divinity, even when only spoken in a metaphorical way. Of course, even the more mundane expressions which occur in human life can be understood as expressions of the divine principles, elements, or divinities, especially if one attunes oneself to this aspect of existence.

While the experiences we categorize as sensational, epic, monumental, profound, and highly moving may be those that most easily render us able to see Heidegger's ideas at work, what he has in mind has its place also in the more commonplace and ordinary parts of existence. Think of the perceptions and feelings that may be had while walking in the forest, while gazing into a loved one's eyes, while listening to the laughter of playing children, while tending to a garden, while watching a colorful sunset, or listening to waves crash on a beach. The divine is present in the ordinary. Divinity is truly immanent. Mortals need only be open to the *presencing* of Being to experience such things.

Keeping in mind Heidegger's assertion that anyone can engage in *meditative thinking* in his or her own way and in his or her own manner on his or her own patch of home ground, it should become increasingly clear as I proceed. Being is omnipresent. And as Heidegger is fond of pointing out, that which is closest to us is that which we have the greatest difficulty recognizing. By looking at language, Heidegger is often able to unconceal truth. Consider what he says in *Parmenides*:

> What shines into beings, though it can never be explained on the basis of beings nor constructed out of beings, is Being itself. And Being, shining into beings, is τό δαίον—δαίμον. Descending from Being into beings, and thus pointing into beings, are the δαίοντες—δαίμονες. The "demons," so understood, are altogether "undemonic": that is, judged in terms of our usual murky representation of the "demonic." But these undemonic δαίμονες are anything but "harmless" and "incidental." They are not casual additions to beings, which man could bypass with no loss of his own essence and could leave aside and could consider solely according to his whims and needs. In consequence of this inconspicuous unsurpassability, the δαίμονες are more "demonic" than "demons" in the usual sense could ever be. The δαίμονες are more essential than any being. They not only dispose the "demonic demons" into the disposition of the horrible and

> frightful, but they determine every essential affective disposition from respect and joy to mourning and terror.[42]

Heidegger tells us in this passage that the *daimones* are more essential to being than any being. The *daimones*, according to Heidegger, are all "affective dispositions" known to mortals. He mentions joy, respect, mourning, and terror. Thus, it is shown how the affective dispositions such as envy, courage, strife, love, and passion mentioned earlier as elements or principles are indeed the very things to which Heidegger is here referring. Heidegger also makes clear that the affective dispositions determined by these *daimones* are not to be avoided, set aside, or otherwise rendered to be without consequence. He stresses that they are not "casual additions" to mortals who could otherwise still fulfill their essence as beings. No, the *daimones* are more essential to being than any being.

The inescapability of the *daimones* as affective dispositions is an idea that sheds light on what was revealed in the lines from Hölderlin's poetry. A given god, as such, can feel nothing in itself, and thus it is said by Hölderlin that he needs a mortal to feel for him, and it is only in the coming together of the two that the fullness of experience is achieved. Heidegger's understanding of this is more nuanced and complex, and it is grounded in what he sees revealed in a close study of ancient Greek thought and language.

Heidegger's own understanding of the thinker is in keeping with that of Aristotle as set forth in his *Nicomachean Ethics* in the discussion of what the achievement of happiness or *eudaimonia* requires and what a life of contemplation looks like. For Aristotle, a thinker, by virtue of his or her being as thinker, is privy to Being in a way that the ordinary person is not since the ordinary person is not engaged in the same type of thinking. The thinker, through his activity as thinker, that is, through the activity of contemplation, is able to achieve *eu-daimonia*, he is able to have *a god good within*.

What is interesting and relevant here is the Greek word *theorein*, most commonly translated as "contemplation" and sometimes as "study," and this is the activity of the thinker or philosopher. It is important to understand that in the Greek this word does not at all involve the idea that there is some problem to be solved or some answer to be discovered. Rather, as translator Terence Irwin explains in his translation of Aristotle's *Nicomachean Ethics*: "*Theorein* is study in the sense in which I study a face or a scene that I already have in full view; that is why the visual associations of *theorein* are appropriate."[43] Thus, the thinker contemplates or studies something that is present to him and able to be viewed, seen, and gazed upon. This is most assuredly Heidegger's own understanding of a real thinker and real thinking, in my view. His never-ending concern with the ways in which he saw modern philosophy as having left behind real thinking are articulated continuously throughout the lifetime of his thinking. Thus in "The Poet as Thinker" does he say, "Three dangers threaten thinking. / The good and thus wholesome / danger is the nighness of the singing / poet. / The evil and thus keenest danger is / thinking itself. It must think / against itself, which it can only / seldom do. / The bad and thus muddled danger / is philosophizing."[44]

The ancient understanding of *theorein*, that is, the idea that the thinker simply holds in view or looks upon something already present to him or her, harmonizes perfectly with Heidegger's ideas of *knowledge* and *tenderness* and the way in which a person possessing those characteristics simply observes what *presences* and mirrors this reality by means of receptive and appreciative capacities. Thus, it seems that the thinker simply engages in a descriptive phenomenology, that is, he or she describes that which is present and such a description no doubt preserves the "mysterious" nature of Being as *a-letheia* and *physis*. Here we do well to remember that, for Heidegger, the very nature of existence entails mystery; *Innigkeit* is a *Geheimnis*. A basic part of his criticism of the modern technologized mode of being prevalent in our age involves the loss of the "mysterious" as such. Thus does he write, "The essence of the latter [the mysterious] has been foreign to man from the moment he "explained" the mysterious simply as the unexplained."[45]

The thinking characteristic of the thinker is undoubtedly a *meditative thinking*. The ordinary person, on the other hand, as Aristotle explains, is chiefly concerned with his or her own perceived good, that is, that which is good for a human being. Thus, that which occupies a true thinker may appear to be astounding or even foolish to the ordinary person. The ordinary person is caught up in what Heidegger calls *calculative thinking*, and therefore he or she has essentially concerned himself or herself with the *merely actual*. Such a person thinks not in terms of the possible or the unhoped-for but thinks in terms of those things with which he or she is presently occupied, the things that are unconcealed and manipulable by a calculative mindset. Such thinking is, of course, in its essence, confining and restrictive, and it ultimately prevents the mortal from attaining to that state in which the good god *dwell*s within. Heidegger says as much when he remarks:

> Aristotle, Plato's disciple, relates at one place (Nicomachean Ethics, Z 7, 1141b 7ff.) the basic conception determining the Greek view on the essence of the thinker, "It is said they (the thinkers) indeed know things that are excessive, and thus astounding, and thereby difficult, and hence in general 'demonic'—but also useless, for they are not seeking what is, according to straightforward popular opinion, good for man." ... What [the average] man is doing and what he pursues, is for the most part without difficulty for him because he can always find, going from one being to the next, a way of escape from difficulty and an explanation. ... Thus "the many" see Being and yet do not see it.[46]

Indeed, that which is closest to us all too often goes unnoticed. Being itself is not in focus for "the many" who are busy organizing and dealing with the "facts." Yet Being is present for the thinker who engages in *theorein*, the thinker who studies that which is in full view but is thought to be somehow "excessive" or "astounding" by the many who cannot see what is right in front of them. As Heidegger emphasizes, the *extraordinary*, although it is that which is closest to us, is that which we too often cannot see, in that it is easily covered over by our tendency to *average everydayness*.

As discussed earlier via Capobianco, the *unheimlich* or *uncanny* or *unhomely* or *unsettled* appears first as part of our very nature as Dasein, yet as Heidegger articulates in *Introduction to Metaphysics*, it signals our richest possibilities. Nonetheless, it is that from which we flee into "the They" (*das Man*) to content ourselves with calculation and the merely actual and thus forego *dwelling*. Aristotle appears to assert the same idea when he writes:

> If reason is divine, then, in comparison with man, the life according to it is divine in comparison with human life. But we must not follow those who advise us, being men, to think of human things, and, being mortal, of mortal things, but must, so far as we can, make ourselves immortal, and strain every nerve to live in accordance with the best thing in us; for even if it be small in bulk, much more does it in power and worth surpass everything.[47]

Aristotle clearly has a conception of human beings as interrelated with divinity in an essential way. Like Heidegger, he sees the highest possibilities as achievable only in purposeful openness to and relationship with divinity, divinity understood as inherent within human being, that is, immanent divinity. Conceptions of divinity that locate divinity outside of and independent of mortals fundamentally misunderstand the nature of the relationship between the two and in displacing divinity necessarily prevent the achievement of *eudaimonia*.

From Aristotle's point of view, mortals cannot fulfill their function without divinity. From Heidegger's point of view, mortals cannot engage in *dwelling* without divinity since *dwelling* requires real thinking that presupposes a recognition of immanent divinity as one of the four of the *Fourfold*. Aristotle even asserts that for a human being to forego this is for the human being to forego what is highest and best in the self. Yet, as both Aristotle and Heidegger understand, all too many do forego it in their excessive occupation with what they conceive as the domain of concern proper to human being. They miss what is right there in front of them, what is right there inside of them.

This ever-present yet extraordinary nature of the daimonic is not to be understood as in any way supernatural or otherworldly, and despite its being extraordinary, it is also exceedingly ordinary. David Farrell Krell describes it as "the nearest of the near, the most intimate and natural thing in the world. It is Φύσις [*physis*] itself."[48] And while the thinker is the one that concerns him or herself with such matters, such matters are continuously available to any who care to see. Once seen, they may be understood as that which they are, that is, as *physis*, as Being. Heidegger says that the *daimones*, as the uncanny or extraordinary, are the "most natural" in the sense of "nature" thought by the Greeks as *physis*.[49]

Heidegger stresses the way in which *physis* is *a-letheia*. They are the same. As discussed in Chapter 2, the Greeks did not "deal with" *a-letheia*; they dealt within it. They understood *a-letheia* by means of, or as, *physis*. We best understand this by seeing that the Greeks' conception of truth as *a-letheia* was determined by their phenomenological experience of nature and its operations. Regarding *physis*, Heidegger writes:

> *Phusis* as emergence can be experienced everywhere: for example, in the celestial processes (the rising of the sun), the surging of the sea, in the growth of plants, in the coming forth of animals and human beings from the womb. But *phusis*, the emerging sway, is not synonymous with these processes, which we still today count as part of "nature." This emerging and standing-out-in-itself-from-itself may not be taken as just one process among others that we observe in beings. *Phusis* is Being itself, by virtue of which beings first become and remain observable.[50]

A helpful way to conceptualize what is meant by the term *physis* is to imagine a time-lapsed video that depicts a patch of ground, a seed falling thereupon, rain taking it down into the dirt, days/weeks passing, the seed sprouting, growing, blossoming, fruiting, withering, dying, and the process then happening again and again.[51] It is the entirety of this dynamic and cyclical process in terms of both that which is available to our sight and that which occurs beyond the scope of our vision, as well as the spirit which animates it all, Being itself, showing forth in such *presencing*, that is indicated by the term *physis*. This is what Heidegger is attempting to explain in the above quotation. Likewise, all cycles that we experience as mortals here on earth beneath the sky and in communion with divinity reveal to us *physis*, truth as *a-letheia*.

These perpetual and unending cycles, such as day into night and night into day, the waxing, full, waning, dark, and new moon, spring into summer into fall into winter, and the cyclical changes the seasons themselves spur within the myriad beings, are all the continuous process of concealing and unconcealing played out endlessly in our view, and in them is revealed that purposiveness that is inherent in the natural world and all its processes, as well as in all beings and things. *Physis* as *a-letheia* as Being. Capobianco describes this when he writes:

> Glimpsed here is what Heidegger glimpsed from the beginning of his lifetime of thinking: the emerging of all beings and things in the ensemble; their holding and lingering and whiling in appearance, carried along by a great giving stream, a stream not hidden exactly, but difficult to see. This great giving flow, this temporal-spatial letting of all things, is Being—but also *physis, aletheia*. Indeed, in our relation to *physis* it is no doubt important to keep in view that it is we mortals who bring into language what emerges and lingers and passes away. There is no overlooking ourselves as "the shepherd" and "guardian" of Being/*physis*. Yet in Heidegger's distinctive vision and version of "phenomenology," we are always called to recall that ours is an *Entsprechung*, a *cor-respondence*. *Physis* first addresses us, and ever so. *Physis* calls forth from us language and saying and meaning. *Physis* opens us so that we may open up a world of meaning. The core matter for Heidegger—and for those inclined to his thinking—is that *physis* is the measure, not Dasein.[52]

As discussed earlier regarding *Logos* as *a-letheia* as Being, it is crucial to a proper understanding of Heidegger that we not shift the locus of truth to Dasein, that we do not seek to make Dasein the measure. Truth, as *a-letheia*, as Being, as *physis*, as *Logos* is independent of human beings. Thus does Heidegger say, "[T]his truth of Being does not exhaust itself in Dasein, nor can it by any means simply be identified with it after the fashion of the metaphysical proposition that all objectivity is as such a subjectivity."[53]

And while Being/*physis*/*a-letheia*/*Logos* comes to manifestation in the *Fourfold*, human beings as Dasein are the clearing where meaning gathers but only in so far as Dasein cor-responds to Being itself. Thus does Capobianco rightly note, "The self-showing that is Being-*physis* is already "*wordable*," we might say, as it comes to us, and we cor-respond in word (and sound and image and movement)."[54] Hence is all myth born.

In thinking of Being as *physis*, again, *physis* is that which permeates all of existence yet exceeds it. *Physis* is Being; it is that from which all other things proceed. In elucidating one of Hölderlin's poems, Heidegger states:

> Nature [*physis*] is present in everything that is real. Nature comes to presence in human work and in the destiny of peoples, in the stars and in the gods, but also in stones, growing things, and animals, as well as in streams and in thunderstorms. … From where does nature [*physis*] take her power then, if she is prior to all that is present? Nature does not have to borrow her power from somewhere else. She herself is that which bestows power. … She is present in everything, even in the gods. … That she is present in all does not mean a complete, quantitative comprehension of

> all that is real, but rather the manner of permeating the real things that, according to their kind, seem to mutually exclude each other. This omnipresence holds in opposition to each other the extreme opposites, the highest heaven and the deepest abyss.[55]

Physis permeates the real. It encompasses the *Fourfold*. All is intimate through it. The divinities get their power from *physis*, as do mortals, earth, and sky. *Physis* reveals to us the concealed/unconcealed nature of Being.

To think further on this, consider that Being is itself made up of the concealed and unconcealed. If the natural world is taken as the unconcealed, we discover when we look at the natural world that it, too, is made up of both the concealed and unconcealed. In looking at some part of the natural world that is unconcealed, say, for example, an oak tree, it is again revealed that the oak tree is both concealed and unconcealed. Moreover, the process of concealing and unconcealing itself can be viewed throughout the seasons of a year or over the course of many years as a given oak tree puts forth leaves, and they turn, fall off, and branches are left bare until the following spring. This pattern is repeated over and over, and in all things.

Keeping in mind this idea about the way in which Being unfolds as layers or levels, each having its own concealed and unconcealed aspect, I want to look at the distinction Heidegger makes between the *gods* and the *daimones*. Heidegger holds that the gods themselves are concealed, but they have their share of unconcealment by means of the *daimones*. The *daimones* are the aspect of the gods that are unconcealed to mortals. Heidegger says:

> Being—ἰδέα—is what in all beings shows itself and what looks out through them, the precise reason man can grasp beings as beings at all … Οί θεοί, the so-called gods, the ones who look into the ordinary and who everywhere look into the ordinary, are οί δαίμονες, the ones who point and give signs. Because the god is, as god, the one who looks and who looks as the one emerging into presence, θεάων, the god is the δαίων-δαίμον that in the look presents himself as unconcealed.[56]

While the *daimones* may be ontologically identical with the gods, they are to be distinguished from them ontically in that they are the *aspect* of the gods or of Being that are unconcealed in the look. Being shines into beings, Heidegger says. Being, as that which looks out through beings, is the gods, but as that which offers itself to be seen, Being is the *daimones*.

The dynamic interplay of the unconcealed and concealed is at work in these ideas about the gods and the *daimones*. This ties in with Heidegger's neo-Aristotelian philosophy; that activity which both Aristotle and Heidegger claim is the province and domain of the thinker involves awareness of and openness to that which offers itself to be looked at, gazed upon, studied, and contemplated. It is best seen by the thinker in the person of the poet or artist since such a person is the richest conduit for this expression, according to Heidegger. This, again, is why he sees as unique and important the special relationship between the poet and the philosopher. Yet, as has been noted, it is available to any mortal willing to think and to see.

Being reveals itself to the Poet, the one who is closest to it. The Poet in turn reveals what he or she sees, and the thinker sees what is revealed and elucidates so as to reveal to others, and so on. If we understand this dynamic properly, we can see how in the ancient world the writers of the tragedies, and the thinkers who explored them, and the performance of these works in theater, and the people's experience of them, and the resultant edification and illumination attained thereby exemplify this process. The importance of myth, art, and the experience thereof is crucial to *dwelling*. Thus does Heidegger emphasize that mythos, ethos, and logos all belong together essentially.[57]

Here I want to look more closely at vision and the visible, this centrally important phenomenon of seeing and being seen. By consulting one's own personal experiences of the phenomenon of eye contact, insight is gained. The important place that eyes and eye contact hold in myriad situations, disciplines, art, and literature, as well as in daily life, is difficult to deny.

A quick look at language reveals a wealth of expressions, clichés, and idioms built upon the phenomenology of eye contact. The phenomenon of eye contact is in human experience a unique and powerful experience thought to be unlike any other. Eyes are the windows of the soul, so the saying goes. A French proverb tells us that the first love letters are written with the eyes. Myriad expressions, such as "turn a blind eye," "eyes in the back of your head," "a roving eye," " the evil eye," "bedroom eyes," "feast your eyes upon," " more than meets the eye," and many others affirm the unique and powerful place of the experience of eye contact.

Heidegger, in his discussion of the nature of the *daimones* and their relation to the gods via an examination of the ancient Greek language, tells us, "Because the god is, as god, the one who looks and who looks as the one emerging into presence, θεάων, the god is the δαίων-δαίμων."[58] Heidegger makes clear that when the Greek language is understood correctly, Being, as the gods, looks out and offers itself to being seen, as the *daimones*, in the look. Thus is sight of the Being of beings made possible.[59]

Silent and sustained eye contact between two human beings is a profound and moving experience that seems often to result in strong surges of emotion. The fact that an important part of training soldiers to kill is to train them to avoid all eye contact is not surprising. In reflecting upon experiences, certain patterns that point us toward Heidegger's ideas are recognizable. Many people agree that the appeal that is made to them in the silent eye contact of a child, for example, is virtually impossible to ignore. Likewise, many people openly acknowledge that they avoid eye contact either because they judge it as intrusive to the other or feel it as the other intruding. People avoid eye contact in an attempt to keep hidden their thoughts and feelings. Often people who work together in various capacities will describe how there is an ability for unspoken communication by means of eye contact. Likewise, in improvisational art forms, eye contact among participating members is often the sole means of communicating. And some people will even acknowledge that they find it exceedingly difficult if not impossible to be overtly dismissive or unjustifiably cruel to someone while looking that person in the eye. And what of that well-known phrase, "It was love at first sight?" Many people describe their experience of eye contact with certain others as jolting, electrifying, soul-stirring, and so on. Perhaps, when under the gaze of another, we sense the presence of Being, the presence of divinity. When gazing at one another, for Heidegger, we are experiencing Being looking out at and back into Being. When we make eye contact and feel the need to look away, perhaps we are retreating so as to avoid the overwhelming *daimon* that is glimpsed in the eyes of the other. When we gaze into the eyes of another person, we inevitably do so either *calculatively* or *meditatively*. If the latter, we are open and receptive to the other and to Being itself. If the former, we are closed off from Being and the other. Much of the work of Emmanuel Levinas and others deals precisely with the encounter with the infinite that is at play in such exchanges.

In thinking further about the *daimones* and the gods, it is interesting to explore how ideas expressed in Plato's *Symposium* are in keeping with an understanding of the *daimones* as either beings in their own right that exist between gods and mortals or as aspects of the gods themselves that might appear to mortals as beings in their own right in that they are that which show themselves to us while the gods themselves do not.

In Plato's *Symposium*, Socrates shares what Diotima told him about the nature of Eros or Love. Diotima said that Eros, being desirous of the beautiful and the good, cannot himself be a god. Rather, he is a very powerful *daimon* that exists halfway between gods and men. About such spirits, it is said:

> They are the envoys and interpreters that ply between heaven and earth, flying upward with our worship and our prayers, and descending with the heavenly answers and commandments, and since they are between the two estates they weld both sides together and merge them into one great whole. They form the medium of the prophetic arts, of the priestly rites of sacrifice, initiation, and incantation, of divination and of sorcery, for the divine will not mingle directly with the human, and it is only through the mediation of the spirit world that man can have any intercourse, whether waking or sleeping, with the gods. And the man who is versed in such matters is said to have spiritual powers, as opposed to the mechanical powers of the man who is expert in the more mundane arts. There are many spirits and many kinds of spirits, too, and Love is one of them.[60]

While in Plato the *daimones* are the intermediaries between the gods and men and would thus appear to be beings in their own right, in another sense, given that it is said that it is they that "weld both sides together," we can fit them into the view expressed by Heidegger in which he sees the *daimones* as the aspect of divinity that communicates or interacts with mortals in that they "point and give signs." This idea of the *daimones* as they that "point and give signs" may be further connected with Plato in that Socrates himself was said to be attended by such a *daimon*. We find references to this in various of Plato's dialogues.[61] Although there is not a great deal of discussion about it in the dialogues, I think that its somewhat regular appearance as a fact about Socrates is significant. Words spoken by Socrates in the dialogue *Cratylus* are in keeping with ideas in Hölderlin's poetry and his description of how the mortal and god are united through mutual need and interdependence.

In *Cratylus*, Plato reports Socrates as saying: "And I say, too, that every wise man who happens to be a good man is more than human both in life and death, and is rightly called a daimon."[62] In proclaiming the good man as more than human, Socrates affirms that there is an intimate relationship between the mortals and the divinities, and Socrates' "good man" appears to be on a par with Heidegger's "demigod poet" in the sense that both are felt to be closer to source and privy to some deeper and more meaningful understanding and modality of being. This is in keeping with Aristotle's ideas, as well, as previously explained. Both thinkers and poets play this role. They are the ones who engage in "pointing and giving signs" to the common people. To be such a mortal no doubt carries with it its own difficulties, burdens, and travails. To explore this idea further, I will look at a few more lines from Hölderlin's poem *The Rhine*, as well as something Heidegger says about them in his work *Hölderlin's Hymn "The Ister."* From *The Rhine*:

> Yet of their own
> Immortality the gods have enough, and if one thing
> The heavenly require,
> Then heroes and humans it is
> And otherwise mortals. For since
> The most blessed feel nothing of themselves,
> There must presumably, if to say such
> Is allowed, in the name of the gods
> Another partake in feeling,
> Him they need; yet their own ordinance
> Is that he his own house
> Shatter and his most beloved
> Chide like the enemy and bury his father
> And child beneath the ruins,
> If someone wants to be like them and not
> Tolerate unequals, the impassioned one.

In elucidating these lines of poetry, Heidegger writes:

> An Other must be, who is other than the gods and in his being other must "tolerate unequals." This Other is needed to "partake in feeling" in the name of the gods. Partaking in feeling consists in his bearing sun and moon, the heavenly, in mind and distributing this share of the heavenly to humans, and so, standing between gods and humans, sharing the holy with them, yet without even splitting it apart or fragmenting it. Such communicating occurs by this Other pointing toward the holy in naming it, so that in such showing he himself *is* the sign that the heavenly need. ... The poet is thus beyond human beings and yet unequal to the gods, and to humans as well.[63]

Focusing first on Hölderlin's words, we see that the immortals, the gods, have need of mortals so that the mortals may feel in the name of the gods since the gods themselves can feel nothing. The very nature of the relationship between gods and mortals is one in which the gods themselves in their relating to mortals "tolerate unequals" for some further good, and it appears, from what Hölderlin tells us, that if a mortal who has been impassioned by a god fails to retain his humility and his recognition of his proper place and wishes to be like the gods yet is unlike them in that he does not "tolerate unequals," he will be made to bring about destruction to his own house, his own kin. That is the ordinance of the gods, says Hölderlin.

Harmony and balance are achieved only when each part of the whole, in doing its own part, does so with an aim toward accepting and tolerating lesser and greater beings, it seems. To avoid the destruction of one's own house, one must, if impassioned by a god, "tolerate unequals." Of course, for Heidegger, the specific role that the poet plays is his primary concern in many of the texts under discussion, along with the ways in which the poet serves, as poet, to "weld together" gods and humans. The poet serves the humans by "sharing the holy with them." The poet is the one who provides access to and experience of the "holy" for mortals. The poet serves the gods by being the sign they need. As Heidegger writes, "The sign ("the besouler") bears everything originarily in mind in such a way that, in naming the holy, the sign lets the heavenly show itself."[64] The poet, as such, being unequal to the gods and unequal to mere mortals, must "tolerate unequals" in his efforts to both offer the mortals an "unfragmented" experience of the holy and be the sign the heavenly require.

The idea that the gods (Gk *Theoi*) as such are hidden or concealed while the *daimones* are unconcealed, as pointed out, fits the pattern of the unconcealing and concealing nature of Being. It preserves truth understood as *a-letheia*, that strange, seeming-antinomy that is truth's simultaneous revelation and hiddenness. About it, Heidegger says, "[C]oncealedness and unconcealedness determine beings as such. That means: disclosedness and concealment are a basic feature of Being."[65] Hence, we are reminded yet again that this feature of reality, this concealedness and unconcealedness, is constant.

The nature of the concealedness itself is given treatment by Heidegger in a discussion about truth and the ways in which the Greek's conception thereof differs from the modern conception that supposes that truth is rightly to be understood in opposition to *falsity*. Heidegger suggests that the *hiddenness* or *concealment* that is a part of the Greek conception of truth should be understood as sanctuary or safe-keeping. He explains, "There is also, however, a kind of concealment that does not at all put aside and destroy the concealed but instead shelters and saves the concealed for what it is. This concealment does not deprive us of the thing, as in cases of dissembling and distorting, withdrawing and putting aside. This concealment preserves."[66] To understand the hiddenness as something inherently good in that it "shelters" is in itself already at odds with the modern conceptualization of truth and its tendency to a scientism of thought that would suppose that only truth that makes known can be understood as good since only what is known can be made useful.

When we apply Heidegger's understanding of the hidden as that which is kept safe and preserved to our understanding of the gods as concealed, we see that it is a concealment that preserves and shelters the gods as the aspect of Being that they are while that which they are does come into expression and unconcealment in the *daimones* who offer themselves to a sighting in their pointing and giving of signs. As Heidegger explains, it is the poet who, as perfect channel or conduit for the *daimones*, becomes the sign the gods need so that their own concealed and preserved essences may come to expression and manifestation in the nexus that is earth, sky, divinity, and mortal.

The little known thinker and Heidegger scholar, Vincent Vycinas, expresses such an idea about this distinction between the unconcealed and concealed in one of his books on Heidegger. There he writes, "Moreover, Maet is not the rays of the sun nor is Ra the sun itself; they merely are manifested by these entities which are backed up by these deities or permeated by them. What really are gods in themselves remains concealed; they break through into disclosure by way of things."[67] This idea that the god as such is concealed yet comes into presence by way of *daimones* or "things" is precisely what Heidegger has in mind when he speaks about the importance of the poet as one by means of which the gods can be made manifest. Being, as such, is both concealed and unconcealed. Being as *physis* and *a-letheia* is understood on the basis thereof. The power that may be said to belong to the gods is itself derived from *physis*, as Heidegger articulated in the earlier quotation, and that power is manifest by means of *daimones*, poets, beings, and things.

The divinities are aspects of Being. The concealed are the gods (*theoi*) and the unconcealed are the *daimones*. The *daimones* may be understood as principles or elements or affective dispositions. The *daimones* are a part of *physis* and derive their power therefrom, as Heidegger has said, and their expression is a phenomenon in an experienced human reality. This understanding appears to be precisely what Vycinas also has in mind when he writes:

> These realities [gods as powers of Being] can be considered as the basic articulation of *logos*, the natural language of *physis*. ... In the worlds of two different gods, a thing is not the same in each because by reflecting a different essence of a god, it itself becomes different … love in the world of Hermes and in that of Aphrodite are different loves. Love in the world of Hermes is a matter of luck or opportunity. It is the kind of love a traveler knows—suddenly coming and going, found, enjoyed, and forgotten. A love in the world of Aphrodite is a blissful unification breaking all bounds and upsetting the former mode of living. Such a love brings a revolutionary change in human life, like a sudden spring in which meadows burst into blossoms overnight. ... Gods as worlds never merely dominate or support a section of reality; they dominate everything whatsoever.[68]

The divinities, operating as elements or principles, determine the affective dispositions of the mortals over which they rule. A lover ruled by Hermes is very different than a lover ruled by Aphrodite. The world of love that is ruled by Aphrodite is a very different world than the world of love ruled by Hermes. And, as Vycinas points out, one mortal's experiences as lover may vary, depending upon in which divinity's *world* his actions as a lover are unfolding. When we keep in mind Heidegger's own distinction between earth and world, earth as hidden, and worlds as manifest, and the idea that earth is inexhaustible while any given world may collapse, it allows for the truth that Vycinas points us toward in the above passage to be seen.

I think that with relative ease it can be imagined how a mortal who may be understood as existing in the world of Hermes happens to meet someone who introduces him to the world of Aphrodite. Thus, there is a collapse of his former world. Also, Vycinas' assertion that "gods as worlds dominate everything" is an idea present in ancient texts, such as Euripides' *The Bacchae* or Aeschylus' trilogy *The Oresteia*, but with the understanding that it is from the point of view of the mortal that such may be said to be true. Here, too, Telemakhos in Homer's epic poems comes to mind. The notion that "gods as worlds dominate everything" makes sense with the unavoidable clash of fates that make up the stories that are the Greek tragedies, as well as much of myth.

In thinking of an individual mortal as being attuned to Being by virtue of the god or goddess being served and thus the world occupied, we see that something such as love could indeed be very different in two lovers or worlds. This makes sense when reflection is given to the phenomenological experience of meeting someone who introduces us to a new way of understanding an old concept. Worlds collide. One collapses and another emerges. A new world is disclosed. One vision dies and a new one is born.

There are many other things besides a conception of love which can be imagined changing in like manner. Such things are indeed conceived differently in different worlds. Any of them may be altered by the various connections and encounters that are possible in the *Fourfold*. Imagine a person, for example, who identifies with the myths of Hermes due to his own phenomenological experience of existence and the resonance that exists between it and the myths of Hermes to which he has been made privy. In acquiring a fuller knowledge and appreciation for myth, his own life is made richer by means of the understanding and insight that is provided by the myth, by the god himself, by Being. The important place of myth, art, and poetry for a mortal seeking to *dwell* in the *Fourfold* is of profound significance.

Again, the importance of the attunement of the individual is not to be underestimated. The divinities cannot express fully through just any mere mortal. Based on what has been established thus far, the divinities require mortals who possess within their finitude and orientation toward Being the capacity for acting as a conduit, a clear channel for the glorious manifestation of divinity. The divinities manifest most beautifully through those who, like Hölderlin, are possessed of what Heidegger calls *knowledge* and *tenderness*, that is, mortals who are open, receptive, appreciative, and able to reflect the reality that is divinity which *presences*. Such mortals, it may be said, are truly loved and favored by the divinities in that they make of themselves a vessel fit for the indwelling and operation of these elements, principles, *daimones*, and divinities. Thus does Heidegger say, "But the gods can come to expression only if they themselves address us and place us under their claim. A word which names the gods is always an answer to such a claim. ... Only because the gods bring our existence to language do we enter the realm of the decision concerning whether we are to promise ourselves to the gods or whether we are to deny ourselves to them."[69]

Such an idea is what Heidegger has in mind when, in reference to the above-quoted lines from Hölderlin's *The Archipelago*, he explains that we should understand the word *glory* as it appears in the poem in the Pindaric sense as a *letting-appear*.[70] In order for glory to manifest, the divinities, the hallowed elements, the gods and goddesses, need mortals, mortals who will *let-appear* their glory. Relevant here, again, are those examples of human greatness mentioned earlier: great musicians, dancers, orators, athletes, and warriors, to name a few. Indeed, the artist who possesses the characteristics of *knowledge* and *tenderness* is the fertile ground for the springing forth of the divinity that itself as principle or element manifests only through the artist in the material world as art. And thus, is answered the guiding question as to what is the proper element allotted to the poet. It is feeling for the gods.

One final point I wish to make here regards the way in which Heidegger emphasized that what the gods are in themselves remains concealed. In his essay, "Building Dwelling Thinking," Heidegger tells us that the mortals "do not make the gods." Vycinas, in his *Search for Gods*, writes, "According to mythical understanding, the gods are not to be seen as founded on wholly human grounds, but *vice versa*: man on the transcendental grounds of the gods. Man's holiness, his beauty, his greatness, his wisdom, are the outcomes of his serving the gods in their play."[71]

While there may be differences to be understood, I believe it is important to emphasize that from the phenomenological point of view, both Heidegger and Vycinas understand the experience of mortals in relation to divinity in this way. Hence Heidegger's assertion in *Parmenides* that "the *daimones* are more essential than any being." Left to grasp as best as able the nature of the inescapable and inexorable bond that holds between divinities and mortals, it is clear that it is most intimate. Such a bond is representative of the relationship that holds between all four of the *Fourfold*. And while the manifest and experiential operation of the *Fourfold* is *physis*, the *Fourfold* is one.

The myths by means of which we attempt to understand the divinities preserve within themselves, albeit in a somewhat hidden way, the various truths of human being, profound phenomenological insights into the workings of Being as it manifests in and through beings and each of the four of the *Fourfold*. The undeniably powerful elements that operate in the lives of all human beings, elements that are referred to as *daimones* by Heidegger, can be recognized, appreciated, understood, and thus reverenced for what they are by the return to and the embrace of myth and art and the acknowledgment of the role, place, and purpose of these in our mortal lives in our pursuit of *dwelling* within the *Fourfold*.

The attunement that opens one up to hearing the truths found in art and myth, as well as in the natural world itself, is indeed an attunement to Being. Through the cultivation of *knowledge* and *tenderness* and engagement in *meditative thinking*, we may achieve harmonious *dwelling* within the *Fourfold* through the building of new and different worlds. Keeping in mind the concealed and unconcealed nature of truth, I will now seek further unconcealment from a different vantage point.

NOTES

1. Martin Heidegger, *Elucidations on Hölderlin's Poetry*, trans. Keith Hoeller (New York: Humanity Books, 2000), 212.
2. Ibid.

3. Ibid., 210.
4. Ibid., 219.
5. Ibid., 9.
6. Ibid.
7. Ibid., 214.
8. Ibid., 213.
9. Ibid., 214–17.
10. Ibid., 214.
11. Martin Heidegger, *Hölderlin's Hymn "The Ister,"* trans. William McNeill and Julia Davis (Bloomington & Indianapolis: Indiana University Press, 1996), 138–9.
12. Erazim Kohak, *The Embers and the Stars* (Chicago & London: University of Chicago Press, 1984), 103.
13. Ibid., 97.
14. Ibid., 102.
15. Ibid., 122.
16. Peter Warnek, "Translating Innigkeit: The Belonging Together of the Strange," in *Heidegger and the Greeks*, ed. Drew Hyland and John Panteleimon Manoussakis (Indianapolis: Indiana University Press, 2006), 79.
17. Martin Heidegger, *What Is Called Thinking*, trans. J. Glenn Gray (New York: Harper and Row, 2004), 19.
18. Warnek, "Translating Innigkeit: The Belonging Together of the Strange," 62.
19. Heidegger, *Elucidations on Hölderlin's Poetry*, 215.
20. Ibid.
21. Martin Heidegger, "Postscript to 'What Is Metaphysics?'" in *Pathmarks*, ed. William McNeill (Cambridge: Cambridge University Press, 1998), 237.
22. Ibid.
23. Martin Heidegger, "The Question Concerning Technology," in *The Question Concerning Technology and Other Essays*, trans. William Lovitt (New York: Harper & Row, 1977), 14.
24. Ibid., 27.
25. Iain Thomson, *Heidegger, Art, and Postmodernity* (New York: Cambridge University Press, 2011), 21.
26. Heidegger, *Elucidations of Hölderlin's Poetry*, 192.
27. Ibid., 92.
28. Ibid., 214.
29. Martin Heidegger, "Letter on Humanism," in *Basic Writings*, ed. David Farrell Krell (New York: HarperCollins, 1993), 247.
30. Ibid., 249.
31. Martin Heidegger, *Discourse on Thinking*, trans. John M. Anderson and E. Hans Freund (New York: Harper and Row Publishers, 1966), 151.
32. Ibid., 152.
33. Ibid., 153.
34. Martin Heidegger, "Building Dwelling Thinking," in *Basic Writings*, ed. David Farrell Krell (New York: HarperCollins, 1993), 362.
35. Ibid.

36. Richard Capobianco, *Engaging Heidegger* (Toronto: University of Toronto Press, 2010), 67–8.
37. Heidegger, *Elucidations of Hölderlin's Poetry*, 171.
38. Friedrich Hölderlin, *Friedrich Hölderlin: Poems and Fragments*, trans. Michael Hamburger (Ann Arbor: University of Michigan Press, 1967), 415.
39. Ibid., 215.
40. Ibid., 227.
41. "*Der Spiegel* Interview with Martin Heidegger," 1966, accessed August 15, 2016, http://web.ics.purdue.edu/~other1/Heidegger%20Der%20Spiegel.pdf
42. Martin Heidegger, *Parmenides*, trans. Andre Schuwer and Richard Rojcewicz (Indianapolis: Indiana University Press, 1992), 106.
43. Aristotle, *Nicomachean Ethics*, trans. Terence Irwin (Indianapolis: Hackett Publishing, 1985), 427.
44. Martin Heidegger, "The Thinker as Poet," in *Poetry, Language, Thought*, trans. Albert Hofstadter (New York: Harper & Row, 1971), 8.
45. Heidegger, *Parmenides*, 63.
46. Ibid., 100.
47. Aristotle, *Nicomachean Ethics*, 1177b30.
48. David Farrell Krell, *Daimon Life* (Bloomington & Indianapolis: Indiana University Press, 1992), 19.
49. Heidegger, *Parmenides*, 101.
50. Martin Heidegger, *Introduction to Metaphysics*, trans. Gregory Fried and Richard Polt (New Haven: Yale University Press, 2000), 15.
51. Iain Thomson, *Heidegger on Ontotheology* (New York: Cambridge University Press, 2005), 37.
52. Richard Capobianco, *Heidegger's Way of Being* (Toronto: University of Toronto Press, 2014), 63.
53. Heidegger, "Introduction to 'What is Metaphysics?'" in *Pathmarks*, ed. William McNeill (Cambridge: Cambridge University Press, 1998), 283.
54. Capobianco, *Heidegger's Way of Being*, 79.
55. Heidegger, *Elucidations of Hölderlin's Poetry*, 75.
56. Heidegger, *Parmenides*, 104.
57. Ibid., 70.
58. Ibid., 104.
59. Ibid.
60. Plato, "The Symposium," in *The Collected Dialogues of Plato*, ed. Edith Hamilton and Huntington Cairns (Princeton: Princeton University Press, 1961), 555.
61. *Apology*, 31c–d, 40a. *Republic*, 496 b–c. *Symposium*, 175.
62. Plato, "Cratylus," in *The Collected Dialogues of Plato*, ed. Edith Hamilton and Huntington Cairns (Princeton: Princeton University Press, 1961), 435.
63. Heidegger, *Hölderlin's Hymn "The Ister,"* 155–6.
64. Ibid., 156.
65. Heidegger, *Parmenides*, 71.
66. Ibid., 62.

67. Vincent Vycinas, *Search for Gods* (The Hague: Martinus Nijhoff, 1972), 21.
68. Vincent Vycinas, *Earth and Gods* (The Hague: Martinus Nijhoff, 1969), 187–8.
69. Heidegger, *Elucidations on Hölderlin's Poetry*, 58.
70. Ibid., 219.
71. Vycinas, *Search for Gods*, 22.

Chapter Four

Our Loss of Dwelling

OUR WORLD

Our world is fraught with crises, disorder, injustice, suffering, exploitation, oppression, degradation, and destruction. Most people, even if unaware of details and specifics, have an abiding sense of things simply not being "right," and many suffer a lack of meaning, hope, happiness, and peace. Whether focusing on individual, collective, societal, or global situations, many long for guidance, direction, or simply for someone to show them a different way. Too many despair. They question whether a different way of existing is even possible.

In the essay, "Ecofeminism: Toward Global Justice and Planetary Health," Greta Gaard and Lori Gruen offer a sampling of statistics gathered in their research. A few of the crises and stats they mention are: 85 percent of the world's' income goes to 23 percent of the world's people, the United States has only 5 percent of the world's population yet uses 33 percent of all non-renewable resources and 25 percent of the planet's commodities, 1.2 billion people lack safe drinking water, the United States has lost all but 10 percent of its ancient forests, 40,000 children starve to death on our planet each day, and animal agriculture produces two billion tons of waste each year.[1]

Additionally, there are all the problems and issues related to fracking, mountain top removal, prison as a for-profit industry, oil spills, coral bleaching, homelessness, ocean acidification, domestic abuse, desertification, hunger, malnutrition, sexual assault, the Pacific ocean garbage patch, neglected veterans, Fukushima, loss of fresh water supplies, colony collapse disorder, debt, drought, disease, rising health care costs, increased poverty, police brutality, war, religious strife, and the list goes on. While my intent is not to elaborate on these particular issues, I simply offer them as examples of the various crises currently faced.

While one may conceive of each and every one of these things as a discrete and separate problem or issue and engage in a thorough going investigation of it, no doubt gaining understanding of details and perhaps even hitting upon things relevant to causation, I contend that a better approach is one that allows for a more holistic understanding. In seeking to understand such things in terms of their interrelatedness, with an aim toward finding the underlying reality or realities that give rise to and/or maintain each of these problems, we are in a much better position to clearly see exactly what types of changes may bring resolution.

Perhaps a metaphor and analogy is useful here to understand this difference in approach I am proposing. In traditional Western medicine, illness and the body have been approached in a very nonholistic way. While you have your general practitioners, most of the heavy lifting is done by specialists who have devoted themselves to the understanding and study of one specific part or system of the human body in isolation from the rest.

Today, more and more people recognize the limitations of this Western approach despite the seemingly entrenched modes of practice that constitute the industry and institution that is medicine. The rise of interest in and appreciation for alternative approaches that view the body holistically and acknowledge the interrelatedness of not only the different systems within the body but the different facets of human being relevant to well-being speak to this shift in conscious awareness of the integral nature of health and well-being.

By conceiving our world in a similar manner it is possible not only to recognize that it is indeed sick and has many, many symptoms, but we gain the ability to acknowledge that while it does have various different systems that operate within it, all the systems are ultimately interrelated. When this reality is acknowledged, the various ways in which any one part is diseased are better understood in terms of the influences and effects that result from its reciprocal relation to other parts. The health and well-being of each part is understood to be undoubtedly integral to the healthy functioning of the whole.

To begin reflecting on these things, I will offer a summary of the philosophy of ecofeminism and examine a few of the most meaningful contributions of this philosophy for the gaining of deeper understanding of our current human situation and our current world. Inherent within the ecofeminist framework is theorizing as to how we arrived at this point, how the current global crises came to be, and how we might best understand the interconnected nature of these crises and their causes which might otherwise be construed as separate and discrete.

As I see it, there is within ecofeminist theorizing an insightful articulation of the interrelated explanations for the present functioning of global oppressions and for what I am calling "a general loss of *dwelling*," as well as many other valuable insights. Perhaps most importantly, however, there is an orientation of openness toward thinking, toward any and all thinking that takes as its concern the health of our planet and human well-being and flourishing. Ecofeminism aspires to think toward the eradication of oppression and exploitation and the cessation of destruction and suffering by cultivating what the Heideggerian ecofeminist Trish Glazebrook calls "an intellectual climate of solidarity, connection and intersection" through the maintenance of an "inclusivity that seeks introduction over reduction, emergent growth over confining and common denominators."[2]

ECOFEMINISM AND WHAT IT UNCONCEALS

Ecofeminism has its roots in the French tradition of feminist theory. Early on, Simone de Beauvoir made the case that patriarchal reasoning relegated both nature and women to the realm of *other*.[3] Later, French feminist Francois d'Eaubonne coined the term "ecofeminism" when she called upon women to bring about ecological revolution in opposition to the overpopulation and destruction of resources that resulted from patriarchal rule. In North America, various writers such as Rosemary Radford Ruether and Carolyn Merchant began to lay the foundation for the much fuller approach that ecofeminism has come to be today. While there is some disagreement among various ecofeminists regarding particular issues, there are some basic viewpoints and ideas shared by virtually all ecofeminists, and it is from those that I will take my start.

As its name implies, the philosophical approach that is known as ecofeminism begins with the supposition that historically there has been a very clear link between the subjection, domination, and oppression of women and the conquest, destruction, and exploitation of nature. As Karen Warren states, "What *all* ecofeminists agree about, then, is the way in which *the logic of domination* has functioned historically within patriarchy to sustain and justify the twin dominations of women and nature."[4] Moreover, what Warren and other ecofeminists have argued and consistently shown is that the logic of domination as such is that which conceptually links and binds together all forms of oppression. Warren writes:

> Ecofeminists insist that the sort of logic of domination used to justify the domination of humans by gender, racial or ethnic, or class status is also used to justify the domination of nature. Because eliminating a logic of domination is part of a

> feminist critique—whether a critique of patriarchy, white supremacist culture, or imperialism—ecofeminists insist that *naturism* is properly viewed as an integral part of any feminist solidarity movement to end sexist oppression and the logic of domination which conceptually grounds it.[5]

In attempting to understand the conditions that gave rise to the mutually reinforcing oppressions of certain humans along with the natural world, specific ideas and institutions continually come to the fore. Within much of the ecofeminist literature, one can discern an important theme: a conceptual and material separation between culture and nature is at the root of our current crises. Conceptually, it seems that the separation between culture and nature is itself a consequence of the prevailing logic of domination that characterizes our current epoch. Materially, it seems that the separation between culture and nature is itself a consequence of both conceptual ideologies and the lived embodied realities upon which those are based. However, such observations, as insightful as they may be, are somewhat vague and abstract and call for further thinking. Many ecofeminist thinkers are responding to that call. One such thinker is scholar Ariel Salleh. Salleh has produced a work of exceptional scholarly research and thinking, *Ecofeminism as Politics*.

Salleh's work aims to undercut the postmodern notion that feminism and environmentalism are both disconnected, single-issue movements. She does this through an examination of science, the body, nature, culture, and politics. Her examination yields the insights central to the ecofeminist critique with a special emphasis on the embodied materialism of ecofeminism. Salleh writes, "The basic premise of ecofeminist political analysis is that ecological crisis is the inevitable effect of a Eurocentric capitalist patriarchal culture built on the domination of nature, and domination of Woman 'as nature'."[6] Of course, Salleh is careful to point out that women are not closer to nature in any kind of ontological sense. Women and men are both in, with, and of nature. However, she explains that "attaining the prize of masculine identity depends on men distancing themselves from that fact."[7]

Additionally, Salleh seeks to make clear, in response to certain critics who misconstrue the project of ecofeminism or who focus in too narrowly on certain aspects of its critical approach, that "By the structural criterion, an ecofeminist is anybody who carries out ecofeminist activities. That is, the term applies to a man or a woman whose political actions support the premise that the domination of nature and domination of women are interconnected. To repeat: ecofeminism is neither an essentialising standpoint nor an identity politics."[8]

Many ecofeminist thinkers, like Salleh, Merchant, Glazebrook, Gaard, Gruen, and others, focus in on four specific things that provide us with a fuller and more in-depth understanding and explanation for most if not all of our current crisis situations. The majority of those claiming to be ecofeminist see each of the four explanations as playing an important role in the unfolding of our global and human situation in that they are historically and culturally intertwined and mutually reinforcing in various ways. Metaphorically, these four things may be conceived as making up the four sides of a frame, the frame of ecofeminism, through which we are better able to see and understand our world and its realities in terms of both accurately diagnosing problems and their causes and offering prognoses. The four things that make up the ecofeminist framework of critique are the scientific revolution and the resultant mechanistic materialist model of the universe, capitalism, patriarchy and patriarchal religions, and *self and other dualisms*.[9]

The first explanation I will look at is that of the scientific revolution and the spread of the *mechanistic universe* worldview.[10] While this shift did not occur overnight, it was an epochal shift that did indeed occur and involved some serious changes in the prevailing mindset of humanity, or at least in those who wielded power over others and over what would come to be understood as conventional wisdom. Prior to this epochal shift, nature was seen as alive. With the shift into the mechanistic materialist model, nature came to be seen as simple, dead, and inert matter. Ever increasingly nature was viewed as a machine whose laws could be known and understood. What was formerly seen as a forest, alive and full of life, came to be seen merely in terms of its usefulness. A former sacred wood became only so many potential square feet of lumber.

Thanks to the work and thought of Descartes, Francis Bacon, and others, both nature and animals, the human body, and the very earth itself came to be understood on the model of a machine. The entire universe was taken to be something that could be comprehended mathematically, its laws discovered and documented, and ultimately manipulated and controlled via analysis, reason, science, and technology. All of the natural world was thereby reduced to something to be conquered, dominated, and controlled. Of course, it followed that nature and all within it existed so as to be used, instrumentalized, and optimized. Under such a mechanistic, materialist conception, the only ethics that were applicable were the ethics of utility and perhaps a Hobbesian egoism.

While there is no doubt that the scientific revolution, and the subsequent scientific and technological innovations that gave rise to the Industrial Revolution, were themselves instantiations of a logic of domination in action, the ideology that advocated, accompanied, and applauded these changes was itself predicated upon the unquestioned assumption of the "rightness" of a logic of domination, of the superiority of *calculative thinking*, and the instrumentalization of both nature and human beings. Salleh writes:

> The Industrial Revolution, by providing a sophisticated machinery for the exploitation of natural and human resources, soon propelled the dream of

mastery forward under the banner of "development." ... But, as Marcuse observed, the self-estranged functional rationality of science would yield only knowledge of "a dead world," apprehended in terms of fungible atomic units, to be reduced and reassembled according to human will. The ideal form for presentation of this knowledge was the neutral algebraic formula, it being poor science, delusion, lies, to intrude value considerations into the generation of pure positive knowledge. For physicists, matter thus faded into mathematical and topographical relations: a vocabulary of events, projections and abstract possibilities was ushered in. The entire methodological trend implied a suspension of inquiry into the nature of reality or "the reality of nature," replacing it with an emphasis on the specific operations to be used in its transformation.[11]

Salleh's observations are indeed echoes of the concerns articulated by Heidegger regarding our technological Enframing and the reduction of *poiēsis* to mere *challenging* [*Herausfordern*]. In his essay, "The Question Concerning Technology," Heidegger writes:

[A] tract of land is challenged into the putting out of coal and ore. The earth now reveals itself as a coal mining district, the soil as a mineral deposit. The field that the peasant formerly cultivated and set in order appears differently than it did when to set in order still meant to take care of and to maintain. The work of the peasant does not challenge the soil of the field. In the sowing of the grain it places the seed in the keeping of the forces of growth and watches over its increase. But meanwhile even the cultivation of the field has come under the grip of another kind of setting-in-order, which *sets* [*stellt*] upon nature. It sets upon it in the sense of challenging it. Agriculture is now the mechanized food industry. Air is now set upon to yield nitrogen, the earth to yield ore, ore to yield uranium, for example; uranium is set upon to yield atomic energy, which can be released either for destruction or for peaceful use.[12]

For many ecofeminist thinkers, there is yet another concerning dimension of the science aspect of the equation, and it has to do with the way in which environmentalism itself, as a movement, too often is complicit in the creation and maintenance of many of the relevant crises that calls it forth in the first place. As Salleh explains, the deep and abiding ways in which scientific technology is bound up with patriarchy and capitalism obscure realities that are themselves the result of this unholy alliance. Salleh writes:

[T]he technocratic thesis that scientific knowledge is central to environmentalism remains very popular. Developers and Greens both use risk analysis, and science-trained experts fill the upper echelons of the ecological establishment. Yet science is neither a necessary nor a sufficient condition for protest against the destruction of livelihood. Commonsense observation of the spread of sickness and plant deformities is sufficient for women and indigenous groups to challenge the capitalist patriarchal growth ethic. More often than not, the scientific fraternity is concerned to suppress dangerous findings in order to protect free enterprise.[13]

The implications of the realities of this observation are clear and will be made clearer as I proceed, and all that results from these interlocking systems of domination, while readily observable by an embodied common sense vision of the visible, are nonetheless veiled, denied, obscured, or otherwise claimed to be invisible by the paradigm that is the nexus of science, technology, patriarchy, and capitalism.

The next or second of the four causal explanations offered in the ecofeminist critique is the rise of capitalism and its accompanying colonialist/imperialist practices. The rise of feudalism in Europe and the enclosing of the commons along with the creation of private property are seen as having brought about the hierarchy that is endemic to the culture/nature division by creating the land-owner class and the landless peasants.[14] Engels himself is often cited, for in 1884 he wrote, "The overthrow of mother-right was the world historical defeat of the female sex. The man took command in the home also; the woman was degraded and reduced to servitude, she became the slave of his lust and a mere instrument for the production of children."[15]

While the role and place of women can certainly be argued to have been fundamentally altered with the rise of capitalism, it was not only women who found themselves oppressed, exploited, and denied equal value. Rather, anyone for whom the designation of "other" seemed to apply fell victim. However, as Salleh makes clear, the exploitation of both women and nature predates the exploitation of the proletariat, and the intellectual emphasis upon the abuse of the proletariat has itself served to obscure these more basic realities. Salleh notes that "[O]n an international scale, women, undertaking 65 per cent of the world's work for 5 per cent of its pay, effectively are 'the proletariat'."[16] Salleh elaborates upon this further when she writes, "Ecofeminists assert that the enclosure and privatization of women, the subsumption of women's time, energies and powers through patriarchal family and public employment alike, parallel or more accurately underwrite the class exploitation of labour by capital. Women's position as 'mediator of nature' constitutes a prior condition for the transaction that takes place between capitalist and laboring men-big men and small."[17]

Regarding the concept of women as "mediator of nature," I want to offer a brief explanation and provide proper context. Across many disciplines, various scholars, researchers, and thinkers have pondered the issue of women's status and standing. As Sherry Ortner wrote in the 1970s, "The secondary status of woman in society is one of the true universals, a pan-cultural fact."[18] However, there does exist a great deal of diversity both among the various cultural conceptions and symbolizations of woman and the ways in which women are treated in different cultures. In her essay entitled "Is Female to Male as Nature Is to Culture," Sherry Ortner explores the relevant questions and provides a very illuminating analysis.

Ortner begins by establishing the criteria by means of which it may be ascertained if indeed women are evaluated as inferior to men, and in employing those criteria she concludes, "I would flatly assert that we find women subordinated to men in every known society."[19] In her attempt to understand how and why this happens, she acknowledges the long-standing explanation of biological determinism and rejects it, noting that this explanation "has failed to be established to the satisfaction of almost anyone in academic anthropology."[20] Her own investigation into the matter, along with her thoughtful analysis and critical assessment, lead her to see clearly the ways in which biological factors, along with various social constructs and their requisite values and ideals, result in this universal ideology. She writes:

> [M]y thesis is that woman is being identified with—or, if you will, seems to be a symbol of—something that every culture devalues, something that every culture defines as being of a lower order of existence than itself. Now it seems that there is only one thing that would fit that description, and that is "nature" in the most generalized sense. Every culture, or, generically, "culture," is engaged in the process of generating and sustaining systems of meaningful forms (symbols, artifacts, etc.) by means of which humanity transcends the givens of natural existence, bends them to its purposes, controls them in its interest.[21]

Ortner's analysis discovers three interrelated reasons why women are seen as closer to nature, and all three are ways in which the physiological facts of the body and its procreative functions operate, albeit on different levels. [22] The first is the merely physiological and the fact that a woman's body and its functions are more involved with maintenance of the species. The second is the way in which these physiological realities place women in particular social roles that are considered lower than men's in terms of cultural process. Caring for home and children, women are "charged with the crucial function of transforming animal-like infants into cultured beings."[23] The third is the way in which the social roles that have been imposed upon women give them a different psychic structure that is seen as closer to nature. "The feminine personality tends to be involved with concrete feelings, things, and people, rather than with abstract entities."[24]

What Ortner uncovers in examining each of these, however, is not that woman is equated with nature but rather that at each of these levels, woman serves as mediator between nature and culture. Ortner writes, "All these factors make woman appear to be rooted more directly and deeply in nature. At the same time, however, her 'membership' and fully necessary participation in culture are recognized by culture and cannot be denied. Thus she is seen to occupy an intermediate position between culture and nature."[25]

This position of women as mediators between culture and nature is a crucial element of the mechanisms that serve to both subordinate and exploit women in the patriarchal capitalist paradigm. As Salleh states, "Women's traditional positioning between men and nature is a primary contradiction of capitalism, and may well be the deepest, most fundamental contradiction of all."[26] As Salleh makes clear, under capitalist patriarchy, the tasks that women, and in particular housewives, perform include but are not limited to: sexual satisfaction for the man; birthing and suckling offspring; caring for the offspring; protecting and socializing them; growing, procuring, and cooking food; maintaining the home; sweeping, cleaning, doing laundry, and dealing with garbage. As Salleh says, "The common denominator of these activities is a labour of 'mediation of nature' on behalf of men, which function continues despite legal recognition of 'female equality' by nation-states. Such legalities are incidental to the underlying accord between governments, capital and labour, guaranteeing each man his own piece of 'the second sex'."[27]

A further consequence of the spread of capitalism and its colonialist-imperialist expansion was the enslavement of indigenous peoples, or in India, the Adivasi, the capturing of land and resources for use and profit by an elite few, along with what came to be a kind of systematic underdevelopment in those places that further perpetuated not only the twin dominations and exploitations of both women and nature but also poor people and people of color. While it is indeed recognized that indigenous and Adivasi men suffer, the practical fact is that the domestic responsibilities in such places fall primarily upon women. Women are the ones responsible for growing and preparing food, gathering wood for heating and cooking, collecting water for the household, and so on, and this means that there is an even greater burden placed upon the women since the changes brought about by the colonizers and imperialists often made these tasks much more difficult, if not sometimes impossible.[28] As Salleh states, "For centuries, women engaged hands-on with habitat to provide food and shelter. But technologically transferred development ruptures this re/productive nature-woman-labour nexus, leaving starvation and ecological destruction in its place."[29]

The pattern that was instituted was one in which indigenous, native, and Adivasi people were forced to stop growing the crops that they had traditionally grown so as to grow cash crops for export, which of course translated into very little compensation for the people themselves, and they no longer were growing the food they needed to survive. Practices such as the clear-cutting of forests so as to increase crop yield resulted in massive erosion of the soil, and growing the same cash crop year after year depleted the soil of its nutrients.

Thus, these people soon found themselves truly poverty-stricken and in debt to their colonial lenders. According to Gaard and Gruen:

> The affluence of the North is founded on the natural resources and labor of the South.... One debtor nation, the Philippines, is among 70 countries which annually remit over $50 billion in interest alone to First World creditors. At this rate, the Third World will be perpetually indentured servants of the industrialized nations, an outcome well-suited to the goals of capitalism.[30]

Perhaps what is most ironic and symbolically telling is that the lifestyle these indigenous, native, and Adivasi peoples had been living prior to the arrival of the Europeans, although viewed as "impoverished" and "uncivilized" by the invaders, was in fact what is now understood as "subsistence living," and the so-called improvements in material existence that were supposed to have followed from the civilization and industrialization foisted upon them by their colonizers have actually resulted in real material poverty far worse than ever known before.[31]

Salleh is careful to point out that even postcolonial endeavors to supposedly assist nations with "development" are flawed in that they are themselves operating under the paradigm that created the problems in the first place. She writes, "International agencies like the United Nations (UN) treat 'development' as postcolonial and emancipatory: progress without subjugation. But import of the technological *a priori* through 'transfer' and 'capacity building' merely carries colonization to a new phase."[32]

Another crucial and important element of the capitalist paradigm is the way in which the West established that a nation's wealth is to be measured by its GNP and GDP. The logic of this method of calculation is: if you consume what you produce, you don't produce. Thus, production must be greater than consumption. This imposition rendered the work and product of most women around the world of zero value in so far as what they produced, they consumed. Marilyn Waring's *If Women Counted* explores this in depth. In an interview, Waring summed it up when she said, "In the mainstream, any movement has always been toward the 'market'. That is, there continues to be the assumption that the only way in which work can be visible or valuable is if you treat it as if it were a market commodity or a market service and you attribute a value to it."[33]

In a like manner, nature's own production and destruction are not accounted for in any way under such a means of measurement, nor are they granted value unless and until they somehow enter the cash economy. As Gaard and Gruen point out, "A clean lake which offers women fresh water supplies has no value in these accounting systems; once it is polluted, however, and companies must be paid to clean it up, then the clean-up activity itself is performed by men and recorded as generating income."[34]

In other words, nature as nature does not factor into equations of worth or value in a capitalist system. Only if a fresh water lake has been polluted and subsequently requires that a company be contracted to clean it up does the lake factor into the current economic paradigm as having any value. When the lake is pristine and people are freely utilizing it, it has no value. The failure of capitalism to accord value properly is well-articulated by Vandana Shiva in many of her books, essays, and articles. She sums it up well when she writes:

> Thus nature's amazing cycles of renewal of water and nutrients are defined into nonproduction. The peasants of the world, who provide 72% of the food, do not produce; women who farm or do most of the housework do not fit this paradigm of growth either. A living forest does not contribute to growth, but when trees are cut down and sold as timber, we have growth. Healthy societies and communities do not contribute to growth, but disease creates growth through, for example, the sale of patented medicine.[35]

It is my firm conviction that once one is rendered able to see what is in clear view, reality quickly comes into focus. While some of these ideas may indeed represent a previously unseen perspective for some, other of these ideas are not foreign in any way to our own popular culture, as evidenced by bumper stickers and memes on Facebook that say, "There is no profit in the cure for cancer." What may be lacking for many people is simply a more thoroughgoing and comprehensive understanding of the ways in which these things are in fact interrelated and mutually reinforcing.

The third ecofeminist explanation offered is the advent of patriarchal religion and the societal structure of patriarchy in general. The advent of patriarchal religion is yet another epochal shift, this one occurring long before the scientific revolution, around roughly 4500 BCE. In that shift, there was a move away from long-standing, earth-based, goddess-worshipping religions, in which both the earth's and women's fertility were seen as sacred and reverenced accordingly, in favor of the worship of sky gods, who were distant and removed from the earth and its people yet believed to rule over them nonetheless. Various cultures that had long existed without gender hierarchies began to esteem man above woman. Cultures in which divinity had been understood as immanent and present within both nature and humanity came to conceive of divinity as merely transcendent.[36]

It is important here to be clear about the distinction between gods understood as immanent and "sky gods" whose divinity is merely transcendent. While there were many so-called primitive religions who worshipped a Sun god or a Moon goddess, it is important to recognize that in doing that, they were not worshipping "sky gods" in the sense used here. Rather, for example, the Sun god that is worshipped in certain North American cultural groups, unlike the "sky gods" mentioned, was a very present and viewable phenomenon. The sun is itself seen by the people and recognized, appreciated, honored, and thus personified. Thus, the Sun god is one of many gods present in most if not all worldviews and religions that would be labeled "animistic" and for whom divinity is immanent. In such systems of belief, trees, rivers, mountains, clouds, moon, and sun are understood as imbued with spirit.

The gods referred to as "sky gods" in this context are not gods who possess an animate form that is visible to people. Rather, they are invisible gods who exist "out there" and whose divinity is not immanent but merely transcendent, such as the Judaeo-Christian god. The overthrow of the Titans by the Olympian gods is another example of the ascension of the sky gods to ultimate power and the rejection of gods of the earth.

Historically, many cultures made the transition from belief in immanent divinity to merely transcendent divinity when they fell under the rule of leaders and/or invaders who possessed such ideologies and religions and who imposed these upon the conquered people, the native tribes of the North American continent and their subordination to invading Europeans and their religious beliefs being perhaps one of the more recent examples of this type of occurrence.

Such patriarchal religious views entailed that the earth and all therein were created by a god or gods who created and ruled from outside. This conception of a distant and masculine authority is thought to have paved the way for the role of the male to be elevated above that of the female in reproduction; the female being compared to a barren field awaiting the planting of male seed.[37] Of course, this change occurred over time and at different rates in different places but certainly was in full effect by the time of both the Jews and the Classical Greeks. Within the Judaeo-Christian tradition, man's dominance over both women and nature is entrenched and, moreover, is reinforced by a mythology of divine command.

In a scathing and insightful critique of patriarchy, patriarchal religion, and its concomitant institutions and practices, Mary Daly explores the overthrow of ancient goddess-worship and its attendant reverencing of women and nature through an examination of history, philosophy, theology, mythology, medicine, and language in her book *Gyn/Ecology*. She writes:

> The rape of the Goddess in all of her aspects is an almost universal theme in patriarchal myth. ... The adequate androcratic invasion of the gynocentric realm can only be total erasure/elimination of female presence, which is replaced by male femininity.[38]

To summarize the many relevant insights found in Daly's work is beyond the scope of this project. However, suffice it to say that many of Daly's observations, including the necrophilic nature of patriarchy and its intersection with techno-scientific advances aimed at eliminating the need for women altogether, are indeed observable in the contemporary quest for the successful creation of a man-made womb, as well as laboratory-created meat grown from cells in a petri dish. These and other such so-called scientific advances are in desperate need of an ecofeminist and Heideggerian critique, for they are just a few of the ways in which science, technology, patriarchy, and capitalism operate together and reinforce one another.

For other thinkers, such as Elizabeth Fisher and Donna Haraway, patriarchy is approached from an anthropological perspective, and thus they see patriarchy itself as the result of developments in human evolution. They argue that once male hominids began hunting for food and interacting with other hominids outside their specific group, the realm of *culture* was conceived, and it was one involving men's death-oriented activities, while women, who were weaker and smaller and whose reproductive capacities and obligations prevented them from engaging in the hunting activities of the men, were relegated to the realm of non-culture, along with animals and nature. This distinguishing of the realm of *culture* from the realm involving domestic and reproductive activities is one that is common to ancient Greek thought, and it is made evident by a study of language, as I will explore in Chapter 5. The emphasis, however, even for those thinkers who approach these issues from the human evolution standpoint, is upon the division between men and women that is intimately linked up with the division between culture and nature.

The fourth and final explanation, that of *self and other dualisms*, is different in that it is a conceptual explanation and is the most abstract of the four. In many ways it is itself an aspect of each of the other three. Nonetheless, it is important enough so as to require being distinguished as a separate idea, for its usefulness as a tool of analysis and criticism is quite considerable.

Self and other dualisms are also sometimes referred to as *value dualisms*.[39] Essentially, these dualisms may be understood as valuations that esteem all things associated with the self and devalue all things associated with the other. Oppression and domination are built in to all such thinking in that the other by means of negation is the means for defining or understanding the self as powerful, good, and so on. The idea that an individual or a group will use another individual or a group as a means to their own identity or "goodness" is not a new idea and is certainly not one confined to ecofeminism or feminism. The writings of various existentialists, for example, as well as other thinkers, contain such discussions. Kierkegaard, Nietzsche, Sartre, Shelby Steele, bell hooks, W.E.B. DuBois, Levinas, de Beauvoir, all explicitly speak to this phenomenon.

From the ecofeminist point of view, women have been systematically rendered as the other and linked up with nature in that designation throughout the epoch of history known as patriarchy. The systematic devaluing of all things deemed nonmasculine or "feminine" has served to create an entrenched mode of thinking that has resulted in the ever-increasing loss of an entire section of the spectrum of the possible.

Dualisms such as self/other, culture/nature, reason/emotion, practical/impractical, civilized/wild, white/nonwhite, heterosexual/homosexual, and many others, have all served to establish value hierarchies and determine what constitutes the norm. Moreover, I contend that in the process of defining what is normative, what may rightfully be understood as being "masculine" actually determines and often constitutes what is seen as being "neutral."

A simple example of this idea is found in the use of typeface or fonts. Fonts that from a critical viewpoint might be termed "masculine" are indeed those most commonly referred to as "standard" or "ordinary" or "business" fonts. Such fonts would include Times New Roman, Garamond, or most of the Serifs. Fonts that are not seen as "standard" are often described as "frilly" "feminine," or "artsy." Such fonts would include Monotype Corsiva, Papyrus, and any of the scripts or "handwritten" fonts.

One particular website devoted specifically to website design notes that "Feminine typefaces are overly curvy and ornamental. There's often lots of extra flourish and usually plenty of contrast between the thicks and thins."[40] This same webpage also states, "Masculine typefaces tend to be fairly light on ornamentation and contain lots of hard corners and edges. They steer clear of exaggerated curves." While none of this may be surprising, what was interesting about this webpage was the fact that although it explicitly discussed both masculine and feminine fonts, the default assumption in the very layout of the webpage itself, along with its section titles, was that masculine fonts are the preferred fonts for business and the fonts with the most persuasive power. The website states, "Now that we've got our minds wrapped around the basic idea of masculinity and how it pertains to design, let's talk about some of the specific characteristics of a typeface and how that translates to the level of masculinity." The three characteristics that are listed are boldness, serifs, and shape and ornamentation.

The idea that there exists an identification between the masculine and the neutral was acknowledged by de Beauvoir when she wrote, "In actuality the relation of the two sexes is not quite like that of two electrical poles, for man represents both the positive and the neutral, as is indicated by the common use of *man* to designate human beings in general."[41]

Here I find it interesting and important to consider something Heidegger says regarding the loss of handwriting that occurred with the rise of the use of the typewriter. I see further definite points of intersection between Heidegger and ecofeminism revealed when he says:

> It is not accidental that modern man writes "with" the typewriter and "dictates" into a machine. ... The typewriter tears writing from the essential realm of the hand, i.e., the realm of the word. ... Today a hand-written letter is an antiquated and undesired thing; it disturbs speed reading. ... In addition, mechanical writing provides this "advantage," that it conceals the handwriting and thereby the character. The typewriter makes everyone looks the same.[42]

Making everyone look the same is of course the essence of a "neutral" means of communication, no doubt, and a "neutral" font would be requisite. The mechanical writing that Heidegger speaks of is itself the result of the implementation of scientific and technological advances, and of course the efficiency of this mechanization is well-suited to the goals and purposes of capitalism. The loss of the embodied aspect of writing, the use of the hand, no doubt further signals our Enframing. Perhaps even more important, however, is Heidegger's assertion that the concealment of handwriting is a concealment of character, for in that assertion we can tie together many of the important ideas that span the breadth of this project. Modern humanity, having been shaped by the ideals of the scientific revolution, patriarchal religion, capitalism, and enslaved by the reigning value dualisms of self and other, not only assents to a reduction to the same via mechanical writing but may well benefit, enjoy, or otherwise require the anonymity and concealment of character that it provides.

For it is my contention that loss of *dwelling* presupposes inauthenticity; it is in a certain sense a loss of self, a loss of attunement to one's own being and connection to Being. Just as one may be all too content to be a merely *calculative thinker*, one may also be content to be merely a facade, an optimized resource, in turn optimizing all resources afforded by successful fulfillment of the role prescribed in the orchestra that is modern existence. Such a shiny exterior, envied and enviable, serves to conceal the absence of awareness of the *Fourfold*. Perhaps it should not be surprising that human beings, subjected from birth to systems of existence that operate primarily on principles of domination and denigration, ultimately opt to forego the depths and tread only on the surface. Such human beings simply await their optimization (*Bestand*).

The idea of would-be individuals reduced to some homogenous state of being is no doubt a crucial part of the operation of *self and other dualisms*, whether it is occurring by means of the loss of handwriting and individual character or through the imposition of ideological structures into which individuals are expected and made to fit. For, "Domination is built in to such dualisms because the other is negated in the process of defining a powerful self," write Gaard and Gruen.[43] Likewise does Warren make clear that oppressive conceptual frameworks presuppose the logic of domination and the need for such value dualisms so as to "justify" subordination of the other.[44]

I believe that an excellent place to begin looking for value dualisms and dualisms of *self and other* that serve the ends of systems of oppression and subjugation is within language itself. When we take a closer, critical look at language with an aim toward analyzing the function and purpose that certain kinds of language serve, certain ideological underpinnings are revealed. Many of the phrases and terms employed regularly in our language are revealed to connect women to nature and/or animals, thereby configuring them as other. Any close critique of language, as Mary Daly has shown in numerous works, may uncover the rampant and widespread use of words and phrases that perpetuate ideologies that serve to reinforce the inferior status of both women and nature. Many, of course, are also revealed to reinforce the diminution of certain kinds of men or groups of men or people. I contend that it is best to examine this phenomenon with an openness to seeing what it reveals, keeping in mind Heidegger's insight and claim that "Man acts as though he were the shaper and master of language, while in fact language remains the master of man."[45]

Heidegger's idea that language is a powerful force that holds sway over human beings is by no means a novel or unheard-of idea. When we recognize that our concepts and thoughts themselves are constructed from words, the power of language is recognized. Thus, it is not untrue to say that the larger a person's vocabulary, the greater is her capacity for thinking. However, unconscious and unreflective use of language too often conceals the very meaning and import of words and language. Much of an individual's use of particular words and phrases may be done habitually and without thoughtful reflection upon the deeper meaning and significance of the words used in terms of the values, beliefs, and ideals embedded within the terms and phrases. In order to unconceal values, beliefs, and ideologies that are operative, whether consciously or unconsciously, it is necessary to analyze not only the definition of any given term but to look also at the way in which a particular term or phrase carries with it a certain value judgment.

Analysis of the matter reveals that any individual or group of people who are deemed as other will be subjected to a process of animalization, feminization, and naturalization via the language employed in reference to them in the process of subordinating them. This process may be observed in an analysis of the metaphors of language that are used to describe a given individual or group. While Gaard and Gruen point out a few instances of this phenomenon in referencing such terms and phrases as "virgin forest," "rape of nature," "bitch," "old hen," and "sow," I think it is useful to continue to think further on the matter.[46]

Upon reflection, I find that there are many animals whose names are applied to humans in the process of attempting to render them subordinate: "cow," "hog," "pig," "chicken," "dog," "cougar," "wolf," "snake," "squirrel," "worm," "rat," "mouse," "alley cat," "fox," "goat," "shark," and "beaver," although that last one is used in reference to a particular body part of a woman and not the woman herself. In each instance, regardless of which animal name is being used and regardless of what traits are being alluded to as existing in the human referent, there is at work in the language employed both the logic of domination and a value hierarchy, the value being implied in the very act of animalizing the human being and its consequent configuring of that human being as other.

There is no doubt that there are a great many terms and phrases employed in a language whose ideological underpinnings call for a closer examination. Here I want to take a look at a couple of very contemporary terms that have since their introduction into common vocabulary struck me as very relevant: "douche" and "douchebag." I noticed the entrance of these words used in their current fashion about five years ago. According to *Merriam Webster online dictionary*, "douche" is defined as "a liquid that a woman squirts into her vagina to wash it; also: an object used to squirt such a liquid into the vagina."[47] I found it interesting that while the online free dictionary called Dictionary.com offered the following definition for "douche bag": "a small syringe having detachable nozzles for fluid injections, used chiefly for vaginal lavage and for enemas,"[48] the *Merriam Webster online dictionary* only provided the current slang meaning for the term: "an unattractive or offensive person."[49]

The contemporary usage of these terms as forms of slang is rampant; a quick googling of the terms shows that undeniably. The slang meaning of both terms is spelled out on urbandictionary.com, a site that itself is a veritable gold mine for further proving ecofeminist theses about language. On urbandictionary.com, "douche" is defined as "a word to describe an individual who has shown themself to be very brainless in one way or another, thus comparing them to the cleansing product for vaginas."[50] Urbandictionary.com also defines "douchebag" as "someone who has surpassed the levels of jerk and asshole, however not yet reached fucker or motherfucker. Not to be confuzed with douche."[51]

By all means, I do want to avoid being "confuzed." To analyze this, first, there is the perhaps obvious misogynistic and degrading putting-to-use of these terms in these new and contemporary ways in order to describe specific persons and attribute to them specific characteristics. There is an entire ideology of the vagina as something "dirty" and "unclean" built into the terms themselves, along with the even more degraded means by which such "filthy things" would be cleaned.

Second, there is the fact that actual douching as a practice is now widely understood and scientifically verified to be not only completely unnecessary but often unhealthy and potentially dangerous. Yet, as is reported by the National Institute of Health, douching continues to be practiced, and even more so by poor women and women of color. From the report:

> Douching in the United States is more common among African-American women. Independently of race, associations between douching and poverty, less than a high school education, a history of pelvic inflammatory disease, and having between two and nine lifetime sexual partners are reported. A lower educational level, many sexual partners, and poverty are also risk factors for sexually transmitted diseases and bacterial vaginosis, making it especially complicated to assess causality since women might douche secondary to infection-related symptoms rather than for routine purposes. [52]

These specific terms then are not only great examples of *self and other dualisms* and their concomitant value dualisms present within language, but these particular terms and their import are also easily linked up with all four of the main areas of concern that constitute the ecofeminist critique: the mechanization and technologization of the body and all natural processes that is part of the *mechanistic universe* worldview, the commodification of the body and its clinicalization so as to render it in need of product and service by a capitalist industry, value dualisms imposed that impart the female body's less-than status, and the patriarchal mindset that feels justified in imposing the other three in so far as women's bodies are considered their territory and ultimately under their purvey and control. Language is indeed the master, as Heidegger says. It is a medium for the sedimentation and consequent reinforcement of these somewhat subtle yet undeniable forms of oppression.

Ultimately, the ecofeminist framework, being comprised of the close and critical examination of the four phenomena of the scientific revolution, capitalism, patriarchy, and *self and other dualisms*, aids in bringing into view the role and function of each of the four phenomena, as well as their mutually reinforcing interrelatedness. It provides a means of surveying our world, bringing into focus more sharply the very real ways in which human beings are experiencing "a loss of *dwelling*."

NIETZSCHE'S INSIGHTS: PATRIARCHAL RELIGION AND THE OTHERWORLD

While Patriarchal Religion is not an explicit theme in Nietzsche's work, I want to examine certain of his ideas from an ecofeminist point of view. I see his ideas as expressing insights to which appeal could be made in a critique of many of the concerns central to the ecofeminist point of view.

In his *Thus Spake Zarathustra, Beyond Good and Evil*, and *Genealogy of Morals*, Nietzsche speaks of the attachment of the resentful to the "other-worldly" (*überirdischen*, literally, the "over-earthly," sometimes translated as "supernatural"). Nietzsche emphasizes that within the Judaeo-Christian worldview, there is an overemphasis upon and an overconcern with a "true world," a place other than this world, a place above, beyond, or outside the earthly realm.

Nietzsche takes serious issue with the fact that what is embraced is a metaphysics that is "hostile to the senses."[53] Nietzsche, speaking as Zarathustra, says, "I beseech you, my brothers, *remain faithful to the earth*, and do not believe those who speak to you of otherworldly hopes! Poison-mixers are they, whether they know it or not. Despisers of life are they, decaying and poisoned themselves, of whom the earth is weary: so let them go."[54] For Nietzsche, those who would focus upon an otherworld and forego this one are betrayers of life, and being decayed and poisoned themselves, they seek to poison others. Here I want to look at the points of intersection between Nietzsche's thought and the ideas of ecofeminism.

Nietzsche's assessment of the Judaeo-Christian worldview as primarily responsible for the rise in attachment to the "otherworldly," and the resultant loss of intimate connection with and care and concern for the earth is much like the ecofeminist idea that the rise of patriarchal religion is responsible for many of the current ills of our planet due to its rejection of immanent divinity and its profaning of both the flesh and nature in its embrace of a belief in a merely transcendent divinity.

The Judaeo-Christian worldview, by overthrowing earth-based, goddess-worshipping religions and emphasizing a male-centered cosmogony, once spread via the Roman Empire and then the Roman Catholic Church, may be understood as one of the most crucial events in history in this regard. Nietzsche argues that those who are focused on the otherworld necessarily become haters or despisers of life itself. In their embrace of and emphasis upon the otherworld, they reject life as its own justification and demand something outside of life to justify it. Nietzsche's idea thus resonates with the ecofeminist assertion that in foregoing a belief in immanent divinity in favor of a belief in divinity as transcendent only, there is a fundamental loss of reverence for life itself and the life-giving power of the earth, nature, and women. Life is no longer intrinsically sacred, but requires sanctification from outside itself.

I also see Nietzsche as coinciding with ecofeminist thinking in terms of concerns about the paradigm created by the scientific revolution and the consequent issues arising therefrom. For, as Nietzsche argued, while religion had formerly provided answers regarding ultimate purposes, science ushered in the doubt and progressive overthrow of religion. And although science may try to fill the void created by the death of god and people may even come to worship science as the new religion, science can never actually achieve that end. Science as such has no consideration for ultimate purposes.[55]

The "death of God" and nihilism may both be understood as this very lack of any ultimate reasons for being. In the opening of his work *Will to Power*, Nietzsche writes, "What does nihilism mean? That the highest values devaluate themselves. The aim is lacking: 'why?' finds no answer."[56] For both Nietzsche and ecofeminist thinkers, the mindset belonging to the mechanistic materialist model of the universe is indeed one that deprives existence of ultimate purposes, denies inherent or intrinsic value, and ultimately reduces everything to meaningless resources awaiting optimization.

I want to further develop this important intersection between Nietzsche and ecofeminism in terms of the ways in which Nietzsche speaks about *self* and *other*. In the *Genealogy*, he states:

> Whereas all noble morality grows out of a triumphant affirmation of oneself, slave morality immediately says No to what comes from outside, to what is different, to what is not oneself: and *this* No is its creative deed. This reversal of the value-positing glance—this *necessary* direction outward instead of back to oneself—is of the nature of *ressentiment*: to come into being, slave morality requires an outside world, a counterworld; first an opposing world, a world outside itself. Psychologically speaking, it requires external stimuli in order to act at all. Its action is basically reaction.[57]

Nietzsche's point in this quotation is an excellent example of the concept central to the ecofeminist critique of *self and other dualisms* or *value dualisms*. Nietzsche argues that the very system of valuation which is contingent upon dualities is itself flawed in that the *self* in such a system does not see itself *first* but only sees itself subsequently and through an other. The existence and conceptualization of the other is the necessary condition for the existence and conceptualization of the self, one might say, at least for those Nietzsche would label "slaves." Additionally, this is also much like Sartre's description of the bigot, as discussed in Chapter 2, as a person who lacks the capacity for introspection and thus can only see himself through the eyes of others and who conceives of himself thus not as an individual but as simply a member of the group, part of a tradition.

Of course, it is this very type of evaluative system that ecofeminists see as operative and at play in the twin dominations of women and nature. Patriarchy, as a way of thinking, I would argue, emerged in the thinking of men who sought to develop their self-understanding by means of contrasting themselves with the other as embodied in both women and nature. In the thinking of men, women are configured as other. Thus, it is in the event of the conceptual linking of women with nature that men conceive themselves as linked to culture.

A less anthropologically oriented ecofeminist assessment may be to see the ascendancy of patriarchy as involving men taking over all determinations of value, and regardless of what their motives may have been, relegating woman to a less-than status in establishing themselves as superior, rational, logical, productive, and conquest-seeking. Men defined themselves in self-conscious opposition to women as they perceived them. Such a tendency to think in terms of *self* and *other* has been argued by some to be basic to the functioning of human thinking. Even de Beauvoir wrote, "The category of the *Other* is as primordial as consciousness itself."[58]

However, this tendency, no matter how primordial, has also been argued to be something that can and should be overcome or at least recognized and resisted, contextualized, and rendered contingent and thus less oppressive, all the more so when it is understood to be motivated from power-seeking impulses such as fear and aggression. Nietzsche's own assessment of the motivation for the thinking typified by the slaves is that they are essentially fear-driven. This fear prompts them to define themselves as good or superior by means of denigrating the other. This is the precise kind of thinking Nietzsche describes when he writes, "Imagine 'the enemy' as conceived by a man of *ressentiment*—and here precisely is his deed, his creation: he has conceived 'the evil enemy', '*the evil one*'—and indeed as the fundamental concept from which he then derives, as an after-image and counterinstance, a 'good one'—himself."[59]

Nietzsche's thinking is applicable here in the sense that it is only in man's defining of "woman" or "the feminine" that he can then define himself as an "after-image." In his defining of woman and nature in this way, he necessitates that both be dominated and controlled, for the after-image created is one of a rightful ruler. With these ideas in mind, I will now turn my attention to look at the mythological figure of Lilith, representative of women and the feminine in the Judaeo-Christian tradition, using as tools for my analysis some enlightening ideas from Giorgio Agamben on how sovereign power is created.

NOTES

1. Greta Gaard and Lori Gruen, "Ecofeminism: Toward Global Justice and Planetary Health," in *Environmental Ethics: An Anthology*, ed. Andrew Light and Holmes Rolston III (Oxford: Blackwell Publishers, 2003), 276.

2. Trish Glazebrook, "Heidegger and Ecofeminism," in *Feminist Interpretations of Martin Heidegger*, ed. Nancy J. Holland and Patricia Huntington (University Park: The Pennsylvania State University Press, 2001), 224.

3. Simone de Beauvoir, *The Second Sex* (New York: Bantam Books, 1952), 114.

4. Karen J. Warren, "The Power and Promise of Ecological Feminism," in *Ecological Feminist Philosophies*, ed. Karen J. Warren (Indianapolis: Indiana University Press, 1996), 23.

5. Ibid., 24.

6. Ariel Salleh, *Ecofeminism as Politics* (London & New York: Zed Books, Ltd., 1997), 13.

7. Ibid.

8. Ibid., 108.

9. Gaard and Gruen, "Ecofeminism: Toward Global Justice and Planetary Health," 277.

10. Ibid., 278.

11. Salleh, *Ecofeminism as Politics*, 58.

12. Heidegger, "The Question Concerning Technology," trans. William Lovitt (New York: Harper and Row, 1977), 14.

13. Salleh, *Ecofeminism as Politics*, 10.

14. See Vandana Shiva, *Staying Alive: Women, Ecology, and Development* (London and New York: Zed Books Ltd., 1989).

15. Friedrich Engels, *The Origin of the Family, Private Property and the State* (New York: Penguin Classics, 1972), 108.

16. Salleh, *Ecofeminism as Politics*, 6.

17. Ibid., 94.

18. Sherry Ortner, "Is Female to Male as Nature Is to Culture," in *Woman, Culture & Society*, ed. Michelle Zimbalist Rosaldo and Louise Lamphere (Stanford: Stanford University Press, 1974), 67.

19. Ibid., 70.

20. Ibid., 71.

21. Ibid., 72.

22. Ibid., 73.

23. Ibid., 84.

24. Ibid., 81.

25. Ibid., 84.

26. Salleh, *Ecofeminism as Politics*, 93.

27. Ibid.

28. Gaard and Gruen, "Ecofeminism: Toward Global Justice and Planetary Health," 279.

29. Salleh, *Ecofeminism as Politics*, 61.

30. Gaard and Gruen, "Ecofeminism: Toward Global Justice and Planetary Health," 281.

31. Vandana Shiva, *Staying Alive*, 13.

32. Salleh, *Ecofeminism as Politics*, 61.

33. "*Aurora* Interview with Marilyn Waring," 1998, accessed July 17, 2016, http://aurora.icaap.org/talks/waring.htm
34. Gaard and Gruen, "Ecofeminism: Toward Global Justice and Planetary Health," 280.
35. Vandana Shiva, "How Economic Growth Has Become Anti-Life," *The Guardian*, accessed August 17, 2016, https://plutopress.wordpress.com/2013/11/06/how-economic-growth-has-become-anti-life-vandana-shiva-in-the-guardian/
36. Gaard and Gruen, "Ecofeminism: Toward Global Justice and Planetary Health," 278.
37. See Merlin Stone, *When God Was a Woman* (New York: Barnes & Noble, 1976).
38. Mary Daly, *Gyn/Ecology* (Boston: Beacon Press, 1978), 84.
39. Gaard and Gruen, "Ecofeminism: Toward Global Justice and Planetary Health," 278.
40. "Leveraging Stereotypes in Design: Masculine vs. Feminine Typography," Joshua Johnson, accessed July 31, 2016, https://designshack.net/articles/typography/leveraging-stereotypes-in-design-masculine-vs-feminine-typography/
41. Beauvoir, *The Second Sex*, 255.
42. Heidegger, *Parmenides*, trans. Andre Schuwer and Richard Rojcewicz (Indianapolis: Indiana University Press, 1992), 80.
43. Gaard and Gruen, "Ecofeminism: Toward Global Justice and Planetary Health," 278.
44. Warren, "The Power and the Promise of Ecological Feminism," 21.
45. Heidegger, "Building Dwelling Thinking," in *Basic Writings*, ed. David Farrell Krell (New York: HarperCollins, 1993), 348.
46. Gaard and Gruen, "Ecofeminism: Toward Global Justice and Planetary Health," 278
47. The website of Merriam Webster, accessed December 31, 2014, http://www.merriam-webster.com/dictionary/douche
48. The website of Dictionary Reference, accessed December 31, 2014, http://dictionary.reference.com/browse/douche+bag
49. The website of Merriam Webster, accessed December 31, 2014, http://www.merriam-webster.com/dictionary/douche%20bag
50. The Urban Dictionary website, accessed December 31, 2014, http://www.urbandictionary.com/define.php?term=douche
51. The Urban Dictionary website, accessed December 31, 2014, http://www.urbandictionary.com/define.php?term=douchebag
52. "Vaginal Douching: Evidence of Risks or Benefits to Health," US National Library of Medicine National Institutes of Health website, accessed December 31, 2014, http://www.ncbi.nlm.nih.gov/pmc/articles/PMC2567125/
53. Friedrich Nietzsche, *On the Genealogy of Morals*, trans. Douglas Smith (Oxford: Oxford University Press, 1999), 468.
54. Friedrich Nietzsche, *Thus Spake Zarathustra*, trans. Thomas Common (New York: Dover Publications, 1999), 425.
55. Friedrich Nietzsche, *Human, All Too Human*, trans. R.J. Hollingdale (New York: Cambridge University Press, 1996), 58.

56. Friedrich Nietzsche, *The Will to Power*, trans. Walter Kaufmann (New York: Vintage Books, 2011), 9.

57. Nietzsche, *On the Genealogy of Morals*, 451.

58. Beauvoir, *The Second Sex*, 255.

59. Nietzsche, *On the Genealogy of Morals*, 452.

Chapter Five

Lilith and Agamben

AGAMBEN'S IDEAS

Taking seriously Foucault's idea that power should be thought of in terms of the concrete ways it penetrates not only the lives of subjects but also their very bodies, Giorgio Agamben develops an interesting set of critical ideas in his book *Homa Sacer: Sovereign Power and Bare Life*. I will explain those ideas and then appropriate them in order to provide an ecofeminist perspective on a seemingly timeless conception of a certain aspect of the feminine as found in the mythological figure of Lilith. The concepts Agamben develops and employs that are relevant to this undertaking are: *zoē, bios, homo sacer, bare life, sovereignty, the state of exception*, and *the hinge*.

In the spirit of Foucault, in terms of looking at power and power structures and the ways in which they directly play upon the very physicality of a subject's being, I shall demonstrate how Agamben's ideas may be appropriated and used to better understand certain ideas surrounding a particular conception of the feminine, particular beliefs and practices that were developed in relation thereto, as well as specific phenomenological experiences that are not confined to any particular place or time but that perpetually recur so long as a given society is under the control both politically and religiously by what, for our purposes, I will refer to herein as *the sovereign masculine*.

This chapter is divided into three sections. In this first section, I will lay out the meaning and use of the relevant terms developed and employed by Agamben, with the understanding that I will take them up again in further discussion and application in the third section of the chapter. In the second section of the chapter, I will introduce and discuss the character of Lilith, an ancient she-demon, found in the teachings and myths of various cultures, but one primarily developed in Judaism and more extensively in the mystical branch of Judaism known as Kabbalah. In the third section of the chapter, I will show how Agamben's ideas may be used in an analysis of Lilith, as well as her counterparts, Adam and Eve, and how the insights gained from that analysis demonstrate further the applicability of the ecofeminist critique.

My intent with the undertaking in this chapter is threefold: I will demonstrate via an examination of a mythological figure the way in which myth does indeed reflect human beings' understanding and interpretation of their lived phenomenological experiences. Exactly whose experiences are being reflected in any given myth will be an important question to ask. I will also demonstrate via an examination of this mythological figure the ways in which the ecofeminist framework, in good Heideggerian fashion, may assist us in seeing something that has been right in front of us all along but was nonetheless unseen. Finally, I will demonstrate how Agamben's ideas, giving us insight as they do into the underlying structure and operation of political power, provide us yet another means of better understanding the way in which the four core areas of concern in ecofeminism, the scientific revolution and its resultant mechanistic materialist model of the universe, capitalism, patriarchal religion, and *self and other dualisms*, intersect and intertwine to bring about real material disempowerment for certain human beings as both bodies in the world and citizens of a polis, this being both relevant in itself and relevant as an integral part of the loss of *dwelling*. Crucial and relevant connections to Heidegger's thought will also be highlighted along the way.

One further thought: From the phenomenological/descriptive point of view, discussions of the feminine, it seems, are often reductive. The feminine, as a phenomenological experience that is concretely described, is seldom recognized as more than one-dimensional in the course of analysis and inquiry. And too often, when an analysis of the feminine is undertaken and the concept of the feminine is approached as something complex or multifaceted, it is done with an aim toward the reintegration of the parts into a neat and tidy unity, a unity that, as such, necessarily conceals certain aspects of the feminine. For, as I will seek to show, it is the very aim of achieving a so-called rational unity and integration that makes possible the usurpation of sovereign power by the masculine.

In the "Introduction" to *Homo Sacer*, Agamben examines two concepts, *zoē* and *bios*, the understanding of which is crucial to the further ideas he develops: *homo sacer, bare life, sovereignty*, the *state of exception*, and *the hinge*. Relying upon his study and understanding of the classical tradition, Agamben explains how the ancient Greeks conceived of life in two distinct and separate ways. He writes:

> [The Greeks] used two terms that, although traceable to a common etymological root, are semantically and morphologically distinct: *zoē*, which expressed the

simple fact of living common to all living beings (animals, men, or gods), and *bios*, which indicated the form or way of living proper to an individual or a group.[1]

Agamben explains that *zoē*, as such, was excluded from the *polis* proper in the Greek tradition and was restricted to the domestic sphere or home in that it was understood as merely reproductive life. *Bios*, on the other hand, is a life that aims toward the good, it is a life with a particular *telos*, a life to be lived and fully realized in the *polis*. *Bios* is the kind of life to which only man can attain in so far as man is that which is able by means of his possession of certain capacities to realize *logos* within himself. Of course, for the Greeks, "man" does here mean "men" only. Women were not included as members of the *polis* thus understood.

This distinction to which Agamben directs our attention is indeed in keeping with the distinction that ecofeminists hold to be so crucially important, that is, the distinction between nature and culture. Additionally, in investigating the terms *zoē* and *bios*, Agamben discovers a division that seems predicated upon what anthropologically minded ecofeminists feel is so important, a division that is predicated upon reproductive activity and the consignment of those caught up therein to the domestic sphere only.

Agamben offers further insight into the interesting way in which these two kinds of life are connected and how they should be understood as a standard pair in the West when he writes:

> The fundamental categorial pair of Western politics is not that of friend/enemy but that of bare life/political existence, *zoē/bios*, exclusion/inclusion. There is politics because man is the living being who, in language, separates and opposes himself to his own bare life and, at the same time, maintains himself in relation to that bare life in an inclusive exclusion.[2]

For Agamben, bare life, in a very real sense, is that which by means of being included through its exclusion forms the very foundation of the entire political system. In other words, bare life is held to be without place in the political realm, but because the very notion of *bios* entails bare life as that to which it opposes and distinguishes itself, it is included as what establishes the fundamental boundaries of the political domain by means of its exclusion. This is a crucial point to be understood. So, it is by the very act of making the distinction between bare life and *bios*, and asserting that only the latter is rightfully to be found in the political realm, that bare life is nonetheless included in the realm of the political by means of its being excluded. Agamben, in speaking further to his point, writes:

> At once excluding bare life from and capturing it within the political order, the *state of exception* actually constituted, in its very separateness, the hidden foundation on which the entire political system rested.[3]

The idea that the *state of exception* constitutes the very foundation for the political system is an important idea I will be looking at often throughout this chapter. Agamben goes on to explain that the very "force" of law is comprised by the ability of law to assert itself in relation to that which is exterior to it.[4] One way to render his meaning here so as to link it up with ideas established thus far is to say that the force of the *same/self* is made up of its capacity to assert itself in relation to an *other*. The *other* is crucial to the operation and function of the *same/self*. Without the *other*, the *same/self* could not exist. This echoes Nietzsche's articulation of the way in which the "slave" defines the self only through and in contrast to the "noble" or "master."

In explaining further the interdependence of and intimate connection between that which is included and that which is excluded, Agamben writes:

> Here what is outside is included not simply by means of an interdiction or an internment, but rather by means of the suspension of the juridical order's validity—by letting the juridical order, that is, withdraw from the exception and abandon it. The exception does not subtract itself from the rule; rather, the rule, suspending itself, gives rise to the exception and, maintaining itself in relation to the exception, first constitutes itself as a rule.[5]

The exception does not subtract itself from the rule; rather, the rule, suspending itself, gives rise to the exception. This idea is both a crucial aspect of Agamben's theory and important and pertinent to the purposes of this work, as well. Agamben asserts that that which gets excluded in no way is excluded by means of something intrinsic to it or as a result of something that it itself does or asserts. Rather, that which gets excluded, for Agamben, is best seen as a non-actor, a non-agent, a pure passivity in the process that unfolds in the sense that what happens to it is precisely *that which happens to it* as a result of the action and agency of something else that asserts itself as the rule. The actor or the agent in this event is that which in action asserts itself as *the rule*. The rule, in suspending itself in relation to that which it seeks to exclude, creates the exception to it. Thus, what is outside the realm over which the rule is operative is rendered so by means of the rule's assertion of itself in its act of excluding. The rule, in maintaining itself in relation to the exception it created, thus establishes itself as the rule. Here, again, is the relevance of Gaard and Gruen's explanation of *self and other dualisms*: "Domination is built into such dualisms because the other is negated in the process of defining a powerful self."[6]

In order to offer an illustration of Agamben's ideas on how the rule makes of itself the rule by establishing the exception, I offer the following analogy: Imagine there are a group of children playing together. Now, imagine that one child determines for whatever reason that he or she no longer wishes to speak or interact with one of the other children. He or she henceforth engages in what we would call *the silent treatment* in regards to the rejected child. In so far as he or she maintains that position and refuses to speak or be engaged by the rejected child that he or she has chosen to shun, under Agamben's theory, he or she simultaneously creates both him or herself as the rule and the other child as the exception. The other child is indeed included in the shunning child's realm of power by means of being excluded. The shunned child in this situation is indeed a non-actor, a nonagent in this unfolding. The shunned child, as Agamben would say, did not subtract him or herself from the rule but was abandoned or made an exception by the actions of the shunning child who asserts him or herself as the rule by means of suspending him or herself in relation to the other child.

Agamben makes clear that the dynamic does not simply end in the rule and its exception. In establishing itself by means of delineating that which is excluded, the rule founds its power so as to make a further distinction. To explain this idea, Agamben makes appeal to the literal historical figure in Roman law known as the *homo sacer*. The *homo sacer*, Latin for "the sacred man" or "the accursed man," must be properly understood here. The *homo sacer* is what he is precisely due to his non-relation to both the divine and the juridical realms, both realms themselves being established by means of the exclusion of the *homo sacer*. By no means is this just some abstract area of intersection between bare life and *bios* to be analyzed in order to understand the concepts. Rather, the *homo sacer* is a concrete and literal historical example through which Agamben's ideas may be understood in that the *home sacer* is the human being who is abandoned, exiled, and cast out.

Drawing upon a number of classical sources, Agamben offers a sketch of *homo sacer* that tells us of his uniqueness in that the *homo sacer* is the person "who may be killed and yet not sacrificed."[7] Agamben speaks of the simultaneous abandonment of the person of *homo sacer* by both the juridical realm and the divine realm by means of the suspension or withdrawal of law in relation to *homo sacer* in each of the two realms by the *Sovereign Power*:

> What defines the status of *homo sacer* is therefore not the originary ambivalence of the sacredness that is assumed to belong to him, but rather both the particular character of the double exclusion into which he is taken and the violence to which he finds himself exposed. This violence—the unsanctionable killing that, in his case, anyone may commit—is classifiable neither as sacrifice nor as homicide, neither as the execution of a condemnation to death nor as sacrilege. Subtracting itself from the sanctioned forms of both human and divine law, this violence opens a sphere of human action that is neither the sphere of *sacrum facere* nor that of profane action. This sphere is precisely what we are trying to understand here.[8]

The figure of *homo sacer*, for Agamben, is one that sheds light on the very structure and nature of politics and the founding and operation of sovereign power. Agamben goes to great lengths to demonstrate how *homo sacer* should not be understood as the result of some ambivalence of the sacred. Rather, *homo sacer*, as a figure, as a person who is beyond both penal law and murder as well as divine law and sacrifice, is "the originary figure of life taken into the sovereign ban and preserves the memory of the originary exclusion through which the political dimension was first constituted."[9] Thus, *homo sacer* is a concrete manifestation of the reality of a dimension of existence that is neither sacred nor profane, a "zone of indistinction" whose very existence is that which allows for the possibility of the distinction itself and the consequent naming and constituting of those two realms in which sovereign power is operative, that is, the juridical realm and the divine realm.

Agamben's "zone of indistinction," in being what allows for distinctions to be made, seems much like the definition of Chaos discussed in Chapter 2 in terms of Chaos being that "gap" which first allows for difference and sameness to come into existence. And just as I linked Heidegger's *peras* with Hesiod's Chaos in Chapter 2, I see all three of these as pointing toward the same idea. This dimension of existence, this "zone of indistinction" between homicide and sacrifice, this zone from which is made the distinction between domestic life and political life, between *zoē* and *bios*, between juridical law and divine law, between the profane and the sacred, between nature and culture, between other and self, is that which constitutes the first content of sovereign power, according to Agamben.[10]

Homo sacer is the one who has effectively been abandoned by both the juridical and the divine orders. The sovereign, who is the sovereign in both of those realms, exercises sovereign authority by virtue of *the withdrawal of the protection afforded by being included in his realm of dominion.* However, the withdrawal of the protection and the resultant abandonment are nonetheless themselves supreme exercises of sovereign power. Thus, the realm in which *homo sacer* finds himself is a realm that, although *a state of exception*, is nonetheless a realm in which *sovereign power is manifest in its own absence*. Doubly excluded from both the juridical and divine realms, *homo sacer* is neither fit for sacrifice nor worthy enough to be considered a victim of homicide. The *homo sacer*, as such, may be killed with impunity.

The realm in which *homo sacer* exists is not a realm merely devoid of law, but is a realm that results from the exercise of sovereign power in its highest form, according to Agamben. *Homo sacer* finds himself abandoned, cast out, excluded, and under ban by means of sovereign power's fullest exercise of power, that is, sovereign power's ability to rule by suspending the very law it creates.

LILITH

Lilith is a character who has appeared in a range of times and places, such as the Sumerian epic poem *Gilgamesh* from around 2400 BCE, the Babylonian Talmud, which was compiled ca. 500 CE, Aramaic incantation bowls that date between the fifth and seventh centuries CE, the Dead Sea Scrolls ca. third century BCE through first century CE, as well as various Kabbalistic sources from the medieval period, including *The Zohar* ca. 1270 CE.

While particular details may vary from source to source, there are nonetheless some central features that are essential to Lilith across place and time. While an attentive and thoughtful student of folklore, myth, and religion will see similarities between Lilith and other feminine mythological figures, for my purposes, I will be offering a sketch of certain of Lilith's central features that render us more easily able to make sense of her in relation to the various concepts and ideas under discussion here in this chapter and in this work as a whole. My purpose here is not to prove that there exists this particular understanding of Lilith or to provide extensive documentation for this understanding of Lilith throughout various times and places but rather to acquaint the reader with the mythological figure in general.

As is well known, in the book of *Genesis*, there are two separate and differing accounts of creation, *Genesis* 1:1–2:3 and *Genesis* 2:4–25. These two accounts differ in that in the first account humans are said to have been created *after* the animals were created, and male and female human beings were *created simultaneously*, both being formed from the dirt of the earth. In the second account of creation, which is the more widely known account, human beings were created *before* the animals, and the female human being was *created after* the male human being. She was created from his very flesh, specifically from his rib.

It is thought that it was this discrepancy in the two biblical accounts of the creation myth that first gave rise to the stories of Lilith. It is thought that Jewish biblical scholars, in an attempt to make sense of the existence of two differing accounts of the creation of woman, developed the understanding of Lilith as the first wife of Adam. Lilith, like Adam, was created by God from the dirt of the earth and was thus equal to Adam. Viewing herself as equal to Adam, Lilith was reluctant to submit to him. When he sought dominion over her, she was quarrelsome and contentious. She did, however, provoke in Adam much desire for her. Yet, she refused his advances and did not wish to lay beneath him for the sex act. The story goes that when Lilith saw that Adam was determined to overpower her, she uttered the name of God, rose up into the air, and flew away to live at the Red Sea, a place full of lascivious demons with whom she was said to have acted out her lust and passion, giving birth to more than a hundred demons daily.[11]

Once Lilith was gone, God made Adam a second wife, Eve. This wife God made from Adam's own flesh, and Adam found her more properly submissive to his authority. However, it was not long before Lilith made her presence felt again in Adam's life. In the Garden of Eden, Lilith appeared to Eve as a serpent and seduced her into eating the fruit of the tree of knowledge of good and evil. Lilith then prompted Eve to tempt Adam with this fruit, as well. It is here that we can see that the aspect of the feminine represented by Lilith in the myth is not without intimate relation to the aspect of the feminine represented by Eve. Although Eve is a version of the feminine that is perhaps "less evil" than Lilith, she is still, in her being as woman, susceptible to the influence of Lilith. Eve must, therefore, be kept under a tight rein, so as to prevent Lilith becoming a further corruptive influence.

Adam, after succumbing to the temptations of Eve instigated by Lilith, and finding himself, along with Eve, cast out from the Garden, separated himself from Eve for 130 years. The story goes that Adam imposed this period of penitence upon himself once he realized that, through the weakness he had experienced as a result of the beguiling and seductive feminine, he had brought the curse of mortality to mankind. During this period in which he abstained from sex with Eve, Adam found that on occasion he would have involuntary nocturnal emissions. Such events were understood to be the result of the work of Lilith, who would visit and seduce him in the night so as to use his semen to create more demons and evil spirits.

It was from this understanding of the biblical text that, in the first century AD, Rabbi Hanina was prompted to issue a warning that forbade men from sleeping alone in a house since, under such conditions, Lilith would likely seduce them.[12] Lilith, as the seductive, lust-inspiring aspect of the feminine, is understood as an ever-present threat to men:

> And she [Lilith] goes and roams at night, and goes all about the world and makes sport with men and causes them to emit seed. In every place where a man sleeps alone in a house, she visits him and grabs him and attaches herself to him and has her desire from him, and bears from him. And she also afflicts him with sickness, and he knows it not, and all this takes place when the moon is on the wane.[13]

The sexually seductive power of Lilith is so strong, so their thinking goes, that there can be no doubt that it has its source in "evil," and, as such, it must be countered by any means necessary. While Lilith succeeds all too easily at seducing men in their sleep, she is also a danger to the wide awake, as well, as is clear in the following:

> She adorns herself like a despicable harlot, and takes up her position at the crossroads to seduce the sons of man. When a fool approaches her, she grabs

him, kisses him, and pours him wine of dregs of viper's gall. As soon as he drinks it, he goes astray after her. When she sees that he has gone astray after her from the path of truth, she divests herself of all ornaments which she put on for that fool. Her ornaments for the seduction of the sons of man are: her hair is long and red like the rose, her cheeks are white and red, from her ears hang six ornaments, Egyptian chords hang from her nape and all the ornaments of the Land of the East, her mouth is set like a narrow door, comely in its décor, her tongue is sharp like a sword, her words are smooth like oil, her lips are red like a rose and sweetened by all the sweetness of the world, she is dressed in scarlet, and she is adorned with forty ornaments less one. Yon fool goes astray after her and drinks from the cup of wine and commits with her fornication and strays after her. What does she thereupon do? She leaves him asleep on the couch, flies up to heaven, denounces him, takes leave, and descends. That fool awakens and deems he can make sport with her as before, but she removes her ornaments and turns into a menacing figure, and stands before him clothed in garments of flaming fire, inspiring terror and making body and soul tremble, full of frightening eyes, in her hand a drawn sword dripping bitter drops. And she kills that fool and casts him into Gehenna.[14]

Clearly, only a fool allows himself to be tempted by the Lilith aspect of the feminine, and he does so at his own peril. For despite alluring appearance and the promise, even fulfillment of sensual delight, this aspect of the feminine is dangerous, deadly, and inherently destructive to man as such.

By no means, however, are we to understand Lilith, as an aspect of the feminine, to only be present in the person of a prostitute or any other woman of so-called "loose morals." For Lilith, as is shown, is always ready to make an appearance when there are any activities of a sensual or sexual nature taking place or even being contemplated, even between a legally wedded man and wife. Lilith, it seems, is responsible for and lurks behind all perceptions on the part of men that are of a sensual, erotically appealing, lustful, or enticing nature. The following illustrates this idea:

And behold, that hard shell, Lilith, is always present in the bedlinen of man and wife when they copulate, in order to take hold of the sparks of the drops of semen which are lost—because it is impossible without such. But there is an incantation for this, to chase away the Lilith from the bed and to bring forth pure souls.[15]

and

Lilith, God preserve us, has dominion over children who issue from him who couples with his wife in candlelight, or with his wife naked, or at a time when he is forbidden to have intercourse with her.[16]

Thus, it is clear that a man who feels sexual desire for his wife, or any other woman, desire that is in any way beyond the scope of what is legally, religiously, or morally permissible, feels such desire because of Lilith. It thus appears that erotic desire in and of itself is the result of Lilith's presence and evil-doing. Lilith then, it seems, is the source and cause of all incarnate and embodied sexual desire and lust.

There is yet another important aspect to Lilith. In addition to her seductiveness and her role as the source of all sexual sin, Lilith is a child-killer. Lilith is seen as ultimately responsible for all barrenness, miscarriages, stillbirths, infant deaths, and any other manner of affliction having to do with failed reproductive capacity, pregnancy, or childbirth. The standard view is that she is motivated to do these things out of spite, hatred, jealousy, wrath, and envy. Women are understood to be especially susceptible to the influence of and harm from Lilith during certain times, such as prior to the loss of virginity, during menstruation, and the hours before childbirth.[17] Thus, it appears that all things uniquely feminine or belonging to woman in the embodied sense are themselves "evil," or at least potentially "evil," in their being intimately connected to Lilith.

Inscriptions found upon many of the Aramaic incantation bowls make evident the perceived power of Lilith. The bowls also illustrate the great lengths to which people would go to try and keep Lilith at bay. Rituals, incantations, amulets, edicts, proclamations, prayers, fastings, and even the drawing up of legal documents, such as a Jewish *get* or divorce document were actions taken against Lilith. Some Rabbis went so far as to pronounce Lilith under ban or *herem* by their respective Jewish community. One such inscription is translated as follows:

> because it is announced to you that Rabbi Joshua bar Perahia has sent against you the ban. ... A divorce-writ has come down to us from heaven and there is found written in it your advisement and your terrification, in the name of Palsa-Pelisa ["Divorcer and Divorced"], who renders to thee thy divorce and thy separation, your divorces and your separations. Thou, Lilith, male Lili and female Lilith, Hag and Snatcher, be in the ban ... of Joshua Bar Perahia.[18]

The scholar Raphael Patai explains in his essay on Lilith that it was believed that Lilith and her entourage of demons would seek to attach themselves to their human hosts by means of sexual seduction in order to produce more demonic offspring. If Lilith or one of her demons was successful in doing so, it was thought that they then acquired all the rights of cohabiting and must therefore be expelled by legal means.[19]

Thus, it seems to me without a doubt that Lilith was conceived of as more than a mere idea or a myth. Lilith was phenomenal. Lilith seems to have been understood as something very much a part of concrete, embodied existence. Lilith was something that, as an aspect of reality, founded by means of her very existence an order and a system that created itself in self-conscious opposition to and separation from her and the aspect of reality she represented.

If Lilith is desire incarnate, that is, embodied sexual longing and lust, in all its reason-defying power and persuasion, then it was Lilith that gave rise to an order and system that constituted itself in purposeful opposition to her as a means of "protecting" itself from her. That order and system would thus indeed deem itself as good, righteous, and moral, having judged her and what she represented to be as evil, frightful, and immoral. Seen operative here, in this method of conceptualizing, are the ideas found in both ecofeminism's critique of *self and other dualisms* and Nietzsche's discussion of slaves and masters.

Lilith was possessed of the ability to inspire great lust and desire, as well as fear and terror. Understanding Lilith as such speaks not only to the tremendous nature of her purported powers, but also to the perceived extreme powerlessness of those who feared her. As I will demonstrate in the next section, the mythology of Lilith, understood through the lens of Agamben, illustrates the way in which this particular aspect of the feminine, of woman, has existed in a perpetual *state of exception* that, once conceived and established by the masculine, founded the masculine as *sovereign*.

STATE OF EXCEPTION

Agamben's view is that the very foundation of political life as such is the distinguishing of a life that may be killed with impunity. It is by means of its capacity to be killed thus that it is politicized.[20] In other words, it is through the drawing of this distinction that the realm of the political itself comes into existence.

Once the rule asserts itself as rule by suspending itself in relation to something, the "zone of indistinction" is established, and it is from within that "zone of indistinction" that the juridical realm is established as such and distinguished from the divine realm that is thereby also established. The *homo sacer* finds himself abandoned in that "zone of indistinction." Thus, for Agamben, *homo sacer* is a *state of exception* due to the rule's suspension of itself in regards to him, due to the withdrawal of protection by the sovereign, due to being abandoned by the ruling power. *Homo sacer* thus can neither be sacrificed nor murdered, but he may be killed with impunity.

The establishing of these distinctions is the founding of sovereign power for Agamben. In the establishment of this power, the unique position of the one who is abandoned or confined to the *state of exception* is one that provides the needed opposite polarity for the pole that is the sovereign. Agamben writes:

> At the two extreme limits of the order, the sovereign and *homo sacer* present two symmetrical figures that have the same structure and are correlative: the sovereign is the one with respect to whom all men are potentially *homines sacri*, and *homo sacer* is the one with respect to whom all men act as sovereigns. The sovereign and *homo sacer* are joined in the figure of an action that, excepting itself from both human and divine law, from both *nomos* and *physis*, nevertheless delimits what is, in a certain sense, the first properly political space of the West distinct from both the religious and the profane sphere, from both the natural order and the regular juridical order.[21]

This fascinating inverted proportionality that exists between the sovereign and *homo sacer* illustrates the complete and total power of the one and the complete and total powerlessness of the other. Moreover, as Agamben points out, it establishes a political space that is unique in that it is neither the divine religious domain nor the human juridical domain. It is a space where neither man's law nor God's law applies. The person who is sent there is in essence beyond any hope, mercy, help, redemption, or care; such a person is abandoned, stripped of all personhood, left for dead. So extreme is the powerlessness of the position of the *homo sacer* that any and every man acts as *sovereign* in relation to him.

In terms of the application of these ideas to Lilith, she is undoubtedly the *homo sacer*. Lilith is exiled, under ban, abandoned, and cast out. The *sovereign masculine* first establishes itself as the rule, as a *sovereign power*, by excluding Lilith, by excluding what she represents. But, as Agamben would stress, she is included in his exercise of power by being excluded. Having thus established Lilith as a *state of exception*, the *sovereign masculine*, from within this "zone of indistinction," makes the further distinction between the two realms in which *masculine sovereign power* rules, the two realms included in his domain: the realm represented by Eve (nature/*zoē*) and the realm represented by Adam (culture/*bios*). The masculine is to Lilith as the *sovereign* is to *homo sacer*. And while Adam represents in embodied form, the masculine itself, it is the ultimate masculine, God, who is behind it all, the supreme *sovereign masculine*.

God, it may be argued, is nothing more than the projection of *sovereign masculine* power onto a supposed transcendent reality. Of course, this ties in with ecofeminism's concern regarding the rise of patriarchal religion and its rejection of immanent divinity in favor of a merely transcendent divinity understood as masculine. However, because there is a need for and the necessity of a woman, of the feminine, the realm of *zoē* is established and the aspect of the feminine as represented by Eve is consigned thereto.

Keeping in mind the ways in which *sovereign power* is established in terms of the structural necessities, I think it appropriate here to call to mind the concept of *value dualisms*. Such dualisms, it seems, are likely dependent upon some third thing that has been rendered a *state of exception*, abandoned, and thereby make possible the very distinction between the two parts of the created duality or binary. In considering the *value dualism* of the *rational/irrational*, I see the rational (identified with the masculine as represented by Adam) and the *irrational* (identified with that aspect of the feminine as represented by Eve) as the two sovereign realms founded by means of excluding what I will call the *non-rational* (identified with that aspect of the feminine as represented by Lilith).

Lilith, in all her *non-rationality*, is wild sexuality, untamed, like nature itself, unpredictable, and therefore threatening. The aspect of the feminine represented by Lilith is, in its essence, and has been described as, beyond comprehension or subordination to reason. Such is the very essence of the affects of *desire* and *lust*. They defy reason, do not submit to it, and as such, they are attributed to Lilith. This, it may be argued, is precisely why she is perceived as so dangerous. Thus, the masculine establishes itself as sovereign in relation to the feminine as represented by Eve by abandoning, casting out, and rendering as a *state of exception* that aspect of the feminine represented by Lilith. My own contention, however, is that Lilith, as an aspect of the feminine, is more correctly understood as actually representative not of woman alone, but of that aspect of embodied human existence that is *non-rational* human sexuality. The masculine seeks not only to distance itself from nature without, but from nature within.

Looking again more closely at the way in which Agamben distinguishes *homo sacer* from *zoē*, more clearly seen is the applicability of his ideas to the distinction that is made between the two aspects of the feminine represented by Lilith and Eve. Consider Agamben's words:

> [L]ife that may be killed but not sacrificed is the *hinge* on which each sphere is articulated and the threshold at which the two spheres are joined in becoming indeterminate. Neither political *bios* nor natural *zoē*, sacred life is the zone of indistinction in which *zoē* and *bios* constitute each other in including and excluding each other.[22]

For Agamben, *homo sacer* is *the hinge* on which each of the two spheres are articulated; it is the *threshold* at which the two spheres are joined. Likewise, the aspect of the feminine that is represented by Lilith, which I contend is best understood simply as the *non-rational* nature of human sexuality, indeed does serve that same function. Lilith, like *homo sacer*, is *the hinge* on which the two distinct spheres understood as represented by Adam and Eve are articulated. Eve, like *zoē*, represents reproductive or biological life, that which is necessary to the continuation of the species. Eve represents the realm of "nature," the irrational aspect of life of the species whose purpose and place is to be distinguished from, but nonetheless made subject to, Adam, Adam being he who represents and exemplifies *bios* or life in the polis or the realm of "culture," that is, *rational* life with a telos more fitting his superior nature and power. Lilith, in being abandoned and rendered a *state of exception*, acts as *the hinge* from which each of the other two is articulated via the rule of *sovereign masculine power*.

The analogy between *homo sacer* and Lilith in terms of their role as *hinge* is a very fruitful one, I believe. Just as *homo sacer* is the *hinge* that joins *domus* and *polis, zöe* and *bios*, nature and state, divine and juridical, so is Lilith the *hinge* that joins Adam and Eve, sacred and profane, good and evil, that which is made by and in the image of God and that which is made by man. Lilith is the "zone of indistinction" from which these distinctions are possible and in which they are joined.

It is by means of the very act that designates the realm of the feminine that is represented by Lilith and makes of her the *state of exception* that *sovereign masculine power* is founded. This same act allows for the establishment of the other two realms, that is, the realm of the tolerated because necessary feminine, represented by Eve, and the realm of the sovereign and superior masculine, represented by Adam. Thus is the sovereign masculine power established, and the nature of the political structure of the three created.

Agamben reiterates the uniqueness and importance of the zone where bare life/*homo sacer* exists, its relationship to the other two realms, and its importance to his theory of politics and sovereign power when he writes:

> The time has come, therefore, to reread from the beginning the myth of the foundation of the modern city from Hobbes to Rousseau. The state of nature is, in truth, a *state of exception*, in which the city appears for an instant *tanquam dissoluta*. The foundation is thus not an event achieved once and for all but is continually operative in the civil state in the form of the sovereign decision. What is more, the latter refers *immediately* to the life of the citizens, which thus appears as the originary political element, the *Urphänomen* of politics. Yet this life is not simply natural reproductive life, the *zoē* of the Greeks, nor *bios*, a qualified form of life. It is, rather, the bare life of *homo sacer* and the *wargus*, a zone of indistinction and continuous transition between man and beast, nature and culture.[23]

While I will address the concept of the *wargus* shortly, let me now carefully attend to the above in terms of its application to the analogy I am making. Evident to me is the applicability and instructiveness of an ecofeminist appropriation of Agamben's ideas. In thinking of Hobbes' "myth of the foundation of the modern city" as analogous to the myth of creation, I see Lilith as analogous to Hobbes' *state of nature*. The assumption of power by the masculine, as represented by Adam, is analogous to the formation of the state or modern city. But of course, from a Hobbesian point of view, this would be in line with the dictates of reason and rationality.

However, if we apply Agamben's insight, we can see that what is posited by Hobbes as a *state of nature*, which he contends precedes the coming into being of the state and is that from which the state sets us free, is really itself a creation of the state and one that founds the state's sovereignty in that the state makes of the *state of nature* a *state of exception*.

Such a *state of exception* is integral to sovereign power itself. As Agamben explains, it is that which establishes sovereign power, in that the sovereign power establishes itself by exercising the power to withdraw or suspend itself in relation thereto. Likewise, the aspect of the feminine represented by Lilith is not really something that precedes and from which the zones of *Adam* and *Eve* help us escape, but rather, it is that which is created and abandoned so as to found the very realms designated by "Adam" and "Eve" and establish *sovereign masculine* power in doing so.

Lilith, like the Hobbesian *state of nature*, is a construct that allows for the foundation of a politics and the establishment of a sovereign power that maintains its sovereignty by means of its very ability to suspend its rule in *the state of exception*, which is that realm of the feminine represented by and personified in the figure of Lilith.

Again, my own idea is that Lilith is actually best understood as that which represents sexuality in its purest form, that is, sexuality as that which exists prior to and independently of the realm of reason as a pure phenomenological experience of an embodied being. Thus, its *non-rational* status. Human sexuality is by its very nature *non-rational*. Merleau-Ponty writes:

> Erotic perception is not a cogitatio which aims at a cogitatum; through one body it aims at another body, and takes place in the world, not in a consciousness. A sight has a sexual significance for me, not when I consider, even confusedly, its possible relationship to the sexual organs or to pleasurable states, but when it exists for my body, for that power always available for bringing together into an erotic situation the stimuli applied, and adapting sexual conduct to it. There is an erotic "comprehension" not of the order of understanding, since understanding subsumes an experience, once perceived, under some idea, while desire comprehends blindly by linking body to body.[24]

This *non-rational* and unreasoned sexuality, this Lilith, does not subtract itself from the rule, but rather finds itself abandoned by the rule, as represented by the *sovereign masculine*. Using Agamben's analysis, it is by the *sovereign masculine's* suspension of itself as reason and rule, and its subsequent maintenance of this relation to the aspect of the feminine represented by Lilith as that which is excluded, that the masculine's sovereignty is founded and maintained.

Just as Agamben tells us that "The foundation is thus not an event achieved once and for all but is continually operative in the civil state in the form of sovereign decision," so do we see the way in which the tensions, generated in the positing of these three distinct realms of Lilith, Adam, and Eve, with Adam in the role of the civil state, continually make themselves felt in terms of the *sovereign decision* that perpetuates and reinforces these distinctions, as evidenced not only by the contents of any number of the sources cited in the second section of this chapter but by a host of contemporary realities that concern feminists and ecofeminists alike, such as unequal pay for equal work for women, the pornography industry, sex trafficking, prostitution, lack of maternity leave for working mothers, continued denial of reproductive freedom for women, rape culture, slut-shaming, rape-victim blaming, domestic violence, and various other afflictions, some far more horrifying than the ones faced by women in the more affluent countries, such as female-genital mutilation and public stoning. The seemingly incessant drive within our culture to always ultimately fault the feminine/victim/woman for any and all acts deemed to be of an abhorrent, violent, criminal, aberrant, or otherwise sexual nature is built into this paradigm.

If it be conceded that erotic perception, desire, lust, and sensual longing are inescapable human realities, then the ways in which these three realms, represented by Lilith, Adam, and Eve once distinguished as such, will interact will indeed be a continual and constant laying and maintenance of this foundation.

Agamben tells us that the "sovereign decision" in the state always refers to the bare life of the citizens; that is, in each sovereign decision, it is asserted either implicitly or explicitly that each citizen is a potential *homo sacer*. In other words, in each sovereign decision there is a threat. Likewise, there is in the operation of the *sovereign masculine*, as represented by Adam in his sovereign power to make decisions, the continually reestablished fact that each woman, as an instantiation of the feminine, is a potential Lilith. As Agamben points out, this is the originary political element, and it is neither *zoē* nor *bios*. It is bare life; it is the *homo sacer*. It is neither Eve nor Adam. It is Lilith.

To return now to Agamben's idea on the *wargus*, he says that the *wargus* is also a *homo sacer*. In true Heideggerian fashion, Agamben excavates the term *wargus* to demonstrate how the *wargus* (*vargr*, werewolf, wolf-man) was originally the bandit and the outlaw, one who had been banned, cast out, and exiled. Agamben explains how such a person upon being banned was considered dead and thus could be killed with impunity. Agamben thus sees the *wargus* as the historical precursor to *homo sacer*. And I contend that Lilith shares much the same fate. I also see in the figure of the *wargus* yet another way in which the ecofeminist critique rings true. For, as Agamben explains, the *wargus*, as wolf-man, is understood to be neither man nor beast but something inbetween, and it is only from within this "inbetween" place that the relevant conceptual distinctions may be made. Lilith, like *homo sacer* and the *wargus*, is representative of a "zone of indistinction" and continuous transition between man and beast, nature and culture."[25]

Agamben's use of the concept of *the ban* in formulating his ideas lends itself to appropriation for my purposes here, as well. In explaining *homo sacer* as he who is abandoned and in explicating the nature of that abandonment, Agamben writes:

> The relation of abandonment is so ambiguous that nothing could be harder than breaking from it. The ban is essentially the power of delivering something over to itself, which is to say, the power of maintaining itself in relation to something presupposed as nonrelational. What has been banned is delivered over to its own separateness and, at the same time, consigned to the mercy of the one who abandons it—at once excluded and included, removed and at the same time captured. ... The ban is the force of simultaneous attraction and repulsion that ties together the two poles of the sovereign exception: bare life and power, *homo sacer* and the sovereign. Because of this alone can the ban signify both the insignia of sovereignty and expulsion from the community.[26]

Lilith, as the aspect of the feminine that represents human sexuality in all its *non-rationality*, is abandoned to the (non)status of the "nonrelational." However, a relationship of power is maintained with Lilith by the *sovereign masculine* in all its rationality, as represented by Adam, by delivering Lilith over to her own separateness. Lilith is consigned to the mercy of the one who abandons her. Like *homo sacer* and the sovereign, the simultaneous attraction and repulsion ties together this aspect of the feminine represented by Lilith and the *sovereign masculine* as represented by Adam. The contemporary phenomenon of slut-shaming is a perfect example of "the ban" in action. While patriarchal capitalist culture has created and maintains the sexual objectification and commodification of women's flesh and sexuality, exploiting and profiting from them at every turn, that same culture puts under "ban" any woman who dares to express her sexuality in a way that is not sanctioned by *sovereign masculine* power, that is, either as a "proper" woman operating in the realm of Eve in ways sanctioned by the *sovereign masculine* or as a sexual object operating as such in the realm of Adam in ways also sanctioned by the *sovereign masculine*. And here is insight into the virgin/whore dichotomy that pervades too much of the thinking regarding women within the paradigm that is patriarchy. The realm that would be woman as neither or both, the realm that would be woman freely expressing her own *non-rational* sexual nature in ways she herself deems fitting, is precisely what has been abandoned and rendered the *state of exception* by the *sovereign masculine*.

Recall that in one of the Aramaic Incantation Bowl inscriptions there was the issuing of the ban against Lilith. The ban, or *herem* as it is called in Hebrew, is an act that clearly indicates the exercise of sovereign power, and, in its employment, there is most assuredly the complete abandonment of the one against whom the ban is issued. To proclaim something or someone to be under ban is to establish it as existing outside both the juridical and the divine realms; it is to deem it as completely and utterly forsaken. In the act of forsaking, however, there is the operation of the sovereign power. Thus, that which is banned is nonetheless included in the rule of sovereign power by virtue of being excluded. Agamben, in quoting from William Robertson Smith's *Lectures on the Religion of the Semites*, notes the relevance of this:

> Another Hebrew usage that may be noted here is the ban (Heb. *herem*), by which impious sinners, or enemies of the community and its god, were devoted to utter destruction. The ban is a form of devotion to the deity, and so the verb "to ban" is sometimes rendered "consecrate" (Micah 4:13) or "devote" (Lev. 27;28ff.). But in the oldest Hebrew times it involved the utter destruction, not only of the persons involved, but of their property.[27]

The aspect of the feminine represented by Lilith, that is, sexuality itself, its power to incite lust and desire, to entice to sensual indulgence, along with one's willingness to engage in such things, is declared thus to be under ban, forsaken, abandoned. It is rendered life incapable of being murdered, yet not capable of being sacrificed, but open to being killed.

Having designated it as such, the foundation is created upon which the respective realms of Adam and Eve, or the *sovereign masculine* and the subjugated feminine, may be distinguished, determined, and developed. The carving out of the realm designated by Lilith is what founds the sexually political. It also establishes the *sovereign masculine* power of Adam, as representative of the masculine and of reason. If Agamben is correct in his analysis, the positing of Lilith as an aspect of the feminine that must be distinguished and consequently abandoned is the necessary condition upon which the sovereignty of the masculine depends. For Agamben says, "The relation of the ban has constituted the essential structure of sovereign power from the beginning."[28]

Keeping in mind what is now unconcealed regarding the way in which sovereign power is established, that is, by the delineating of a realm that is abandoned and treated as a *state of exception* so as to found sovereign power and draw a further distinction that establishes the relevant binary as such, we turn back to Nietzsche and Heidegger for further unconcealment.

NOTES

1. Giorgio Agamben, *Homo Sacer* (Stanford: Stanford University Press, 1998), 1.
2. Ibid., 8.
3. Ibid., 9.
4. Ibid., 18.
5. Ibid.
6. Greta Gaard and Lori Gruen, "Ecofeminism: Toward Global Justice and Planetary Health," in *Environmental Ethics: An Anthology*, ed. Andrew Light and Holmes Rolston (Oxford: Blackwell Publishers, 2003), 278.
7. Agamben, *Homo Sacer*, 8.
8. Ibid., 83.
9. Ibid.
10. Ibid.
11. Raphael Patai, "Lilith," *The Journal of American Folklore* 77:306 (1964): 296.
12. *Babylonian Talmud*, Seder Mo'ed, Tractate Shabbath, 151a.
13. *Zohar* (Mahwah: Paulist Press, 1983), 19b.
14. Ibid., 148a–b.
15. Naftali Hertz Bachrach, *Sefer Emek HaMalekh* (HebrewBooks, 2013), 19c.
16. Bachrach, *Sefer Emek HaMalekh*, 84b.
17. Patai, "Lilith," 298.
18. James Montgomery, *Aramaic Incantation Texts from Nippur* (New York: Cambridge University Press, 2010), 155.
19. Patai, "Lilith," 298.
20. Agamben, *Homo Sacer*, 89.
21. Ibid., 84.
22. Ibid., 90.
23. Ibid., 109.
24. Maurice Merleau-Ponty, *Phenomenology of Perception* (New York: Routledge, 2012), 157.
25. Agamben, *Homo Sacer*, 109.
26. Ibid., 110.
27. Ibid., 76.
28. Ibid., 111.

Chapter Six

Beyond the Binary

ECO-PHENOMENOLOGY: TWO DIFFERENT REALISMS

Thus far it has been established that the positing of the inferior other and the establishment of the superior self is undoubtedly at work in the establishment of all systems of domination and all systems of human intercourse that center on power and control. Contemporary discussions, dialogues, and debates regarding the environment and environmental issues often are *hinge*d on a distinction between approaches that are said to be *ecocentric* or *biocentric* as against approaches that are said to be *anthropocentric*.

In taking what has been revealed by Agamben's ideas, in particular, the need for that which constitutes the *hinge* as that which allows for the distinction to be made between two established realms, I propose that in the case of *ecocentrism* and *anthropocentrism*, there is a third perspective to be unconcealed as having founded this binary. That third perspective, I contend, may be understood as something of a reconciliation between the idea of human beings as separate/unique/superior to nature and the idea of human beings as merely part of nature. While I will return to this idea explicitly and more thoroughly in the third section of this chapter, I think it is important to first examine a few other relevant conceptual distinctions.

One important conceptual distinction is found in an examination of some of the ideas of Nietzsche and Heidegger through the lens of eco-phenomenology and ecofeminism. In looking again at Nietzsche and Heidegger, there is occasion to put to further use the insights of Agamben in an analysis of certain important concepts and their intersection with ecofeminism.

The central aim of the eco-phenomenology movement in environmentalism is the undoing of those metaphysical presuppositions that have brought us to our current state of environmental devastation. In an examination of the lines of thought within eco-phenomenology, scholar Iain Thomson uncovers two different approaches, approaches that result in two different realisms. His distinctions and insights are highly relevant to this project.

Returning to the insights Nietzsche provided us regarding humanity and its orientation toward the earth discussed in the third section of Chapter 4, I see Nietzsche as very concerned with what he perceived as an emphasis on the "otherworld" and its entailed demeaning of this world; the otherworld is superior, this world inferior.

This binary way of thinking that Nietzsche criticizes is yet another example of the *self and other dualisms* that concern ecofeminists; in this instance, the analogy would be that the *self* (understood as transcendent in its true essence, a disembodied "spirit") is being identified with the otherworld. This world, Nietzsche's "earth," is being identified as the *other*. This conceptualization in which *self* is identified with the otherworld is very relevant from an ecofeminist point of view in that the otherworld is conceived of as a world of spirit, a world free from the flesh, while this world, the inferior world, is a world of flesh and matter. Such conceptualizations that result in the desacralization of the flesh, of women, and of nature are a chief concern for ecofeminists. A similar concern appears to be at work in Nietzsche's own thought when he says, "Lead back to the earth the virtue that flew away, as I do—back to the body, back to life, that it may give the earth a meaning, a human meaning."[1]

As previously explained, Nietzsche's conviction was that in the esteeming of the "otherworld," there was a loss of esteem and proper reverence for this world, for our very human, bodily existence. Such a dualism clearly devalues this world, our humanity, and our bodily existence. This resonates with something said by Ariel Salleh when she notes, "In the West, feminine and other abject bodies are split off and positioned as dirt, Nature, resource, colonised by masculine energies and sublimated through Economics, Science and the Law."[2] I would add "Religion" to her list of colonizers. Moreover, when we consider the change that occurred in the predominant mindset of humanity in the wake of the scientific revolution, that is, the arising of a mindset in which this world is conceived of as a machine and is thus held to be inherently inferior to an otherworld, we can see how such a mindset could indeed lead to the nihilism that Nietzsche saw as being the inevitable result. If we employ Agamben's analysis of *sovereign power* in examining these dualisms and binaries, even more is unconcealed.

Agamben's idea is that *sovereign power* is predicated upon an abandoned realm that is itself a *state of exception* serving as a *hinge* for the two created spheres in which sovereign power rules. Agamben's conceptualization can be understood as operative in Nietzsche's scenario. The abandoned realm or *state of exception* is the very one to which Nietzsche calls for us to return, that is, Nietzsche's "earth," and the two sovereign realms created by means of this *state of exception* are the otherworldly realm and the mechanistic-scientific world of mere matter and resource. As it turns out and I will soon show, Agamben's analysis may be applied in a critique of Nietzsche's own views, as well. That critique will help elucidate the superiority of Heidegger's view.

While Nietzsche provides some extremely important insights into the devaluation of this world that is entailed in the esteeming of an "otherworld," his ideas, when viewed through the lens of eco-phenomenology, still fall short of offering an understanding that could lead to an amelioration of contemporary ills. Heidegger, however, may be understood as offering something much more promising. If the ideas of these two thinkers are approached from the point of view of eco-phenomenology, a clearer understanding of their thinking is achieved, and Heidegger's thinking is shown to provide a solution.

In a paper titled "Ontology and Ethics at the Intersection of Phenomenology and Environmental Philosophy," Iain Thomson distinguishes between two competing approaches within eco-phenomenology. Thomson begins by setting forth what can be understood as a "vision and mission statement" of eco-phenomenology: By undermining the theory/practice distinction, mind/world dualism, and the division between facts and values, eco-phenomenology seeks to dig up and replace those ethical and metaphysical presuppositions that are the conceptual roots of our environmental crises.[3]

Having recognized that all eco-phenomenologists are ultimately committed to some form of ethical realism, Thomson discerns two different approaches within eco-phenomenology, and he spells out what it is that sets the two approaches apart in terms of both their attendant metaphysics and the consequences thereof, both practically and conceptually understood.

Thomson labels the two approaches as *naturalistic ethical realism* and *transcendental ethical realism*. The means by which Thomson very thoughtfully lays out these key distinctions is primarily through the juxtaposing of the views of Heidegger and Nietzsche regarding "earth." By carefully exploring the two philosophers' use and understanding of the term, Thomson uncovers what can be seen as the very essence of the distinction between the two competing ethical realisms at issue. It is as if Nietzsche first pointed the way for us but yet fell short of forging the path due to the limitations inherent in *naturalistic ethical realism*. In the thinking of Heidegger and the tools with which his thought provides us, that is, through what Thomson calls *transcendental ethical realism*, the path forward may be cleared.

The approach and methodology that is employed in arriving at both kinds of ethical realisms, that is, *naturalistic* and *transcendental*, is phenomenology. As mentioned earlier, it is understood by eco-phenomenologists that this approach can uproot the problematic concepts that underlie our current environmental crises. How will this occur, by means of which ethical and metaphysical principles? Thomson writes, "The 'metaphysical' principle holds that phenomenological approaches reunite mind with world, or, more precisely, that phenomenology's descriptive approaches begin from—and so return us to—the experience of a pre-differentiated mind-world unity."[4]

The ethical principle is connected to the metaphysical principle in that it is only when the mind/world dualism is overcome that we are able to see our environmental "values" as already existent in the world. As Thomson puts it, "certain pro-environmental values are 'always already in the world'," and this grounds our approach to discovering these values and acknowledging them as the basis for a new environmental ethics.[5]

In other words, it is in what Merleau-Ponty would call our "unreflective experience of the world around us," an experience and awareness that is itself indicative of the intimate connection between the human being and the world, that the inherent values of this unity are encountered. Such values are all the more readily apparent when we are properly attuned to our environment and possessed of the appropriate comportment. It is in reflecting upon that unreflective experience and awareness that such values are made able to be articulated, given that they are only then understood to be that which they are, more than mere facts.

According to Thomson, although "earth" is central to the thought of both Nietzsche and Heidegger, it signifies something very different for each of the thinkers. In the earlier quote in which Nietzsche admonishes us to "remain faithful to the earth," Nietzsche called for a return to the earth. He called for us to remain true to it, to serve its meaning, to keep our gift-giving love and knowledge directed there.

Again, for Nietzsche, the earth is to be understood in contrast to the "otherworldly" in that the earth is what is real and the otherworldly only a poisoning illusion that robs us of our willingness and ability to make the most of what we have here on earth. The ultimately unattainable goal of the otherworldly, to Nietzsche's way of thinking, serves to only cripple humanity further by causing the resentment that leads to nihilism. Thus, Nietzsche beseeches us to "remain true to the earth," as Thomson explains, by "maintaining ourselves within the bounds of the knowable."[6]

According to Thomson, it is this very notion of "maintaining ourselves within the bounds of the knowable" that grounds the conceptualization of a Nietzschean eco-phenomenological approach as one that results in a *naturalistic ethical realism*, for in such an approach, "good" and "bad" are ultimately matters of fact, and values should be based thereupon.

Thomson explains that a Nietzschean eco-phenomenological approach is quite different from a Heideggerian eco-phenomenological approach, an approach that yields what he terms a *transcendental ethical realism*. Thomson writes:

> [Here] we can discover what really matters (hence *ethical realism*) when we are appropriately open to the environment, but what we thereby discover is neither a "fact" nor a "value" but rather a transcendental source of meaning that cannot be reduced to facts, values, or entities of any kind (hence *transcendental* ethical realism).[7]

Thus, unlike the Nietzschean approach, or any other approach for that matter in which the discovery of the ethical is something grounded in facts, reason, or utility, and so on, *transcendental ethical realism* sets forth the idea that in order for the meaning to be experienced, there is the prerequisite and necessity for persons to be possessed of a proper attunement or comportment toward their environment as a necessary condition for the experience of meaning to occur.

Such an idea, upon reflection, does make perfect sense. For example, if we wish to determine what should or should not be done with a particular forest, the first step in answering such a question will be to make sure that we are *open* to the forest in the requisite manner: Are we able to *sense* the possible meanings that are present within the forest? This notion of attunement to or comportment toward environment is a centrally important idea. On the surface level, one could explain what it means to be *open* to an environment by means of certain ideas that are quite commonplace, such as *paying attention, being present, not being distracted.* And while those phrases do indeed point us in the right direction, the concept of attunement is best and more thoroughly explained in terms of Heidegger's own ideas of *knowledge* and *tenderness* (*Wissenschaft* and *Zärtlichkeit*).

As I explained in the final section of Chapter 2 and throughout Chapter 3, *knowledge* and *tenderness* involve both the capacity for open receptivity and a kind of meditative/reflective thinking that itself may be understood as a thinking that reflects or mirrors what *is*, what is *presencing*, this being in keeping with Aristotle's conception of the thinker as engaged in *theorein*, as explained in Chapter 3. Such a modality of being is gratitude-laden and appreciative; it recognizes the difference between *meditative* and *calculative* thinking.

Anyone can encourage or cultivate an enhanced or increased perceptual sensitivity that in turn allows for the discovery of something in nature already present but heretofore unnoticed. This idea is in perfect keeping with ideas discussed early on in terms of the concealed and unconcealed nature of both truth and nature itself. The notion that often there is more to something than may initially meet the eye and that we can actively cultivate better powers of sight, so to speak, is an idea embraced by many thinkers, philosophers, and scientists, and across different disciplines. One such thinker is Roger Walsh. Researching for over thirty years in areas including neuroscience and the effects of meditation, Roger Walsh, M.D. and Professor of Psychiatry, Philosophy, and Anthropology writes:

> As human perceptual sensitivity increases beyond a certain threshold, we penetrate beyond the realm of our ordinary experience of the world and its concomitant "reality" and obtain a fundamentally different view of nature. This view may be obtained through any of the epistemological modes of acquiring knowledge: sensory perception, intellectual conceptual analysis, or contemplation. Heightened sensitivity may be obtained either through direct training of awareness as in meditation or other consciousness disciplines, through refinement of conceptual analysis, or by augmentation and systematization of sensory perception through instrumentation and experiment as in advanced science. But no matter how it is obtained, enhancement of sufficient degree may reveal a different order of reality from that to which we are accustomed.[8]

The idea that perceptual sensitivity may be increased and thereby reveal a different order of reality is precisely what is involved in the notion of attunement and the modes of being indicated by Heidegger's *knowledge* and *tenderness* and his concept of *meditative thinking*. This brings to mind again Heidegger's assertion that "Analysis of reality is possible only on the basis of an appropriate access to what is real," as quoted in the introductory chapter of this work.

In my own experience teaching at Green Mountain College from 2008 to 2015, I witnessed firsthand the dramatic difference in perception that is possible from even the simplest of alterations done with an aim toward heightening sensitivity. As part of every environmental ethics class I taught, regardless of fall or spring semester, I had my students participate in what I called a "phenomenology walk." This walk would take place on Cerridwen Farm, a small working farm that is a part of this environmental liberal arts college. I and the students would walk through the farm, stopping at different locations, and often walk along the back field which is bordered by the Poultney River. It was not uncommon for some students to already be familiar with the farm, field, and river. Some students worked on the farm either as part of other coursework or as work–study students. While we did not read any material in the environmental ethics class that would be considered straightforward phenomenology, I nonetheless would always take the time to briefly explain phenomenology at the point in the semester when we began to read material on *ecocentrism*, deep ecology, and ecofeminism.

I would explain to the students that phenomenology may most simply be understood as the practice of approaching experience such that the aspect of the mind that is geared toward evaluation and judgment is first recognized and then "bracketed" off to whatever extent possible so that a fuller openness to simple experience with an aim toward pure description thereof could occur.

Armed only with this most simple of understandings of phenomenology, we would go for our "phenomenology walk" on the farm, field, and river's edge, purposely spending time encountering nature and the different animals there on the farm. Students were not allowed to speak during this entire practice. Without fail, students reported an incredible difference in their experience of the animals, the trees, and the river, and they reported dramatically increased perceptual sensitivity to not only the animals they encountered but also to the environment in general, often citing things such as noticing sounds and smells not noticed before, noticing the movement of tree limbs or leaves, as well as noticing relationships among parts of nature that they had not noticed before, such as how the sheep tend to gather at the bottom of the hill where the grass is greener and thicker due to the creek that runs there. Some students even reported that in carrying out this exercise, they felt they encountered certain animals as *beings* for the very first time. "I have never experienced goats in that way before. I felt like they were trying to communicate with us. That was amazing," a student once said, after our class had stood silently for several minutes watching a small herd of goats, various members of which were insistently bleating at us in different ways with different pitches of voice.

Likewise, in a course I created and taught for curriculum at the college called Body and Being, the curriculum for which included explicit study of phenomenology, in addition to other philosophy, as well as yoga, dance, and movement, I would have students participate in a couple of different "phenomenology exercises" that I created. The response from students in terms of their experience and their awareness of alteration and enhancement of their perceptual sensitivity was quite amazing.

In one of the phenomenology exercises, I would first have everyone engage in ten minutes of silent, slow, deep breathing so as to lower their heart rates and calm their minds. I would then have the students pair up, sitting cross-legged on the floor, knees almost touching, facing one another. For the span of a 4–5-minute song that is ambient and soothing, I would have them maintain with one another silent and unbroken eye contact. I explained to them that in the act of truly holding eye contact, the looker gazes directly into one eye of the face of the other person, and thus should they not be shifting their gaze from eye to eye since that necessarily breaks the gaze. I would tell them that after the exercise I want to hear from them a description of their experiences. In the course of doing this for several years with many different sets of students, I found that some fascinating occurrences were quite commonplace and others nearly universal. Not only did the students report seeing and feeling things they had never seen or felt before, and achieving a state of heightened perceptivity (many went on to reproduce the experience with other people on campus outside of class, so struck were they by the profundity of the experience), they described certain interesting phenomena time after time.

Most students reported that during the exercise they felt the desire or urge to laugh, giggle, and break the gaze. They described the desire as arising from feeling nervous and feeling uneasy at first (inevitably now and then someone would giggle or break the gaze, but I was always impressed with how many students fulfilled the directive and remained silent while holding the gaze). The students reported that in holding the gaze they would begin to experience surges of emotion, especially love and sadness. They reported that, although they were looking straight into the eye of the other person, in their peripheral vision it would appear that the other person's face would begin to morph. The changes most commonly reported as observed were that the person's face appeared to reflect different emotions such as fear, sorrow, surprise, and joy. Many also reported that the person's face would appear to age and then become young again, over and over. Students invariably reported that in participating in these phenomenology exercises they felt a bond with the other person, even when the person was a stranger. Many reported feeling what they often referred to as a feeling of "universal love."

The other phenomenology exercise in which I had students participate involved the same setup, but instead of having them hold eye contact, I would ask that they close their eyes and take turns giving and receiving touch from elbow to fingertips. Many students inevitably reported that they had never before realized just how soothing simple soft touch could be. Many reported that the exercise put them in awareness of their own mind, their own thinking, and that in doing so, they were made aware of personal judgments, issues, and blocks surrounding touch and intimacy. Many students described the exercise as feeling good, but found themselves struggling to just be present with the sensation due to biases and judgments surrounding flesh to flesh contact. Ultimately, the insights gained were powerful and many.

My own understanding of the various things that were taking place within these phenomenological exercises carried out with students is one that indeed involves Heidegger's notions of *knowledge* and *tenderness*. The phenomenological receptivity and openness with which the students entered into the experience allowed them to have an experience that they would not have had otherwise. Their attunement, whether it be to their environment, to animals, or to another person, opened up a dimension of perceptual sensitivity and experience that revealed something that was indeed already there but that likely would have otherwise been missed. In carrying out these exercises, the students were able to perceive what would *presence*, and to appreciate that reality. These ideas, of course, are in keeping with the earlier discussion of the meaning, importance, and powerful nature of eye contact in Chapter 3. Ultimately, however, the most relevant point to this is the fact that perceptual sensitivity can indeed be augmented and enhanced. Human beings can indeed attune themselves so as to approach their environment and their world in a more profoundly phenomenological manner and thus indeed encounter "a transcendental source of meaning that cannot be reduced to facts, values, or entities of any kind."[9]

According to Thomson, this transcendental source of meaning is what Heidegger refers to as "earth." Understanding the earth as the transcendental source of meaning is revealed when we look at the way in which Heidegger understands "earth" as contrasted with Nietzsche's understanding of "earth." As previously explained, Nietzsche's definition of "earth" is developed through the contrasts he articulates between "earth" and the "otherworld." In those expressions, Nietzsche makes clear that the earth is that which may be known by means of the five senses. For Nietzsche, in "remaining true to the earth," we will be "maintaining ourselves within the bounds of the knowable."[10]

Heidegger's own understanding of "earth" is quite different from Nietzsche's, and Heidegger articulates it in contrast to his own understanding of "world." Thomson explains that Heidegger's understanding of "world" is that it is "not the totality of physical objects, but rather the holistic nexus of intelligibility organized by our identity-constituting life projects."[11] Understood in this way, it is clear how one's world could change or collapse in myriad ways and a new world emerge. One day a man is married to a particular woman and holds a particular job, and he has a particular understanding of his life and its purpose. The next day, any one or all of those things could change. His world could collapse. A new world could emerge. Likewise, an inner-city youth who has only ever seen a forest on television could experience a new world emerge the first time he walks in an actual forest. The very possibility of a new world emerging is due to the nature of earth, according to Heidegger. Thus, it is this very difference between "earth" and "world" that allows for the transcendental ground of inexhaustible meanings to be discovered. Thomson explains:

> For Heidegger "earth" refers to something cognitively unattainable, or something that can never really be *known* ... *Earth*, on his analysis, both sustains this meaningful world and resists being interpretively exhausted by it. ... "Earth," in other words, is one of Heidegger's names for that which gives rise to our worlds of meaning without ever being exhausted by them, a dimension of intelligibility we experience primarily as it recedes from our awareness, eluding our attempts finally to *know* it, to grasp and express it fully in terms of some positive content. Heidegger contends, nevertheless, that we can get a *sense* for the "earth."[12]

That very thing which we are unable to ever fully grasp yet can undeniably get a sense for is that which becomes available to us when we practice phenomenology with both *knowledg*e and *tenderness*. This "realm," if you will, is precisely the realm missing from Nietzsche's view. Its absence is why the *naturalistic ethical realism* that results therefrom is inadequate to the tasks at hand.

If Agamben's analysis is applied to Nietzsche's own ideas, Nietzsche's binary of "earth" and "otherworld" may itself be understood to be founded upon the very realm he excludes or abandons. That *state of exception* is the realm Heidegger embraces and calls "earth." I will explore further in the third section of this chapter the importance of this particular *state of exception*, this *hinge*, in terms of moving beyond the binary in pursuit of fuller *dwelling*.

A further aspect of *transcendental ethical realism* that is relevant to how meaning arises in experience is explained by Thomson as the way in which Heidegger historicizes Kant's *discursivity thesis*. The idea is that intelligibility is the result of a subconscious process in which there is a spontaneous organization of input from a "sensibly overwhelming world to which we are fundamentally receptive."[13] Heidegger understands that the implicit organization that takes place, however, is not achieved by means of historically fixed categories as Kant would have it but rather by means of a dynamic and changing historical understanding of the being of entities, which is itself established and stabilized by the reigning metaphysics of a given era or epoch.[14]

This understanding of the dynamic and non-static nature of "categories" is also central to ecofeminist thought, as I will explore further in the next section. The notion of a dynamic and changing historical understanding of beings is in keeping with the relevant and important distinctions Heidegger makes between "earth" and "world" in that it is in the nature of "earth" as source of inexhaustible meaning to allow for the emergence of different "worlds" over time. "Earth," as that which both overflows, exceeds, and withdraws, makes possible the changing historical understanding of the being of entities in that it makes possible the different and various eras and epochs themselves by allowing for changes in the metaphysics that shape a given era or epoch as such.

Given these features of existence, the importance of a perpetual and continual attunement to being, along with a comportment of openness and appreciation toward those things by means of which Being reveals itself, things such as art, poetry, and myth, things that can assist us in our pursuit of fuller *dwelling*, are shown. For it is the multilayered and polysemic nature of myth that allows for its "adaptability" to changing circumstance and thereby renders it able to retain its relevance throughout different epochs in that it is, like Heidegger's "earth," a source of inexhaustible meaning. These traits of myth, like nature, are revelatory of *a-letheia*, Being, *Logos*, and *physis*. Thus, they are an essential part of what the pursuit of *dwelling* entails.

As has been shown, the trait of "earth" to remain always partially hidden, always somewhat out of reach, is what constitutes the very essence of truth understood as *a-letheia*. Heidegger's own understanding of "understanding" as something conditioned by and occurring within time is clear when he writes:

> Historical science may thoroughly explore a period, for instance, in every possible respect, and yet never explore what history is. By way of history, a man will never find out what history is. … The essence of their sphere—history, art, poetry, language, nature, man, God—remains inaccessible to the sciences. … The essence of the spheres I have named is the concern of thinking.[15]

Each of the areas mentioned by Heidegger is conditioned by time and the reigning metaphysics of the given epoch or era in which it is operative. Each is constrained in the sense of being what it is by virtue of existing within a larger context and configuration of realities and metaphysical presuppositions that are themselves subject to something greater that is itself mutable, transitory, and in flux.

Thomson captures this nicely: "Metaphysics, as ontotheology, temporarily secures the intelligible order both ontologically, from the inside-out, and theologically, the outside in (so to speak), thereby supplying the most basic conceptual parameters and ultimate standards of legitimacy for each of history's successive *epochs* or constellations of intelligibility."[16] Thus, when Heidegger says that a man will never find out what history is by way of history it is much like saying that a fish will never find out what water is by way of water. Why? The fish exists in the water. Only if the fish somehow escapes the water can the water itself be conceptualized.

Only if there is access to a given thing from outside of the given thing is it even possible to gain access to any greater understanding of the thing. This *outside* may only be had via thinking, specifically *meditative thinking*. To suppose that one can be *outside* in this way is to recognize the mutability of what may seem immutable from inside, it is to acknowledge the essence of *a-letheia* as the concealed and unconcealed in flux.

The differences recognized in making the distinctions that Thomson does between the two realisms and between Nietzsche's and Heidegger's understanding of "earth" are crucial to various elements of this project. Such a vision of the very nature of truth and understanding is indeed the one embraced by Heideggerian ecofeminist thinker Trish Glazebrook in advocating that we forego the model of truth as immutable, objective, and universal in favor of a model of truth that is organic, dynamic, and natural. Thus does she write about the differences between "eco-logics" and "phallic logic."

PHALLIC LOGIC AND ECO-LOGICS

In an essay entitled "Gynocentric Eco-Logics," Trish Glazebrook articulates ideas that are both Heideggerian and ecofeminist, and she focuses a great deal on the nature of truth and the limits of scientific objectivity as paradigm of truth. On the notion of truth and its applicability to understanding nature and hence environmental issues, Glazebrook writes:

> For Heidegger, truth is never complete; rather unconcealment always has concealment at its heart. Applied to the question of nature, Heidegger's *a-letheia* suggests any interpretation of nature cannot be exhaustive but rather is a partial insight in which other possibilities for understanding are precluded. Nature is never present to the thinker as a totalized whole but is experienced in a play between concealment and revelation.[17]

Glazebrook illustrates what she means through the example of the practice of dissection. She explains that while the informative scientific practice of dissection yields us knowledge of the inner workings of the subject under study, the principle of life itself withdraws in the face of dissection. She then posits this as analogous to the way in which one cannot cut open a stone in an attempt to understand why it is affected by gravity. The ultimate point is that in a pursuit of unconcealment, and even success in attaining a measure of it, there is yet still something that remains concealed. In this way of thinking, she concurs with other thinkers, all of whom agree that the truly astute thinker will always remain mindful of the limitations of his approach and subsequent findings and remain open to other possibilities.[18]

By taking a look at some of Glazebrook's ideas, insights are gained that both enhance understanding of relevant issues and enable a clearer vision of how those issues plague and impede full *dwelling*. Understanding the ways in which a return to *dwelling* may be accomplished and what such a return may look like are also achieved. Certain of her central contentions are captured when she states:

> I suggest therefore that nature can be eco-logically understood as that which always exceeds interpretation, that which is always more than the account to which it is reduced. Accordingly, scientific and technological interpretations of nature have no epistemological privilege as the final word, as complete understanding, as the "real" truth. They are truths, but not the only ones. Hence their logic is not a tumor that needs to be cut out, but an excessive infestation that needs to be cut back to make room for other logics, especially eco-logics that promote wholeness and balance in this epoch of eco-destruction, that make the physical environment relevant to knowledge claims by modeling themselves upon its diversity and inexhaustibility.[19]

Glazebrook's conception of nature as that "which always exceeds interpretation" is of course in keeping with Heidegger's distinction between "earth" and "world," and it does entail those characteristics specific to Thomson's *transcendental ethical realism*. Glazebrook's main argument in her essay is that "phallic logic" is, as a disease of modernity, a root cause of most current environmental crises. She sees the cure for this not in the complete foregoing of phallic logic but rather in there being made an adequate space and place for eco-logics.

The way in which Glazebrook construes eco-logics is via specific ideas of Heidegger. The term "phallic logic," as she explains, is the logic of modernity. The term "logic" is not being used in the sense of a discipline in which rules are employed to manipulate abstract statements. "Logic" is being used, rather, as an epistemological term, that is, it is a description of the way understanding is structured.

Glazebrook's claim is that phallic logic is what undergirds and reinforces patriarchy. Another way to conceive of this is to say that patriarchy as the model of *sovereign power* makes appeal to objective truth as that which founds its power. It is interesting to note here how we can apply Agamben's analysis and see that the binary realms of "subjective" and "objective" which are operative in modern and patriarchal thinking may well be analogous to Agamben's binaries of the "divine" and "juridical" realms or the binary realms represented by *bios* and *zoē* in that they are the two realms established by means of the exclusion or abandonment of another realm, the abandonment of that realm being what founds *sovereign power* in Agamben's analysis. Agamben's abandoned realm or *state of exception* in this case is the phenomenological realm, the realm that actually precedes any division between subject and object and whose exclusion makes possible the distinction between and founding of those realms. The reclamation of the phenomenological realm can indeed bridge the fact/value divide and, as Thomson put it, "undermine the theory/practice distinction."[20]

In her essay, Glazebrook explains that phallic logic takes scientific objectivity as its paradigm, thus ultimately imposing upon all phenomena limitations and structures that themselves obscure or otherwise distort our perception of reality such that truth itself is corrupted, damaged, limited, or otherwise rendered incomplete. Glazebrook argues that it is due to the exclusive use of this phallic logic that we are facing many of our current crises. She makes very clear that the call for alternative "logics" comes from within the scientific community as well as from without. Quoting various scientists, ecologists, geologists, and others, Glazebrook makes the case that there is little doubt within the scientific community that the objective model of modernity does not provide us with all that we need and require. In summing up the thoughts and ideas of these various scientists and thinkers to which she makes appeal, Glazebrook says:

> Science is therefore best practiced as phenomenological conversation … environmental science uncovers natural processes in order that human being can

> adjust to them and be at home in the world. … Our knowledge of the environment is not just rational but also involves responsive, emotional engagement. … [Many scientists are] arguing for ecologically functional models to replace dispassionate objectification, for emotional and spiritual connection to the earth, and for an epistemological validity to knowledge that cannot be fully articulated according to the demands of objectivity, they appeal to the limitations of knowledge and its fragmentary situatedness.[21]

Glazebrook points out that there is a call from within the sciences themselves to make room for new approaches to understanding nature that take into account the limitations of human knowledge, our continuously unfolding experience, and observation of nature and natural processes, as well as our intimate connectedness to nature as manifest in the physical, emotional, and spiritual realms. Knowledge that cannot be fully articulated according to the demands of objectivity remains knowledge and should be accorded epistemological validity.

Many of the issues with which I am concerned in this project are brought into sharper focus via Glazebrook's ideas. The concept of truth understood as *a-letheia*; that is, truth understood as being in its very essence beyond full and total apprehension by finite human beings and manifesting itself in the continuous movements of unconcealment and concealment, is key. Present within her thinking are important connections to the monumentally important endeavor of human *dwelling*, as well as the relevance of Heidegger's two kinds of thinking, *meditative* and *calculative*, and the building that results therefrom. Made clearer also is the recognition and understanding of the place and purpose of the human being as mortal in relation to each of the other three parts of the *Fourfold*. The important power and purpose of art and myth and their role in the realization of *dwelling* is further established. The mechanisms of power by means of which certain aspects of our lived reality are abandoned and exiled and thereby made the grounds for the establishment of a *sovereign power* that excludes them and thus prevents our attainment of full *dwelling* is further elucidated. All of these things, when viewed through the framework of a Heideggerian ecofeminism, provide us the means by which thinking differently about our current realities, long-standing modalities, and future possibilities may begin.

The approach Glazebrook sets forth in the concept of "eco-logics" is an approach grounded in certain explicitly Heideggerian theses. In explaining eco-logics, she states, "I propose that such new eco-logics, that is ways of thinking about nature, take their guidance from the physical environment. If nature informs knowledge claims, then knowledge itself is construed organically: it is finite and changing rather than fixed and eternal."[22] Knowledge is alive, we might say. It will grow and alter and change. All of that which can be known does not remain static, fixed, eternal, and unchanging. Wisdom acknowledges this. As Glazebrook says, "The claim is not that truth and falsity are irrelevant, but that they are insufficient."[23] Truth will reveal itself in the actions of concealment and unconcealment through nature and over time. In this way, the conceptual link that Heidegger makes between Being, *a-letheia, Logos*, and *physis*, as discussed in Chapter 2, is made clearer.

Nature is the greatest teacher of both truth and the nature of truth. Heidegger emphasizes that if we attend to nature, we learn about truth. Just as a given oak tree unconceals and conceals different aspects of itself, all of which may be said to be "true," over time and throughout the seasons, so, too, does Being. This is precisely why truth and falsity are insufficient. They presuppose the nature of truth as fixed and static, as Heidegger makes clear in different places, including "On the Essence of Truth." And anyone engaged in a phenomenological encounter with reality sees that the understanding of truth as mere truth and falsity is insufficient.

Just as the view articulated by Thomson, which he termed *transcendental ethical realism*, does recognize and gives place to the realm that is constituted by "facts" while maintaining that reality ultimately exceeds it, so, too, do the "eco-logics" for which Glazebrook advocates give place to the realm properly governed by phallic logic while maintaining that reality ultimately exceeds what that realm can provide us. Glazebrook states, "Rather than simply inverting phallic logic, they [eco-logics] instead orchestrate an openness to and respect for differences that displace any logic of domination. Thus they make a place for phallic logic, but resist its excessive claim to universality."[24]

The idea of resisting phallic logic's excessive claim to universality is central to this project. In fleshing out her point of view, Glazebrook makes reference to early thinkers who conceived themselves as operating under the paradigm of objectivity, yet who were clearly from our current understanding and point of view engaged in this phallic logic of homogenization, conquest, and domination in the very ways explained in chapter 4's discussion of the ecofeminist critique.

Francis Bacon's alignment of women with nature, his use of the pronouns "she" and "her," and his description of his undertaking as one in which he hopes to "conquer nature in action" are examples.[25] Glazebrook is careful to make clear that she is not in any way arguing for the abandonment of phallic logic or for throwing out Bacon's taxonomy or Newton's physics or any other such thing, nor is she simply assuming that they are somehow useless or wrong; rather, she is arguing that their claim to exclusive access to truth is in error, that it is a dangerous scientism that eclipses a broader and more encompassing understanding of the matters at issue.

In contrast to those thinkers whose claims to universality ultimately undermined their quest for truth, Glazebrook highlights Goethe's practice of science and the way in which it is now understood as a phenomenology of nature that refuses to leave the connection between subject and object behind. In the book *Goethe's Way of Science: A Phenomenology of Nature*, editor David Seamon, writes:

> Goethe's method teaches a mode of interaction between people and environment that involves reciprocity, wonderment, and gratitude. He wished us to encounter nature respectfully and to discover how all its parts, including ourselves, belong. In this way, perhaps, we come to feel more care for the natural world, which answers back with meaning.[26]

Seamon speaks of Goethe's practice of science in such a way that the relevance of ideas in eco-phenomenology, Heidegger's *knowledge* and *tenderness*, and Thomson's idea of *transcendental ethical realism* are able to be seen as at play. Again, the concepts of *knowledge* and *tenderness* have crucial importance for Heidegger in terms of his understanding of what is required for full *dwelling*. Glazebrook expounds upon this:

> *Denken* and *Besinnung* are thoughtful, respectful, and thankful relations to nature, rather than its reduction to object and resource. Heidegger's vision is an ethic of reciprocity and care, the very vision for which ecofeminists call, a vision that stands in marked contrast to what has been diagnosed and rejected as a logic of domination by both.[27]

Such an approach toward nature is the one attributed to Goethe by both Glazebrook and Seamon. Goethe's approach to nature seems to exemplify Heidegger's ideas in that the hallmarks of the approach are a continual receptive openness and an abiding care for that which is being encountered and received. The nature of nature, as something that exceeds any in-the-moment phenomenological experience thereof, and is the means by which our understanding of *a-letheia* is best understood, is respected as such by the scientist who, like Goethe, conceives of the self as part of what is being encountered and observed. This inclusion of the self as part of that which is under observation is central to what it means to allow natural phenomena to speak for itself. As Glazebrook puts it, such a scientist, "[M]ust guard against the danger that hypothesis may hinder reconsideration of the object under study."[28]

To engage in such a guarding is to acknowledge the dynamic and non-static nature of nature, it is to be open to a continuous concealing and unconcealing that is received with gratitude, it is to practice a descriptive phenomenology, and so, to distinguish *meditative thinking* from *calculative thinking* and pursue the former both for its own sake and for the proper application of the latter in building, and it is to practice a *transcendental ethical realism* that makes full *dwelling* possible.

When we understand the binary of *anthropocentrism* and *ecocentrism* that looms so large in the environmental debates and discussions of our present day in light of this different way of thinking that itself reveals to us how this binary actually obscures a third point of view, a point of view that may be understood as an Agambean *hinge* upon which the two parts of the binary of *anthropocentrism* and *ecocentrism* hang, we are made able to see what has been hidden in plain sight. This *hinge*, this *state of exception*, is the descriptive eco-phenomenological approach that yields a *transcendental ethical realism*.

THE HINGE

> Thinking is precisely the relation that is at stake in ecofeminism. … Human being has carved out for itself a special role among beings: no other creature is capable of realizing such wide-scale manipulation of its environment. Acknowledging how human being, though itself part of nature, has singled itself out as steward is the first step in re-establishing that role ethically rather than in the domineering destruction and exploitation that are characteristic of the West. For if human being has a privileged role in the knowing of nature, the Heideggerian account also points out that this human role is made possible by something larger, the very ground upon which human being stands.[29]

It is only in the recognition of this "something larger," which itself makes possible our unique and privileged human situation, that we can escape the confines of modernity's dualism, move beyond the binary, inaugurate an epochal shift, and begin building a new world in which all human beings may fully *dwell*. I hold that *transcendental ethical realism* is the way in which we do recognize this "something larger." For if we give ourselves over to thinking, to *meditatively* thinking about the very ground upon which we stand, we can see clearly that a thinking relation to nature that is characterized by *knowledge* and *tenderness* grounds us firmly and properly in our place in the *Fourfold*.

If space is made for the consideration of all that can be understood by means of the various logics, that is, phallic logic, gynologic, and eco-logics, then we will be that much more equipped to bring about the changes that are needed. From our place as mortals in this nexus of the *Fourfold*, consciously embraced, we are able to perceive what is without a doubt present to us, and we can respond to it as the truth that it is, honoring both that which is unconcealed and that which is concealed, and become aware of its flow and flux.

Remaining fundamentally attuned to this continuous flux and change both without and within, we are rendered ever increasingly able to modify and adjust so as to flow more and more harmoniously with the unfolding of existence. There should be little doubt for rational and well-informed beings that a fundamental shift in our paradigm is what is required if we wish to make real changes. Patriarchy and patriarchal religions, capitalism, the mechanistic model of the universe, and entrenched *self and other dualisms* must all be transformed, abolished, or otherwise rendered without the *sovereign power* and totalitarian rule they have thus far exercised in the modern epoch.

The vision I have articulated is, I believe, a vision of a possible future in which there is both the survival and flourishing of beings, nature, as well as things held dear uniquely by human beings. The explorations and excursions into the various areas of thought that have been part of this project have in no way been without solid, practical relevance to the true telos of the project, and every idea and possibility discovered or imagined has served to flesh out and more fully articulate the vision.

If we put on our Agambean glasses and take a fresh look at some things, the importance of such a perspective in our attempt to move beyond the binary is shown. In the first section of the present chapter I attempted to show how Agamben's analysis may be applied to Nietzsche's ideas in that the binary that is the *mechanistic world* and the *otherworld*, conceived as the two sovereign realms, is itself possible only on the basis of the abandoning of a third realm that serves as the *hinge*. That abandoned third realm is the one Nietzsche referred to as "earth" and to which he called for us to return. I then attempted to show how we could use Agamben yet again, from a Heideggerian standpoint, to see Nietzsche's conception of "earth" as that which is comprised by facts, along with his "otherworld," as the two sovereign realms that are themselves founded upon the abandoned third realm as represented by Heidegger's "earth." Additionally, I attempted to show that the binary of "subjective" and "objective" may be understood as the two sovereign realms founded upon the abandoned third realm that is the phenomenological realm.

Again, Agamben's brilliant and insightful idea is that the very nature of sovereign power is such that it establishes itself by means of excluding, denying, abandoning, or otherwise exiling something. The something that gets excluded Agamben terms the *state of exception*. He says that this *state of exception* is the *hinge* on which the established sovereign realms thereby established connect to one another. His own concrete and historical examples of the *hinge/state of exception* are the *homo sacer* and the *wargus*. From these *hinge*s hang the established realms in which sovereign power operates, realms he distinguished as the juridical realm and the divine realm, nature and culture, homicide and sacrifice, the profane and the sacred. Agamben showed how this system was operative in ancient history with the *homo sacer* serving as *hinge* and the *state of exception* for the two realms of sovereign power thereby established, those of *zoē* and *bios*. The uniqueness of the *hinge* or the *state of exception* is that neither of the two sovereign realms thereby established protect, serve, or otherwise acknowledge that abandoned realm which is the *state of exception*. That which is *the state of exception* or the *hinge* is only included by being excluded.

In examining the application of Agamben's ideas in Chapter 5 to the mythological figure of Lilith, I attempted to illustrate how we can appropriate Agamben's ideas and gain a deeper understanding of some important realities related to patriarchy, the experience of women, the concept of woman and the feminine, and simple human sexuality, and more, all of these things being relevant to the ecofeminist critique that is informing this project. Thus, I contend that if we take this concept of Agamben's and use it as a tool of analysis and a structure for understanding, things that may have eluded us before are seen, and further means are discovered for liberation from the confines of modernity. I see Agamben's ideas on the nature of the structure and operation of *sovereign power* as a powerful means of unconcealing truth.

In my own years of experience researching and teaching environmental ethics, I found myself perpetually ambivalent and legitimately torn when it comes to the ideas of thinkers who propose that ethics require us to completely forego our *anthropocentrism*. On the one hand, I am always moved by the strength of their arguments regarding the way in which human beings are indeed a part of nature. And there is no doubt, from an ecofeminist point of view, that most of the tendencies that have followed from the *anthropocentric* worldview as operative within a capitalist patriarchy have not in fact been ethical and have not been conducive to the survival and flourishing of either humanity in general or our ecosystems.

Most of the views and arguments of various thinkers like Aldo Leopold, Arne Naess, Warwick Fox, and Paul Taylor, among others, are virtually irrefutable in my estimation and no doubt have an important place in discussions of what it will take to achieve full *dwelling*. Yet, on the other hand, I have never felt fully convinced that *ecocentrism* is the complete and proper response. There seems to exist some kind of serious tension between the idea that human beings are the ones who have brought the world to its current crisis situation and the idea that it is only in the complete abandonment of most if not all of our merely human projects and interests that harmony may be restored. Thus, in long consideration of the ideas articulated by thinkers such as Heidegger, Thomson, Glazebrook, and others, ideas that clearly acknowledge the unique position human being holds while simultaneously acknowledging also that which holds human being, coupled with the insights gained through Agamben, my own ambivalence regarding the *ecocentrism/anthropocentrism* binary has finally been resolved.

I see that the realms of *anthropocentrism* and *ecocentrism* must indeed hang on an Agambean *state of exception* or *hinge*, and it is this *hinge* that is the realm abandoned by *sovereign power* so as to establish these two realms of *sovereign power*. Moreover, I believe that only in recovering that abandoned realm may we finally be on our way to full *dwelling*.

I see this *state of exception*, this *hinge*, as the very space or place from and in which thinkers like Heidegger, Thomson, and Glazebrook are located. I know of no one who has articulated a distinct name for this realm, the realm whose exclusion founds the very designations with which we are most familiar, those of *anthropocentrism* and *ecocentrism*. Perhaps no one has even proposed that there is such a third realm, but some thinkers have observed that neither *ecocentrism* nor *anthropocentrism*, commonly construed, really gets the job done. Thus, I shall here deem this realm, this *state of exception*, this *hinge*, this seemingly new yet formerly abandoned realm and way of thinking, *Daseincentrism*.

The name does seem quite fitting, but it is the concept that matters most, and it matters quite immensely. For it is only in this realm of *Daseincentrism* that we find eco-phenomenology and *transcendental ethical realism*, as I have been discussing them. I believe that the realm of what I am calling *Daseincentrism* is the *state of exception*, the *hinge*, upon which hang the two sovereign realms of *ecocentrism* and *anthropocentrism*. It is a realm that was abandoned and exiled in the founding of the *sovereign power* that is the nexus of science, technology, patriarchy, and capitalism, in short, the *sovereign power* of modernity.

If we return to thinking about the concept of *transcendental ethical realism*, that is, the idea that we are able to discover what truly matters only when we are properly attuned to our environment, we are able to see how, on the one hand, it is indeed our very being as Dasein, our being as *beings* for whom being itself is an issue, that allows us to experience the unconcealment of Being in the various phenomenological ways that indeed do lead us to posit certain things *as mattering*, and how, on the other hand, it is also in our being as Dasein that so much more than the typical and stereotypical narrow and selfish human interests of *anthropocentrism* also show up to us *as mattering* a great deal.

Thomson, in the context of discussing *transcendental ethical realism* and distinguishing it from *naturalistic ethical realism*, explains how the Nietzschean metaphysics result in a mechanistic, telos-lacking view of Being that is the filter through which reality is conceptualized. As Thomson points out, eco-phenomenologists who embrace a *naturalistic ethical realism* unwittingly reinscribe this modern metaphysics into their environmentalism, and we end up with *ecocentric* views that simply do not give place to human being or human interests and values as such and may in fact advocate for such things as "active population control" and therefore court the charge of "eco-fascism."[30]

Thomson explains that the Nietzschean metaphysics of late modernity views the being of entities as nothing but eternally recurring will-to-power with no real telos other than unlimited self-augmentation.[31] Such a metaphysics is one that mechanizes being and deprives it of any final causes. Everything and everyone become mere resources to be optimized. Heidegger's own analysis of modern science reveals that once causation is reduced to mere efficient cause and all notion of final causes is lost, nature itself becomes purposeless and is rendered a mere means and instrument for human ends. On this very issue Glazebrook notes that "This Heideggerian tale about the modern ideological and technological exploitation of nature is consistent with the deep ecologist's diagnosis of anthropocentrism as causal rather than merely symptomatic of contemporary environmental crises."[32]

The *anthropocentrism* that deep ecologists and others see as a causal part of our current human and environmental crises is better and more deeply understood when we look at the metaphysics operative therein, as Thomson makes explicit. This is Thomson's point when he offers his critique of *naturalistic ethical realism* as leaving behind the place, purpose, and power of human beings, the very place of Dasein, in the all-too-human desire to find solutions to our crises.

What Thomson is able to show is that the very metaphysics that gave rise to the kind of *anthropocentrism* seen as causally responsible for our current ills is the same metaphysics operative within the *naturalistic ethical realism* of eco-phenomenology that is part of the *ecocentric* views in question. Both Thomson and Glazebrook make clear that there are problems with *ecocentrism* from both a theoretical and practical perspective. They both endeavor to show that while the answer is certainly not in a continuation of *anthropocentric* business-as-usual, it is not found in a complete foregoing of all aims and interests of human beings as Dasein either.

As Heidegger himself makes clear, that truth cannot occur without a thinker, and as Glazebrook points out, "Human being is always present in the account it gives of nature, for it is human being giving the account."[33] Thus, one of the theoretical difficulties for *ecocentric* views is the role and place of the human being as the one holding or articulating the view. Glazebrook sees Heidegger's ideas, including the concept of Dasein, as capable of responding to the concerns of *ecocentric* theorists without displacing human being.

Thomson, in arguing for the Heideggerian approach in eco-phenomenology and thus the *transcendental ethical realism* it involves, sheds light on both the theoretical and practical when he says:

> *Being and Time's* revolutionary conception of the self not as a thinking substance, subject, ego, or consciousness, but as a Dasein (a "being-here," that is, a temporally-structured making-intelligible of the place in which I happen to find myself) promises us a philosophically-defensible non-speciesist way of making the ethically-crucial distinctions ... missing from the ecocentric views. Without such distinctions, these positions, we have seen, tend to generate anti-human consequences that render their widespread acceptance extremely unlikely, leading to a practical dead-end.[34]

As Thomson points out, the practical difficulties seemingly inherent to *ecocentric* views that deny human beings and their aims and values any special status in the overall environmental scheme are the ones that are not only detrimental to human beings but may ultimately work against the environmental aims and goals of *ecocentrism* itself. It is one thing to assert that human beings are not superior to the rest of nature and should therefore not be allowed to play the role of conqueror, but it is another thing entirely to say that the lives of human beings, along with their capacities, hopes, and desires, merit no special recognition.

The reasoning and principles that are part of *ecocentric* views are very often understood to lead directly to such "anti-human" consequences. Clearly, while there may be some who embrace an *ecocentric* viewpoint that dismisses the notion that human being is somehow more relevant than any other living thing or that the things most distinctively human and meaningful to humans merit no special consideration, the insights provided by Heidegger's philosophy open up an alternative way of understanding such things. Such insights shed light upon the mechanistic metaphysics that Thomson, Glazebrook, and others see as being at work in such an *ecocentric* view.

If it is considered that the relevant metaphysics of modernity is precisely the way this particular binary is generated in the first place, this binary that is the very presupposition that there are only these two particular approaches of *ecocentrism* and *anthropocentrism* (typically understood), it is recognized that this metaphysics needs to be supplanted by a much different view, and that view is the one I have termed *Daseincentrism*. For it is in this clearing created for us in our thinking by Heidegger's own thinking that we discover the place from which we may begin the pursuit of full *dwelling*. The *transcendental ethical realism* that is revealed through a Heideggerian eco-phenomenological approach to our current situations and crises, as well as our environment, an approach I am terming *Daseincentrism*, serves the aims and ends of *ecocentrism* while avoiding its pitfalls and safeguards the role and place of Dasein.

The view I term *Daseincentrism*, understood as an Agambean *state of exception* or *hinge*, is the realm that, in its exclusion, allowed for the establishment and sovereign rule of the two realms of *ecocentrism* and *anthropocentrism*, realms between which discord and tension may carry on unceasingly. An examination and embrace of the *hinge* that is the view I term *Daseincentrism* yields us an alternative that is far more promising. Consideration of *transcendental ethical realism* via the ecofeminist viewpoint results in a clearer understanding of what it would both mean and look like to fully *dwell* in the Heideggerian sense. Such *dwelling* relies on and is made possible by the phenomenological mode of being-in, being-with, and being-toward that is Dasein correctly understood. Such an understanding holds the potential to overcome all the difficulties inherent within both *anthropocentrism* and *ecocentrism*.

While *Daseincentrism* grants human beings their unique capacities and values, it entails that other non-human beings be recognized appropriately, for the differences in being between beings, for Dasein, is rightly understood not as a difference in kind but only as a difference in degree, for in this view Being itself is understood as the source of all beings while necessarily exceeding them. Final conclusions that may be drawn regarding the way in which I understand the implications, both practical and otherwise, for the various insights gained thus far as well as their implementation in an ethos and an ethic, the goal of which is the attainment of full *dwelling*, I shall set forth in what follows.

NOTES

1. Friedrich Nietzsche, *Thus Spake Zarathustra*, trans. Thomas Common (New York: Dover Publications, 1999), 188.
2. Ariel Salleh, *Ecofeminism as Politics*, (London: Zed Books, 1997), 54.
3. Iain Thomson, "Ontology and Ethics at the Intersection of Phenomenology and Environmental Philosophy," *Inquiry* 47:4 (2004): 381.
4. Ibid.
5. Ibid., 383.
6. Ibid., 387.
7. Ibid., 385.
8. Roger Walsh, "Emerging Cross-Disciplinary Parallels: Suggestions from the Neurosciences," *Journal of Transpersonal Psychology* 17 (1995): 175.
9. Thomson, "Ontology and Ethics," 385.
10. Ibid., 387.
11. Ibid., 384.

12. Ibid., 387.
13. Ibid., 396.
14. Ibid.
15. Martin Heidegger, *What Is Called Thinking*, trans. J. Glenn Gray (New York: Harper and Row, 2004), 33.
16. Thomson, "Ontology and Ethics," 396.
17. Trish Glazebrook, "Gynocentric Eco-Logics," *Ethics & the Environment* 10:2 (2005): 85.
18. Ibid., 86.
19. Ibid.
20. Thomson, "Ontology and Ethics," 381.
21. Glazebrook, "Gynocentric Eco-logics," 79.
22. Ibid., 76.
23. Trish Glazebrook, "Heidegger and Ecofeminism," in *Feminist Interpretations of Martin Heidegger*, ed. Nancy J. Holland and Patricia Huntingon (University Park: Pennsylvania State University Press, 2001), 243.
24. Glazebrook, "Gynocentric Eco-Logics," 77.
25. Ibid., 81.
26. David Seamon, ed., *Goethe's Way of Science: A Phenomenology of Nature* (New York: State University of New York Press, 1998), 10.
27. Glazebrook, "Heidegger and Ecofeminism," 243.
28. Glazebrook, "Gynocentric Eco-Logics," 83.
29. Glazebrook, "Heidegger and Ecofeminism," 239.
30. Thomson, "Ontology and Ethics," 405.
31. Ibid., 397.
32. Glazebrook, "Heidegger and Ecofeminism," 228.
33. Ibid., 237.
34. Thomson, "Ontology and Ethics," 401.

Chapter Seven

Dwelling in a New World

So, we have come round again near to where we started. A line from the movie *Swimming with Sharks* comes to mind. Kevin Spacey's character says, "And now try to follow me, because I'm gonna be *moving* in a kind of *circular* motion, so if you pay attention, *there will be a point*!" I hope you have been paying attention because there have been many points. That's the thing about a circle. The absence of angles, depending on point of view, renders it either pointless or full of an infinite number of potential points. I've tried to keep the points to a manageable number and allow their mutually reinforcing organization to draw them together.

While my positive proposals help resolve some of the problems I have critiqued, I suspect that were I or others to continue to think on these things, given the very nature of some of the most central ideas, further and possibly inexhaustible points do remain to be discovered. And while such a prospect is indeed awe-inspiring, it is now hopefully understood that it need only be daunting and overwhelming if one is operating under a view that presupposes the realm of thinking as a finite totality to be grasped in its entirety.

In the previous chapter (Chapter 6), I set forth how a Heideggerian application of phenomenology via the eco-phenomenological approach that posits a *transcendental ethical realism* yields what I term a *Daseincentrism* that itself may be understood as a third alternative to the traditional binary of *ecocentrism* and *anthropocentrism*.

In examining this third alternative, as fleshed out through ideas of Glazebrook and Thomson, I established further the superiority of Heidegger's view in his embrace of truth as *a-letheia* and what such an embrace reveals. In understanding the limitations imposed upon us by the metaphysics of modernity that takes scientific objectivity as the paradigm of truth, a vision beyond those limits was revealed. And such a vision is precisely what is called for by many thinkers and across many disciplines. That vision makes clear the role and place of phenomenology and phenomenological being-in-the-world in the pursuit of truth, truth understood as something necessarily not finite but organic and changing, as well as its necessity in the recovery of full *dwelling* as the cure for our current personal, environmental, and global crises.

The distinction between *naturalistic ethical realism* and *transcendental ethical realism* was made by Thomson, and in it was revealed the ways in which *transcendental ethical realism* preserves the knowledge manifest as "facts," had by means of *naturalistic ethical realism*, while at the same time opening up a space or clearing for perception, awareness, and value that result from a proper attunement that is itself necessarily excluded by *naturalistic ethical realism* and the mechanistic materialist metaphysics inscribed therein.

Transcendental ethical realism and my approach of *Daseincentrism* have been shown to have the ability to both preserve the place and purpose of uniquely human interests, projects, and values while also acknowledging and addressing the problems and issues that constitute the central concerns of an *ecocentric* approach and their criticism of *anthropocentrism*. In *Daseincentrism*, the difficulties *ecocentrism* necessarily entails, difficulties that, as shown, are both theoretical and practical, are overcome. The crucial importance of attunement and comportment toward being that are so central to a Heideggerian phenomenology have also been made clear. Heidegger's *meditative thinking*, what it is and the role it should play, has been explored, and the importance of its distinction from *calculative thinking* made clear. The limitations of the logic of modernity were shown through an examination of "phallic logic," and the concept of augmentation via "gynologic" and "eco-logics" revealed the means of escape from those limitations. I have shown that through conscious awareness and implementation of the modes of being signified by Heidegger's *knowledge* and *tenderness*, a *meditative thinking* follows that allows for a move beyond the binary that has been the legacy of modernity.

I contend that to move beyond the binary is indeed to embrace Heidegger's understanding of truth, which does entail a rejection of phallic logic as *the* logic and a rejection of truth understood merely in terms of "falsity." While such things have their place, their claim to exclusivity in relation to truth is undoubtedly in error. To move beyond the binary entails going beyond the *self and other dualisms* that makes up so much of our modern conceptualizing. To move beyond the binary is to embrace *meditative thinking* as that which is fundamentally required for the attainment of full *dwelling* in that it is only by means of *meditative thinking* that we can understand what in fact constitutes full *dwelling*, for only then, as Heidegger makes clear, are we able to engage in proper and appropriate *calculative thinking* as the aspect of *building* that it is, whether in the form of cultivation or construction, all of which, as he says, is to be done for the sake of *dwelling*.[1]

As Thomson and Glazebrook made clear, Heidegger's approach does not exclude facts or science or technology or phallic logic, but rather, when understood properly, shows that there is a way of being in, toward, and with the world that acknowledges and makes a place for "earth," for Being itself, that which is the inexhaustible source of meaning, of worlds, of truth, and of value, while still allowing a place for the knowledge had by those other means. Such an approach recognizes truth as *a-letheia* and respects the reality of the concealed and unconcealed. As I have argued, this recognition and respect for truth as *a-letheia* is crucial to any truly effective response to our current crises. All of these things are necessary if human beings are to attain to full *dwelling* in a new world of our own caring and thoughtful making.

I contend that recognizing the reality of the concealed and unconcealed is to understand Heidegger's *Law of Proximity* and how it operates. In considering the ideas of Agamben in conjunction with Heidegger, that which was abandoned by *sovereign power* and thus concealed from view is brought into unconcealment as that which may indeed be closest to us. I propose that, upon proper examination, virtually any given binary that may be analyzed will reveal the way in which the two sovereign realms of the binary are founded upon the abandonment of some third realm.

Applying Agamben's analysis to the deeply entrenched constructs of thinking that may be said to constitute the binary as such is a way to look for what is hidden, to look for what is being concealed by the very approach (or epoch and its given "categories") that makes the initial reduction to the binary in its very act of abandoning and exiling. To purposefully and consciously engage in such analyses would be to put into practice our theoretical understanding of *a-letheia* in such a way that what occurs may be seen as a form of deconstruction that is simultaneously a creative dialectic in its revealing of that which was hidden. Utilized as a way to examine *self and other dualisms*, Agamben's analysis, as I am using it, promises an expansion of our understanding by looking for that which is hidden, concealed, abandoned, and exiled, and understanding it as that which serves as *state of exception* or *hinge* for the binaries or dualisms.

But make no mistake. Such an endeavor will in no way allow us to achieve some totalized and complete understanding, as if truth were something finite. The essence of truth, understood as *a-letheia*, remains. To suppose otherwise would be to fall back into old metaphysics, that modern habit of thinking which has been shown via the explorations of this project to ultimately yield only a partial and limited understanding and is all too often detrimental to pursuit of full *dwelling*.

Pursuit of the Agambean *hinge* may indeed help bring forth a new world or epoch and set us on the path to full *dwelling*, but it will not reveal to us the earth. "*Earth*, in his [Heidegger's] analysis, both informs and sustains this meaningful world and also resists being interpretively exhausted by it," Thomson reminds us.[2] Heidegger's earth, like Being, *a-letheia, Logos*, and *physis*, is inherently beyond full comprehension and cannot be totalized. Human beings assume their rightful place in and in harmony with the *Fourfold* only when this is understood. And thus do I stress that I am in no way proposing that Agamben's analysis or its use can somehow overcome the fundamental nature of "earth" or *a-letheia's* nature as concealment and unconcealment. Rather, I propose that using Agamben's analysis is indeed a way to better understand our current world and the structures that comprise it, this being a necessary condition for real change. By analyzing in this way the myriad *self and other dualisms* and the many binaries that constitute so much of modern thinking, I believe we can uncover alternatives that till now have eluded us and in eluding us have thwarted attempts to achieve full *dwelling*.

In thinking a bit more deeply about this intersection of thought between Heidegger and Agamben and the crucial significance of the *hinge*, it is best to keep in mind that it is in no way arbitrary or random that certain specific things are concealed while others are unconcealed. As Heidegger's understanding of understanding has it, that which shows up for us as unconcealed has a specific relationship to that which does not show up to us in its concealment in that the "categories" which are determining our ways of conceptualizing, and thus determining what is unconcealed to us, are themselves determined by the dominant metaphysics of a given era or epoch. This point is not to be underestimated in its importance.

Thus, if we successfully undertake to unconceal at least some of what is presently concealed from us by means of an Agambean analysis of that which is presently unconcealed to us, with an aim toward discovering the *hinge*, we are, at least in some sense, a part of a new era, epoch, paradigm, or world, or, at the very least, one appears to us possible. Thus, can we indeed hope for the unhoped-for. If in looking out upon our present world we attempt to see what is right there in front of us but somehow occulted, we may well discover that which has been purposely exiled or abandoned, and, in uncovering the *hinge*, we may begin a process of reclamation. Such a reclamation, I hold, is precisely what is needed in order to resume our proper place in the *Fourfold* and commence full *dwelling*, for such a reclamation would involve both the explicit recognition of the polysemic and dynamic nature of reality and a conscious foregoing of the mindset of modernity that in all our undertakings and understanding put upon us the yoke of monosemic exactitude.

In an edited collection of Heidegger's essays, David Farrell Krell notes that when Heidegger delivered his tripartite lecture "The Origin of the Work of

Art" in Frankfurt in 1936, a reviewer for the *Frankfurter Allgemeine Zeitung* compared Heidegger's lectures to "an abandoned landscape."[3] I found this very meaningful (and even took it as a *sign*), for if we consider the era in which Heidegger was working, thinking, and lecturing in light of ideas discussed in this project, we can see how a great deal of what Heidegger was attempting to convey may very well be understood as ideas and concepts that had been "abandoned" and "exiled" by and in the founding of the *sovereign power* of modernity. Hence, we understand more deeply Heidegger's passionate engagement with ancient Greek thinking.

I want to consider again briefly a few of the Greek concepts discussed earlier in the project. Our earlier discussions of Chaos may now be linked up with insights and ideas gained from Agamben. Recall how in Chapter 2 I looked at Drew Hyland's analysis of Chaos (as in Hesiod's *First of all came Chaos* dictum) and the way in which Hyland proposed that Chaos best be understood as "difference." When considering the idea of Chaos as *the gap, yawn*, or *separation*, Hyland said, "The *between* somehow precedes the binaries which it distinguishes." In this statement it is clear that the binary is dependent upon something else. The "*between*," as *hinge*, precedes the two parts of the binary which it itself makes possible.

In examining the arguments made by John Bussanich on the matter, Chaos was understood not as difference itself but as that which allows for the emergence of both difference and sameness. Bussanich says, "Since its function is cosmogonic, Chaos must be defined as undimensional or principial space, an articulated nothing: it is the barest indication that there is a qualitative something, from and in which cosmic differentiation occurs."[4]

While there are no doubt ways in which the concept of Chaos differs from Agamben's *hinge* or *state of exception*, I find the similarities very striking and worth noting and considering. As we saw in Chapter 5, Agamben sees realms in which power operates as being made possible only by the abandonment or exiling of some other given realm. His explanation of this involves the idea that it is only from this abandoned realm, what he calls the *state of exception* and refers to as *hinge*, that the realms of power thus established may be delineated. Agamben's examples are all binaries, whether speaking of the realms of divine and juridical law or the realms of *zoē* and *bios*. Agamben's description of the *homo sacer* as one who may be killed, but neither murdered nor sacrificed, exemplifies the way in which *homo sacer* is neither part of the divine realm, nor part of the juridical realm. Were he part of the juridical realm, he could indeed be murdered. Were he part of the divine realm, he could be sacrificed. But, as Agamben explains, the *homo sacer*, being the *state of exception* and thus not part of either of the two sovereign realms founded by his own existence and abandonment, may be killed with impunity. The *homo sacer*, in essence, as such, is nothing. But, like Chaos, he may definitely be said to be an "articulated nothing," an "articulated nothing" from and in which differentiation occurs.

Agamben's characterization of the *state of exception* as the *hinge* upon which the two realms hang and from which they may be articulated posits the *hinge* as the necessary condition for the delineation and articulation of the two relevant parts of the binary. Agamben says, "Life that may be killed but not sacrificed is the *hinge* on which each sphere is articulated and the threshold at which the two spheres are joined in becoming indeterminate." [5] The idea that the *hinge* is the threshold at which the two spheres are joined in becoming indeterminate is profoundly similar to Bussanich' rendering of Chaos in that both "sameness" and "difference" depend upon it, that is, without it, one cannot distinguish them as such. Thus, Chaos, understood in this way as the gap, yawn, or separation, functions like Agamben's *hinge*.

To what end do I make these connections? Only to the end of further thinking. When Heidegger talks of Chaos, "Nothing that is real precedes this opening, but rather always only enters into it," I believe we are prompted to consider that an exploration of these ideas and the ways in which they intersect may yield insights otherwise missed.[6] For it seems to me that in thinking about things in this way, as I have explained, that is, with an eye toward an Agambean analysis of binaries, we can look for what is concealed and seek to understand it as that whose abandonment and exile make possible the very delineation of the two parts of the binary.

In thinking about Chaos in light of Agamben, I am intrigued also by the idea that what is signified by the term Chaos may be more than uncovered thus far, given the operation of concealment and unconcealment coupled with this notion of exile and abandonment. Likewise, in thinking more about the Greek term *peras* and the way Heidegger defines it as "that from which something begins its essential unfolding," further connections to Agamben's ideas appear.[7] The simple consideration of these ideas appears to me as central to thinking, for even a path of thinking that leads to no particular place is still a *clearing*, and in the *clearing* a new world may emerge and *dwelling* may commence.

In thinking about the *clearing* and how it may serve us in our pursuit of *dwelling*, something Glazebrook notes is helpful, "When he [Heidegger] renamed the open region which he associated with the truth 'the clearing' he talked of it as a forest clearing into which the light may come."[8] Each of us, hopefully, has had the phenomenological experience of walking through dense woods and coming suddenly into a clearing. The brightness may be temporarily blinding, but there is no doubt that the clearing makes possible things not possible outside of it, such as the possibility of full *dwelling*. It is in the clearing that thinker and thing come together making truth possible. There is for Heidegger a very definite way in which Dasein's way of being in the world, Dasein's capacity for thinking, both *meditatively* and *calculatively*, can bring "dwelling to the fullness of its essence." Heidegger tells us:

> The proper dwelling plight lies in this, that mortals ever search anew for the essence of dwelling, that they *must ever learn to dwell* ... But how else can mortals answer this summons than by trying on *their* part, on their own, to bring dwelling to the fullness of its essence? This they accomplish when they build out of dwelling, and think for the sake of dwelling.[9]

My own thinking is that it is in a synthesis of the ideas and concepts explored in this project and thoughtfully applied with gratitude and openness that a fundamental shift may occur such that the goal of full *dwelling* may be attained. Thus, I contend that the embrace of a descriptive phenomenological approach, whose metaphysics reflect the infinitude of Being as well as the central place of Dasein therein, is the approach required in this venture. For it is only through such an approach and its *transcendental ethical realism* that the crucial place and purpose of human projects is recognized and safeguarded as that which can promote full *dwelling* by helping us to better understand our place in the *Fourfold* by means of that phenomenological comportment toward existence that is characterized by *knowledge* and *tenderness*. For, as I have shown, such comportment is the one that allows for the broadest and deepest understanding of existence. Only such a comportment makes possible the very experience of embodied participation in the *Fourfold*. It is by means of the enhanced perceptual sensitivity that is gained thereby and the gratitude-laden openness to what those perceptions reveal that full *dwelling* may be attained. To practice our existence in this way is to *dwell* poetically.

My concept of *Daseincentrism* and its emphasis upon Dasein and *transcendental ethical realism* presupposes human beings as a central area of concern as both agents and ends, but it also precludes the reduction of all else to a mere means for human ends. It staunchly opposes such an idea. Thus, *Daseincentrism* overcomes the problems inherent to both *anthropocentrism* and *ecocentrism*. I hold that a proper understanding of Heidegger shows us that what it is to be perfectly human is to be in such a way that value, value*s*, are re-cognized, having their source in that which is inherently beyond any complete and totalizing comprehension; they are emergent in the being-in, being-with, and being-toward that constitutes our existence. The being-toward is what is represented in its optimum form as *knowledge* and *tenderness* as proper attunement and comportment. This requisite being-toward is that which opens up possibilities of intelligibility through greater and enhanced perception and through reflecting upon that unreflective experience and awareness in a way that does in fact honor Heidegger's idea that "higher than actuality stands possibility."[10] Within such an understanding, truth, that "thing of indefinite approximation," is indeed granted its infinitude.[11]

To enact the idea that the possible ranks higher than the merely actual is to forego limiting structures that impede our ability to exist in such a phenomenological openness to Being. It is to consciously allow ourselves that unreflective experience and awareness that necessarily precedes reflection, leaving us free to experience without bias or prejudice, so that meaning and value manifest. We are then rendered able to exist in our bodies, to *dwell* creatively in the *Fourfold* in receptivity, wonder, and gratitude, open to the full spectrum of affective dispositions that may emerge and express, open to the play of those transcendental realities best understood through myth as divinities or gods.

Such a way of existing is the one Heidegger attributes to the poet; it is the way of existing that I propose is possible to each and every one of us to some degree or another via *meditative thinking* and *knowledge* and *tenderness*. It is a poetic way of being, a sacred intersection of Being and human being. Heidegger says, "Only because there are those who divine, are there those who belong to nature and correspond to it. Those who co-respond to the wonderfully all-present, to the powerful, divinely beautiful, are 'the poets'." [12]

In recalling how Heidegger's esteem of the poet is predicated on the poet's being as such rather than on any poetic product produced, understood better is the nature of poetic *dwelling*. Poetic *dwelling* is the achievement at which all ideas in this project aim. It would be the synthesis and fulfillment of the aims of ecofeminism as well as an eco-phenomenological *transcendental ethical realism*. It would give proper place to myth and art. It would set us to thinking in such a way that we could rightly be said to be building out of *dwelling* and thinking for the sake of *dwelling* by restoring us to our place in the *Fourfold* of earth, sky, divinity, and mortal.

Perhaps we are presently in the midst of our encounter with that which is foreign to us, that which has brought on our feeling of homelessness. But a god does wish to save us. "The historical spirit of the history of a humankind must first let what is foreign come toward that humankind in its being unhomely so as to find, in an encounter with the foreign, whatever is fitting for the return to the hearth. For history is nothing other than such return to the hearth."[13]

NOTES

1. Martin Heidegger, "Building Dwelling Thinking," in *Basic Writings*, ed. David Farrell Krell (New York: HarperCollins, 1993), 349.

2. Iain Thomson, *Heidegger, Art, and Postmodernity* (New York: Cambridge University Press, 2011), 90.

3. David Farrell Krell, Introduction to “The Origin of the Work of Art,” in *Basic Writings* by Martin Heidegger (New York: HarperCollins, 1993), 140.
4. John Bussanich, “A Theoretical Interpretation of Hesiod’s Chaos,” *Classical Philology* 78:3 (1983): 214.
5. Giorgio Agamben, *Homo Sacer* (Stanford: Stanford University Press, 1998), 90.
6. Martin Heidegger, *Elucidations on Hölderlin’s Poetry*, trans. Keith Hoeller (New York: Humanity Books, 2000), 85.
7. Heidegger, “Building Dwelling Thinking,” 356.
8. Trish Glazebrook, “Heidegger and Ecofeminism,” in *Feminist Interpretations of Martin Heidegger*, ed. Nancy J. Holland and Patricia Huntingon (University Park: Pennsylvania State University Press, 2001), 240.
9. Heidegger, “Building Dwelling Thinking,” 363.
10. Martin Heidegger, *Being and Time*, trans. John Macquarrie and Edward Robinson (New York: Harper and Row, 1962), 63.
11. Jean-Paul Sartre, *The Anti-Semite and the Jew* (New York: Schocken, 1995), 19.
12. Heidegger, *Elucidations on Hölderlin’s Poetry*, 78.
13. Martin Heidegger, *Hölderlin’s Hymn “The Ister,”* trans. William McNeill and Julia Davis (Indianapolis: Indiana University Press, 1996), 125.

Bibliography

Agamben, Giorgio. *Homo Sacer*. Stanford: Stanford University Press, 1998.

Aristotle. *Nicomachean Ethics, trans*. Terence Irwin. Indianapolis: Hackett, 1985.

Babylonian Talmud. Seder Mo'ed, Tractate Shabbath.

Bussanich, John. "A Theoretical Interpretation of Hesiod's Chaos." *Classical Philology* 78:3 (1983): 212–19.

Capobianco, Richard. *Engaging Heidegger*. Toronto: University of Toronto Press, 2010.

———. *Heidegger's Way of Being*. Toronto: University of Toronto Press, 2014.

Carman, Taylor. *Heidegger's Analytic*. Cambridge: Cambridge University Press, 2003.

Cherubin, Rose and Mannucci, Mirco A. "A Very Short History of Ultrafinitism." In *Set Theory, Arithmetic, and Foundations of Mathematics*, ed. Juliette Kennedy and Roman Kossak. Cambridge: Cambridge University Press, 2011, 180–99.

Daly, Mary. *Gyn/Ecology: The Metaethics of Radical Feminism*. Boston: Beacon Press, 1978.

De Beauvoir, Simone. *The Second Sex*. New York: Bantam Books, 1952.

Engels, Friedrich. *On the Origin of the Family, Private Property and the State*. New York: Penguin Classics, 1972.

Fox, Warwick. "Deep Ecology: A New Philosophy of Our Time." In *Environmental Ethics: An Anthology*, ed. Andrew Light and Holmes Rolston III. Oxford: Blackwell Publishers, 2003, 252–61.

———. *Toward a Transpersonal Ecology: Developing New Foundations for Environmentalism*. New York: State University of New York Press, 1995.

Gaard, Greta and Gruen, Lori. "Ecofeminism: Toward Global Justice and Planetary Health." In *Environmental Ethics: An Anthology*, ed. Andrew Light and Holmes Rolston III. Oxford: Blackwell Publishers, 2003, 276–93.

Glazebrook, Trish. "Gynocentric Eco-Logics." *Ethics & the Environment* 10:2 (2005): 75–99.

———. "Heidegger and Ecofeminism." In *Feminist Interpretations of Martin Heidegger*, ed. Nancy J. Holland and Patricia Huntingon. University Park: Pennsylvania State University Press, 2001, 221–51.

Heidegger, Martin. *Being and Time*, trans. John Macquarrie and Edward Robinson. New York: Harper and Row, 1962.

———. "Building Dwelling Thinking." In *Basic Writings*, ed. David Farrell Krell. New York: HarperCollins, 1993, 347–63.

———. *Discourse on Thinking*, trans. John M. Anderson and E. Hans Freund. New York: Harper and Row, 1966.

———. *Elucidations on Hölderlin's Poetry*, trans. Keith Hoeller. New York: Humanity Books, 2000.

———. *Hölderlin's Hymn "The Ister,"* trans. William McNeill and Julia Davis. Indianapolis: Indiana University Press, 1996.

———. *Introduction to Metaphysics*, trans. Gregory Fried and Richard Polt. New Haven: Yale University Press, 2000.

———. "Introduction to 'What Is Metaphysics.'" In *Pathmarks*, ed. William McNeill. Cambridge: Cambridge University Press, 1998, 277–90.

———. "Letter on Humanism." In *Basic Writings*, ed. David Farrell Krell. New York: HarperCollins, 1993, 217–65.

———. "On the Essence of Truth." In *Basic Writings*, ed. David Farrell Krell. New York: HarperCollins, 1993, 115–38.

———. *Parmenides*, trans. Andre Schuwer and Richard Rojcewicz. Indianapolis: Indiana University Press, 1992.

———. "Postscript to 'What Is Metaphysics.'" In *Pathmarks*, ed. William McNeill. Cambridge: Cambridge University Press, 1998, 231–8.

———. *The Question Concerning Technology*, trans. William Lovitt. New York: Harper and Row, 1977.

———. "The Thinker as Poet." In *Poetry, Language, Thought*, trans. Albert Hofstadter. New York: Harper & Row, 1971, 1–14.

———. *What Is Called Thinking*, trans. J. Glenn Gray. New York: Harper and Row, 2004.

Hölderlin, Friedrich. *Friedrich Hölderlin: Poems and Fragments*, trans. Michael Hamburger. Ann Arbor: University of Michigan Press, 1967.

Hyland, Drew. "First of All Came Chaos." In *Heidegger and the Greeks*, ed. Drew Hyland and John Panteleimon Manoussakis. Indianapolis: Indiana University Press, 2006, 9–22.

Kohak, Erazim. *The Embers and the Stars*. Chicago: University of Chicago Press, 1984.

Krell, David Farrell. *Daimon Life*. Indianapolis: Indiana University Press, 1992.

Leopold, Aldo. *A Sand County Almanac*. Oxford: Oxford University Press, 1949.

Liddell, Henry and Scott, Robert. *An Intermediate Greek-English Lexicon*. Oxford: Oxford University Press, 1889.

Merleau-Ponty, Maurice. *Phenomenology of Perception*. New York: Routledge, 2012.

Montgomery, James. *Aramaic Incantation Texts from Nippur*. New York: Cambridge University Press, 2010.

Nietzsche, Friedrich. *Human, All Too Human*, trans. R.J. Hollingdale. New York: Cambridge University Press, 1996.
———. *On the Genealogy of Morals*, trans. Douglas Smith. Oxford: Oxford University Press, 1999.
———. *Thus Spake Zarathustra*, trans. Thomas Common. New York: Dover Publications, 1999.
———. *Will to Power*, trans. Walter Kaufmann. New York: Vintage Books, 2011.
Ortner, Sherry. "Is Female to Male as Nature Is to Culture." In *Woman, Culture & Society*, ed. Michelle Zimbalist Rosaldo and Louise Lamphere. Stanford: Stanford University Press, 1974, 67–88.
Patai, Raphael. "Lilith." *The Journal of American Folklore* 77:306 (1964): 295–314.
Plato . "The Apologyiln *The Collected Dialogues of Plato*, ed. Edith Hamilton and Huntington Cairns. Princeton: Princeton University Press, 1961, 3–26.
———. "Cratylus." In *The Collected Dialogues of Plato*, ed. Edith Hamilton and Huntington Cairns. Princeton: Princeton University Press, 1961, 421–74.
———. "Republic." In *The Collected Dialogues of Plato*, ed. Edith Hamilton and Huntington Cairns. Princeton: Princeton University Press, 1961, 575–844.
———. "Symposium." In *The Collected Dialogues of Plato*, ed. Edith Hamilton and Huntington Cairns. Princeton: Princeton University Press, 1961, 526–74.
Roszak, Theodor. *Where the Wasteland Ends*. New York: Bantam Books, 1973.
Salleh, Ariel. *Ecofeminism as Politics*. London: Zed Books, 1997.
Sartre, Jean-Paul. *The Anti-Semite and the Jew*. New York: Schocken, 1995.
Seamon, David, ed. *Goethe's Way of Science*. Albany: SUNY Press, 1998.
Shiva, Vandana. *Staying Alive: Women, Ecology and Development*. London: Zed Books, 1989.
Thomson, Iain. *Heidegger, Art, and Postmodernity*. New York: Cambridge University Press, 2011.
———. *Heidegger on Ontotheology: Technology and the Politics of Education*. New York: Cambridge University Press, 2005.
———. "Ontology and Ethics at the Intersection of Phenomenology and Environmental Philosophy." *Inquiry* 47:4 (2004): 380–412.
Vycinas, Vincent. *Earth and Gods*. The Hague: Martinus Nijhoff, 1969.
———. *Search for Gods*. The Hague: Martinus Nijhoff, 1972.
Walsh, Roger. "Emerging Cross-Disciplinary Parallels: Suggestions from the Neurosciences." *Journal of Transpersonal Psychology* 17 (1995): 1–32.
Warnek, Peter. "Translating Innigkeit." In *Heidegger and the Greeks*, ed. Drew Hyland and John Panteleimon Manoussakis. Indianapolis: Indiana University Press, 2006, 57–82.
Warren, Karen J. "The Power and Promise of Ecological Feminism." In *Ecological Feminist Philosophies*, ed. Karen J. Warren. Indianapolis: Indiana University Press, 1996, 19–41.
Zohar. Mahwah: Paulist Press, 1983.

Index

About the Author

Susanne Claxton has been teaching philosophy around the United States at the college level since 2000. She earned a PhD in Philosophy from the University of New Mexico, an MA in Philosophy from Oklahoma State University, and a BA in Letters from the University of Oklahoma. While teaching for seven years at a small liberal arts college in Vermont, she created a tribal dance and spirituality program called Shakti Tribal Dance as well as a general education course for a curriculum called Body and Being that combined dance and philosophy, body and mind. She has enjoyed creating events for charitable causes, performing with students, and leading workshops in various places, including Yale University and Montreal. While in Vermont, she began giving regular public lectures for the Vermont Humanities Council, as well as other organizations. Susanne is active in the profession attending and presenting at professional conferences while continuing to pursue her calling to educate and empower in the traditional classroom, online, and in the wider community. In her spare time, Susanne enjoys nature, traveling, and making art from bones.

Made in United States
Orlando, FL
03 May 2022